A
SOLDIER
KING

A SOLDIER KING

MONARCHY AND MILITARY IN THE THAILAND OF RAMA X

SUPALAK GANJANAKHUNDEE

 YUSOF ISHAK INSTITUTE

First published in Singapore in 2022 by
ISEAS Publishing
30 Heng Mui Keng Terrace
Singapore 119614

E-mail: publish@iseas.edu.sg
Website: http://bookshop.iseas.edu.sg

ISEAS Library Cataloguing-in-Publication Data

Name(s): Supalak Ganjanakhundee, author.
Title: A soldier king : monarchy and military in the Thailand of Rama X / by
        Supalak Ganjanakhundee.
Description: Singapore : ISEAS-Yusof Ishak Institute, 2022. | Includes
            bibliographical references and index.
Identifiers: ISBN 9789814951548 (soft cover) | ISBN 9789814951555 (pdf) |
            ISBN 9789814951562 (epub)
Subjects: LCSH: Monarchy—Thailand. | Thailand—Armed Forces—Political
        activity. | Thailand—Politics and government.
Classification: LCC DS586.15 S95

Photograph of His Royal Highness The Crown Prince of Thailand, Vajiralongkorn Mahidol, 1972, on the book cover courtesy of the National Archives of Australia. NAA: A6135, K19/6/72/1.

Book cover concept by author and executed by Lee Meng Hui
Index by Raffaie Nahar
Typeset by International Typesetters Pte Ltd
Printed in Singapore by Markono Print Media Pte Ltd

CONTENTS

PREFACE

Monarchy and military have sat at the centre of Thai politics for a long time—since a king first created the armed forces to protect the crown and national interests at the beginning of the country's modern history. The Thai military claims that it helps the monarchy fight for the survival of the nation; many historians and other scholars think otherwise. They have in innumerable works explained that the military in fact acts mostly to ensure its own survival and maintain its power and leading role in domestic politics, since Thailand has rarely faced external threats or wars. Two military coups in the first two decades of the twenty-first century have confirmed the fact that Thai politics is manipulated by the union of monarchy and military. These two institutions manipulated politics to ensure their own security and maintain the status quo of a hierarchical regime during the transition period before the ascension of a new sovereign to the throne.

As King Vajiralongkorn's succession has been achieved smoothly under the military's guardianship, exploring how the nexus of the crown and the armed forces will operate to maintain the status and roles of the two institutions is important. The new monarch, who took the throne after his father, King Bhumibol, passed away in late 2016, took many steps to secure his reign and ensure his own safety. Like many other kings in the past, King Vajiralongkorn badly needs to win over the men under arms, who present what is potentially the greatest danger to the new reign. There is no reason to expect that armed men will obey an unarmed one, or that an unarmed monarch will remain safe and secure when his servants are fully armed.

In this book I look into the relationship between, and interplay of, monarchy and military during the first five years of King Vajiralongkorn's reign, but I have been able to see only some parts of the picture since this nexus is opaque. Not many people are willing to open their doors to discuss the matter openly and candidly—for fear of legal consequences as Thailand has draconian laws and regulations to prohibit free expression on matters relating to the royal institution. Ongoing political struggles and division are also major obstacles to the study of the monarchy, as rightist-royalists seem easily to smear anybody who tells unflattering stories about the palace with allegations of disloyalty or anti-monarchism. In the meantime, the military claims that it has a duty to act against what it deems offences to the monarchy.

However, discussion of the monarchy is no longer a taboo, as the royal institution's fairy tale has been over for a long time—since the 1932 revolution to bring it under the constitution. Like other political institutions, the monarchy and military in Thailand also are accountable to the people since they obtain huge budgets from public coffers. It is therefore my obligation to shed some light on the monarchy-military nexus, and this is the reason that I have compiled this book. Mistakes and errors, if any, are all my responsibility.

Supalak
June 2020, Singapore

ACKNOWLEDGEMENTS

This book would never have become a tangible reality without the assistance and contributions of many people. May I express my gratitude first and foremost to Puangthong R. Pawakapan, who has inspired me to work on the most important issue in Thai politics and also helped shape my ideas and approach, and to Thongchai Winichakul, who kindly helped shed light on the historical background. The book would never have appeared without the time and energy over days and nights that Michael Montesano devoted to working with me on this project, from the initial draft through to the final manuscript. I also thank Kittipong Soonprasert, Thanapol Eawsakul, Yiamyut Sutthichaya, Sarayut Tangprasert, Bhatchara Aramsri, Fahroong Srikhao and Chularat Saengpassa for providing me with materials, documents, contacts and many other kinds of assistance. General Sonthi Boonyaratglin, Lieutenant General Pongsakorn Rodchompoo, Nattawut Saikua and a number of anonymous informants who shared information on military affairs deserve my special thanks. The leadership of, and my colleagues at, the ISEAS – Yusof Ishak Institute provided resources and support of all kinds during my visiting fellowship in 2019–20 and thus made it possible for my ambitions for this project to be realized, even in the midst of the COVID-19 pandemic, which hit Singapore severely. Last but certainly not least, I owe all members of my family, friends and colleagues much for their moral support and for logistical assistance in making my work go smoothly.

A NOTE ON THAI NAMES AND TERMS

The romanization of Thai terms in this book follows the Royal Thai General System of Transcription set by the Office of Royal Society, Thailand, with the exception of proper names. Some of the latter, used here in the individual's preferred or most common form, may seem inconsistent although they are the same in the Thai language (as in the case, for example, of the surnames of Plaek Phibunsongkhram and Pradap Pibulsonggram, who are closely related). In referring to the king's favourite aides and his bodyguard units, the book follows the palace and military in using the romanized form *rajawallop* in place of *ratchawanlop*.

The ranks of military officers mentioned in the book are given only the first time that they occur in the text of each chapter; these are the ranks that officers carried at the time of writing. An exception in this regard is the case of General Sonthi Boonyaratglin, whose rank is repeatedly mentioned to distinguish him from the civilian of the same given name whose full name is commonly transliterated as Sondhi Limthongkul.

Names of military units also change from time to time, and the English names of a unit and the position of its commanders may not be the same. For example, the Supreme Command has been renamed the Royal Thai Armed Forces Headquarters, but the position of its chief, previously known in English as Supreme Commander, is now Chief of Defence Forces.

Kings of the Chakri dynasty are often also known as "Rama" in numerical order of their respective reigns. For example, Phra Phutthayotfa Chulalok, the founder of the House of Chakri, is also known as Rama I and King Vajiralongkorn as Rama X. The book generally refers to Thai kings by their given names, which are already well known internationally.

1

ROYAL SUPREMACY

Colonel Pitakpol Chusri, then the chief intelligence officer of a task force in the Northeastern Thai province of Khon Kaen, deemed it his duty to file a law suit against student activist Jatupat Boonpatararaksa from Khon Kaen University. For the officer saw that the student activist had shared an unflattering *BBC Thai* article carrying a personal profile of the newly enthroned King Vajiralongkorn.

Jatupat, better known as Pai Dao Din, was arrested on 3 December 2016. More than 2,600 people reportedly shared the same article when it appeared online on the occasion of the new king's accession to the throne, but Jatupat was the only one prosecuted for *lèse majesté*. He was sentenced to two and a half years' imprisonment under Article 112 of the Penal Code, but was freed after a royal pardon in May 2019—only forty-one days short of his prescribed jail term. He was among 50,000 persons granted royal pardons on the occasion of King Vajiralongkorn's coronation. This total included six royalist Yellow Shirt leaders who had been jailed for occupying Government House during a 2008 protest—for the sake of monarchy, they claimed.

Wearing a yellow T-shirt symbolic of loyalty to the monarchy on the day he received his freedom, Jatupat spoke outside the prison in Khon Kaen Province in which he had been held. He said that he was grateful for the king's kindness and his pardons to prisoners.

But he insisted that he would continue fighting for human rights and democracy.[1] Both the media and young activist himself observed that he had in fact been targeted since the National Council for Peace and Order (NCPO) junta took power in May 2014, both for his protests against the junta's authority and for his campaign for rejection of the military-sponsored draft constitution. A military prosecutor filed charges against him and seven other activists in October 2016 for organizing a public forum at Khon Kaen University to discuss the draft charter. The prosecutor deemed the act a violation of the NCPO orders.

After he was freed in 2019, Jatupat had a chance to confront in person the military officer Pitakpol when the Law, Justice and Human Rights Committee of Thailand's House of Representatives invited the two men to give testimony on 27 November 2019. Under the chairmanship of Piyabutr Saengkanokkul of the subsequently dissolved Future Forward Party, the committee held the hearing at which the two men appeared to explore the human rights situation in the country. "Who caused the loss in my life [freedom]", Jatupat asked the colonel. "Please answer me one question, who ordered the detention?" Pitakpol said in reply, "the court". The colonel went on to say that he did not take up the case in a personal capacity, but that he had performed his duty as the officer who oversaw law and order in the area. "Once I saw the post [on Jatupat's Facebook page], I had to report it to my superiors and ask for their decision about what to do", the officer said, "but as a citizen I would not tolerate any offence to the monarchy, either".[2]

Jatupat's story revealed an important dimension of Thai politics: the military saw protection of the royal institution as its main and highest priority. Its officers would use all means, including staging coups like those of 2006 and 2014 and arresting people considered enemies of the nation—in the case of Jatupat apparently a made-up "pseudo" enemy. Its objective was not only to secure but also to uphold and uplift the crown. Military leaders believed that the monarchy and the armed forces could stand together and that their relationship was unique.

The modern Thai armed forces, when established by King Chulalongkorn (r. 1868–1910) during the era of absolute monarchy in the nineteenth century, belonged to the crown. The great king had a small personal guard unit to provide safety for himself. He assigned his brothers and sons to command other military units for purposes of national security. However, the main duty of the military at this early stage was not to use its strength to fight wars against external enemies. Instead, its duty was mostly to demonstrate the modernization of Thailand, then known as Siam, at a time when it faced the threat of colonization from the Western imperial powers—notably Britain and France. The early Siamese army could not compare with the advanced militaries of the West. Although modernization aimed to establish a professional army, relations between the monarchy and military were then still like those between master and servant—ties in which the monarch had absolute power over, and was also respected and revered by, the armed forces. The monarch used the power of the military to protect and support his reign.[3]

The ties of King Vajiravudh (r. 1910–25) with the armed forces were different from those of his father: King Vajiravudh failed to maintain absolute power to command the entire armed forces. The latter could have become a threat to his rule since he was not widely respected or admired by them. It was the late King Chulalongkorn's men who mostly controlled the military during King Vajiravudh's reign. It is true that "a prince who does not understand warfare, as well as misfortune he invites, cannot be respected by his soldiers or place any trust in them".[4] The establishment of a unit under King Vajiravudh's own direct command—the *Suea Pa* or Wild Tiger Corps—as a personal army caused alienation between the military and royal institutions,[5] rather than proving a demonstration of his military leadership. While historians have seen many factors leading up to the attempted 1912 army rebellion against King Vajiravudh, it was the sour relationship between the monarchy and military that significantly contributed to the revolt.

Monarchy-military ties grew even worse during the reign of King Prajadhipok (r. 1925–35). Indeed, the military became the main force responsible for the end of absolute monarchy and the inauguration of constitutional monarchy in 1932.

The short reign of King Ananda Mahidol (r. 1935–46), which the king spent largely overseas, had little influence over the military. But the young king's mysterious death by gunshot took place against the backdrop of a struggle between royalists and their opponents—if not republicans—in which the military elite was at the core of conflict.

The longest reign in Thai history, that of the late King Bhumibol Adulyadej (r. 1946–2016), reflected the real love-hate relations between the monarchy and the military with its many factions. The former managed to establish asymmetrical ties with the latter from the late 1950s until the end of the reign. It was only during the nine years of the militarist regime of Field Marshal Plaek Phibunsongkhram (1948–57) that one saw the armed forces overshadowing the monarchy. That situation is partly explained by the fact that the monarch was relatively young when he ascended to the throne, while the field marshal and premier, better known as Phibun, was not only far more senior and experienced but also a man who championed militarized nationalism and nation-building rather than a royalist ideology. Phibun's government was consistently accused of undermining the royal institution by royalists who sought to rally forces to unseat the military dictator.[6] Nattapoll Chaiching argues that King Bhumibol fully supported the royalist clique in the military led by Field Marshal Sarit Thanarat and its successful coup of September 1957 to topple Phibun's regime.[7] The coup and Field Marshal Sarit's regime (1958–63) were a milestone for the establishment of what Duncan McCargo calls the "network monarchy".[8] It served to enhance systematically the role of the monarchy in order to legitimate the Thai state, Sarit's own power and the anti-communist war. Sarit's style of ruling continued during the premiership of Field Marshal Thanom Kittikachorn (1963–73), until a student uprising to oust the regime in 1973. The student uprising would have not ended in spectacular victory if military cliques and the palace had not also played roles in the move against Thanom. To quote one recent analysis of the episode, "First, the refusal of key military officers to continue the street fighting against the students led to the erosion of the Thanom clique's authority in the government. Second, the king's criticism of Thanom's handling of student demonstrations undercut Thanom's moral authority and contributed to his eventual abdication and flight from the country."[9] While King Bhumibol used civilian advisors—Sanya Thammasak in 1973 and Thanin Kraivixian in 1976—to serve as his proxies to intervene in politics during this troublesome period, the connection between the palace and the entire armed forces never soured. The military spearheaded the suppression of leftists and whoever might be deemed threats to the throne. In the wake of the student massacre at Thammasat University in 1976, it staged a coup to oust the civilian government then in place and initially supported the king's choice of Thanin as premier.

Since the 1976 Thammasat University massacre, the victory of the royalist faction in politics has united the Thai armed forces ideologically—even though disunity within the military has persisted, as seen in the roles of cliques and factions and of military academy classes. Although Thanin was the king's man, the palace supported a 1977 coup to oust him from the premiership as his ultra-rightist government had proved too repressive. The military-led network monarchy thus had a mechanism to correct itself when Thanin's hawkishness crossed an acceptable line. More importantly, the palace preferred working with men in green. It endorsed Army commanders like General Kriangsak Chamanand (1977–80) and General Prem Tinsulanonda (1980–88) as premiers until the end of the Cold War.

The monarchy and the military became more inseparable in this period, but the tie that bound them was still asymmetrical, as the crown played the role of master while the military's roles were those of guardians and loyal servants. In recent times, Thailand has faced no major external threat. Protection of the king has become the grand duty of the Thai military, one perhaps more important than functions like defending the country and protecting the national interest.

All constitutions of Thailand say the same thing, that the king is the head of the Thai armed forces, but in fact the charters have not authorized the constitutional monarch to command troops directly. Going by the book, it is the duty of the government to command the military and to allocate a number of soldiers for the royal guard to provide safety for the monarch, the queen and members of the royal family.

However, the union of the Thai monarchy and military has worked in different ways from what the charters have set out, since the government kept changing in response to the demands of growing civil society for more participation in politics and government. Elected politicians intervened in military affairs in order to ensure that the armed forces and military leaders supported their governments. In order to undermine the role of popularly elected politicians and maintain royal supremacy in the political sphere, the palace therefore needed to exert influence over the military. It always connected with the armed forces through proxies. As Thongchai Winichakul puts it, the military, notably the Army, has been the key to the monarchy's power over elected governments and the bureaucracy.

Since 1973, the palace has been actively involved in the appointment of almost every army commander-in-chief. Although the palace's choice has not always prevailed, every army chief must at least meet the palace approval. This approval is often by proxy. Prem, the palace choice for Army chief in 1978–80 and former prime minister (1980–88), was a member of Privy Council from 1988 until his death in 2019. Prem, in representing the palace, had a say in the selection of the country's army chief ever since the early 1980s.[10]

In McCargo's view, King Bhumibol's chief adviser Prem served as the manager of the network monarchy, but this network was not a fixed system. It adapted and adjusted itself to changing circumstances. The monarchy included not only the king himself but also the queen and other members of the family. While Prem may have been considered a charismatic figure, his power was not unchallenged by military factions and elected politicians.

The chapters that follow explain how the monarchy in the reign of King Vajiralongkorn has conducted its relations with the military. They also discuss the preparations during the transition period from the reign of King Bhumibol to that of King Vajiralongkorn, before exploring the monarchy-military nexus and the (new) network monarchy.

Chapter 2 indicates that the military coup in September 2006 to topple the elected civilian government under Thaksin Shinawatra and that of May 2014 to oust a government under his sister, Yingluck Shinawatra, were staged for the same purpose: to maintain royal supremacy over politics and indeed over the entire society. The establishment and military leaders claimed that both coups were staged for the sake of peace and order after social divisions evident in conflict between the royalist Yellow Shirt movement and pro-poor protesters. But the chapter argues that the palace and military leaders plotted and planned military intervention to enhance royal supremacy in politics because Thaksin's populist and egalitarian politics from the time he assumed the premiership in 2001 challenged that supremacy and the status quo. From the establishment's point of view, Thaksin had made a mistake as he exploited the popular mandate obtained from his electoral victories to intervene in the reshuffling of military officers, which had long been in the hands of proxies of the palace. Former police officer Thaksin put his cousin General Chaiyasit Shinawatra in the top position in the Army and his favourite classmates from the Armed Forces Academies Preparatory School in many key positions in the armed forces. The network monarchy led by Prem then struck back by putting its own men in high positions to counter balance Thaksin. More importantly, Thaksin's experience proved a truth about power games: that one cannot trust one's favourites. The military leaders who were the architects of the two coups to topple Thaksin's government and that of his sister were officers whom Thaksin had supported and whose careers he had nurtured. From this point of view, Thaksin's troubles began when he bitterly kicked his cousin Chaiyasit upstairs to pave the way for General Prawit Wongsuwan to take the position of Army chief in 2004.

Prawit was one of the crucial figures in the political changes of the past decade since he was the big brother of a major clique in the Army known as the *Burapha phayak* or Eastern Tigers, which dominated that service branch since Prawit's tenure as its commander in 2004–5—the years preceding the coup to topple Thaksin. The Eastern Tigers clique represented the monarchy-military nexus since there was a unit known as Queen's Guard under its command. The Queen's Guard mattered: King Bhumibol's consort, Queen Sirikit, took her honorary position as commander of what was formally the 21st Infantry Regiment seriously, as if she were the unit's actual superior. Men in green who served in the unit also claimed the privilege and special status of being the queen's soldiers.

Many members of the intellectual elite and pro-military figures who had supported the 2006 coup came to feel disappointed by the performance of the government installed in that seizure of power. The Council for National Security junta under General Sonthi Boonyaratglin was in power for only one year, and it failed to block the return of a pro-Thaksin political party to Government House in the elections of December 2007. But what was true of the government was not true of the military. General Sonthi may have failed to prevent Thaksin's proxies from returning to power in the political realm, but Prawit managed to bar Thaksin's allies from dominating the armed forces. Prawit implanted Eastern Tigers—notably his beloved protégés General Anupong Paochinda and General Prayut Chan-ocha—in positions that gave them full control of the Army. Military reshuffles between 2008 and 2016 put men from the Queen's Guard and Eastern Tigers into the dominant positions in the Army. The military under the leadership of officers from the Queen's Guard paralysed the governments of

Thaksin's proxies and terrorized the Red Shirt movement before eventually staging another coup, in 2014.

The palace apparently took a stance against Thaksin, as Queen Sirikit presided over the funeral ceremonies for both a royalist protester in 2008 and a prominent Eastern Tigers officer in 2010. Both had died during battles ostensibly to protect the monarchy and against Red Shirt protesters, whom their opponents regarded as anti-monarchist. The palace's support indicated that the union of monarchy and military would do what it took to maintain the status quo, with the crown sitting at the top.

The 2014 coup had dual functions. One was to keep elected politicians, and notably Thaksin's allies, at bay during the transition period when King Vajiralongkorn was about to ascend to the throne. The other was to secure a newly designed political system for the new reign. The NCPO junta, under Prayut's leadership, used its five years in power before the March 2019 elections to promulgate a constitution and a number of laws to grant the monarch crucial powers over the government and the military.

Chapter 2 also spotlights the network monarchy's *modus operandi*. Military leaders from the Eastern Tigers faction of the Army shared with Prem the goal of securing the transition period of succession to the throne and uplifting the royal stature. But one faction's domination of the Army could cause problems, in the form of deep divisions and disunity within the armed forces. Prem moved to discontinue the dominance of the Eastern Tigers by intervening in the 2016 military reshuffle and seeing to it that former Special Force commander General Chalermchai Sitthisart served as Army chief throughout the critical period of succession in 2016-17.

As King Vajiralongkorn ascended the throne after the death of his father King Bhumibol in late 2016, he maintained these networks and relations with the armed forces, but he adjusted and restructured them to take more power under his direct command. In effect, this gave him absolute control over sizeable units of troops. The new king thus essentially commanded a private army outside the constitution and at the same time created a new network to connect to and control the rest of the armed forces.

Chapter 3 covers King Vajiralongkorn as head of the armed forces. He projected to the public the understanding that he was the actual commander-in-chief of the military, rather than someone in a merely ceremonial role. The palace and Thai media have presented the new monarch as a career soldier, as he had undergone military training domestically and internationally, was put in a position of command over royal guard units and had direct experience on the battle field when he encountered communist insurgents in the late 1970s upon return from military college in Australia.

The king also loves to turn people around him into soldiers. Whatever their background, talents or gender, persons attached to the king have been required to undergo military training, and he has bestowed ranks and positions upon them. The monarch's two daughters, the queen, royal consorts and close aides must undergo military training. Aviation skill has also been a required qualification for the queen and consorts since the king himself is a licensed pilot.

The chapter addresses the promotions and demotions of people close to the king, as well as the treatment they received during their periods of service to him. But it leaves many questions unresolved, given that the workings of the palace are opaque and that many unclear rules such as palace customs and norms apply to these people.

The king meant business in his involvement with the military. He had trained and commanded a military unit with a strength of some 5,000 soldiers since he was the crown prince. The unit known in code as "904" was commissioned to provide safety for the crown prince and for other members of royalty upon request, but it looked very much like his private army. As king, Vajiralongkorn expanded his army in 2019, when he took two infantry regiments from the Army into his direct command. The transfer of combat-ready regiments was part of a restructuring of the palace administration under the new reign that had begun quietly during the transition period in 2016. The new arrangement transferred the Royal Security Command from the Ministry of Defence and saw it become an agency under palace auspices, accountable directly to the monarch. The Royal Security Command included under its command the royal bodyguard, the aides-de-camp unit, and the royal police guard.

The king has used the royal guard under his command as a model as he sets about moulding the armed forces in accordance with his standards and preferred style. He commissioned a royal guard school in one of his palaces as a training centre to produce prototype soldiers who will then teach and train soldiers in the rest of the armed forces. He selected a number of senior military officers, mostly from the Army, to form a special task force under the name "904" as well. This elite squad would be trained and indoctrinated with loyalty and monarchist ideology. Its members would later take key positions in the Army. Army Commander-in-Chief General Apirat Kongsompong was picked as the head of the task force, and all the members of this special unit were regarded as the king's men in the army.

Chapter 3 discusses the political implications of these arrangements, but it does not offer any judgement or prediction on whether they would be good or bad for Thailand's political development. Transferring two infantry regiments to the palace and subjecting them to palace jurisdiction has some political implications since the two units, the 1st and 11th Infantry Regiments are located in the capital and have been used as power bases for many if not most of the military coups in Thai history. Having them under the king might protect the political system from another *coup d'état*—unless it was a coup mounted by the palace itself.

The Thai royal institution and its relations with the military faced a major challenge in 2020, when students and youthful protesters across the country called for reform of the monarchy. In particular, the young people demanded that the monarchy restrict itself to an appropriate role in the country's politics and maintain proper relations with the Thai armed forces. The protesters broke a taboo and set a precedent by openly criticizing the monarch, calling for the king to refrain from endorsing military coups in the future and to return to government jurisdiction the two military units over which he had assumed direct authority. The protesters also made clear their wish that relations between the monarchy and the military should operate under the principle of constitutionalism, not royal absolutism.

Chapter 4 discusses relations between the monarchy and military under the framework of the so-called "network monarchy". It argues that the old network no longer works to serve the palace as well as it did during the previous reign. The new monarch has therefore created his own network by picking a number of senior military officers to play the role of king's men in helping him deal with the armed forces; in its early stage this effort has involved only the Army. This chapter provides details on such officers and their positions as well as their career paths in the military.

The network monarchy involved a symbiotic combination of the palace, the military and the Privy Council, the king's advisory body.

But the Privy Council has not worked well with the other two parts of the old network because Vajiralongkorn does not give much importance to it. Its members are mostly elderly figures appointed during the previous reign. Furthermore, they have less influence over the military than in the past. Therefore, the council could no longer be a good proxy in the palace's dealings with the armed forces.

In the asymmetrical relations between palace and armed forces, the military has a budget of billions of baht of tax revenue allocated by the government to protect and provide safety for the royal institution and at the same time to promote and glorify the reputation and stature of the monarchy. It also spent money to respond to and retaliate against any offences to the monarchy.

The fourth chapter also deals with ideology, as the military has launched a campaign to remove memories of what it deemed anti-monarchist—at least from its barracks and camps in the campaign's early stages. To that end, a memorial honouring the Boworadet Rebellion was installed within Army headquarters to remind soldiers that the monarchy's loyalists should be promoted. Prince Boworadet was the leader of a coup attempt to reinstall absolute monarchy a year after the 1932 revolution had brought it under the constitution. The promotion of royalism has been enhanced at the same time that anti-monarchist memory has been deconstructed. Statues of two military leaders—*Phraya* Phahon Phonphayuhasena and Field Marshal Plaek Phibunsongkhram, who helped the People's Party topple the absolute monarchy in 1932—were removed from a military camp in Lopburi Province. A pair of military camps in the province named after the two officers were also renamed. They now bear the names of the late King Bhumibol and of his queen, Sirikit.

This book is not an academic work, but it borrows the concepts of network monarchy and monarchization to help explain the relations of monarchy and military in contemporary Thailand. The network monarchy has been defined as "semi-monarchical rule: the Thai king and his allies have forged a modern form of monarchy as a para-political institution".[11] While "network monarchy" could include civilians, in this book the term is used only in the context of ties between military and monarchy. Meanwhile, "monarchization", or sometimes "monarchized military", simply means implanting monarchist ideology and ritual in the military; it does not mean turning the military into a monarchy. "Royal supremacy" is defined as a state of affairs in which the monarchy is put at the top of a hierarchical structure and in which it directly or indirectly controls and commands the military.

NOTES

1. "Pai Dao Din Released Early on Royal Pardon", *The Nation*, 10 May 2019, https://www.nationthailand.com/news/30369158 (accessed 10 December 2019).
2. "Khadi min: Pai Dao Din nam thim ko mo tho sak adit mue chaengkhwam kho so cho khadi khwammankhong" [*Lèse Majesté*: Pai Dao Din leads a team in the House committee to grill military prosecutor in security case], *BBC Thai*, 27 November 2019, https://www.bbc.com/thai/thailand-50573578 (accessed 10 December 2019).
3. Atcharaphon Kamutphitsamai, *Kabot ro so 130: kabot phuea prachathippatai naeokhit thahan mai* [The 1912 Rebellion: A Rebellion for Democracy, New Military Thinking] (Bangkok: Amarin Printing, 1997), p. 13.
4. *The Prince by Niccolo Machiavelli*, trans. George Bull (New York: Penguin Books, 2005), p. 62.
5. Thep Boontanont, *Kanmueang nai kanthahan thai samai ratchakan thi hok* [Politics in the Thai military during the reign of Rama VI] (Bangkok: Matichon Books, 2016).
6. Sutthachai Yimprasert, *Phaen chingchat thai* [The plan to usurp Thailand] (Bangkok: Samaphan, 1991), pp. 363–64.
7. Nattapoll Chaiching, "The Monarchy and the Royalist Movement in Modern Thai Politics, 1932–1957", in *Saying the Unsayable: Monarchy and Democracy in Thailand*, edited by in Søren Ivarsson and Lotte Isager (Copenhagen: NIAS Press, 2010), pp. 170–72. Nattapoll indicates in the chapter that King Bhumibol's royal command to approve Sarit's coup was legally problematic, and perhaps unconstitutional, since it was issued without being countersigned by an authorized person. For the text of the order, see "Prakat phraborommaratcha-ongkan tang phuraksa phranakhon fai thahan" [Announcement on the appointment of a military commander to protect the capital], *Royal Gazette*, vol. 74, Section 76, Special Edition, 16 September 1957, http://www.ratchakitcha.soc.go.th/DATA/PDF/2500/A/076/1.PDF (accessed 1 February 2020).
8. Duncan McCargo, "Network Monarchy and Legitimacy Crisis in Thailand", *Pacific Review* 18, no. 4 (2005): 499–519.

9. J. Stephen Hoadley, *Soldiers and Politics in Southeast Asia: Civil-Military Relations in Comparative Perspective, 1933–1975* (New Burnswick and London: Transaction Publishers, 2012), p. 34.

10. Thongchai Winichakul, "Thailand's Royal Democracy in Crisis", pp. 282–307, in *After the Coup: The National Council for Peace and Order Era and the Future of Thailand*, edited by Michael J. Montesano, Terence Chong and Mark Heng (Singapore: ISEAS – Yusof Ishak Institute, 2019), pp. 291–92.

11. McCargo, "Network Monarchy and Legitimacy Crisis in Thailand", p. 501.

2

COUPS FOR THE CROWN

Former Army Commander-in-Chief General Sonthi Boonyaratglin, who led a military *coup d'état* in the first decade of the twenty-first century to topple the elected civilian government of former police officer and billionaire-tycoon-cum-politician Thaksin Shinawatra, said that his 2006 military intervention was necessary to fulfil the four obligations of the Thai armed forces. In his view, the Thai military has the duty to defend the country, to maintain domestic security, to help the government in times of crisis such as natural disasters, and—more importantly—to protect the monarchy.[1]

In order to explain his coup, the retired general turned to events late in the last century, when a 1980 policy shift initiated by Prime Minister General Prem Tinsulanonda allowed the return of communist insurgents from the jungle and permitted national reconciliation.[2] Communism has been considered a great threat to the Thai establishment since the middle of the twentieth century, given that its egalitarian idea challenges the very basis of a hierarchical regime, at the peak of which sits the monarchy.

"Among the ex-communist insurgents who returned to the legal fold to help develop Thailand, there are two groups: one agreed with democratic regime with the king as the head of state and the other one does not want the monarchy", General Sonthi said in an interview.[3]

Thai military intelligence believes that anti-monarchists have never given up on the ideology implanted in them when they were young and participated in guerrilla warfare with the Communist Party of Thailand (CPT), whose goal was undermining the revered institution, the retired general said. Many of them became academics, politicians and social activists working with non-governmental organizations and political parties. Among the most watched groups were those who joined with Thaksin Shinawatra to establish the Thai Rak Thai Party and won two elections, in 2001 and 2005. "In my personal view, Thaksin himself was not then a real threat to the monarchy since he was an ex-police officer and an alumnus of the Police Academy and Armed Forces Academies Preparatory School (AFAPS) who swore to protect the monarchy with his life. Like many other police and military officers, he was implanted with such an ideology when he was young. There was no way for him to think about overthrowing the monarchy, but I don't trust the people around him", General Sonthi said.[4]

According to this line of thought, ex-communists exploited their influence and the powerful positions that they held in Thaksin's administration to slowly change Thailand into a democratic regime without the monarchy. "Intelligence reports circulated within the inner circles of the military made clear their plan. We knew where they met and what they talked about", General Sonthi said while declining to give specific details of times, places and persons. "To that end, I warned Thaksin once, when I was serving as the Army chief, against doing anything that could have implications for the royal institution and against trusting the people around him", the general went on.[5]

While General Sonthi's narrative was well known in the military and the establishment, the Army commander initially was not confident enough to risk staging a military coup without public support, as Thaksin was popular and his government had a record of effective policy delivery. Further, unlike many others in the establishment elite, the general himself did not view Thaksin as the source of all evil. He even told the cabinet that he installed after the coup, "many things done by the previous government [under Thaksin] are not all bad; we should continue the good ones."[6]

It was Thaksin's former ally and media mogul Sondhi Limthongkul who helped paint a negative picture of Thaksin's regime as a serious threat to the royal institution after Sondhi's business interests were damaged with the removal of his talk show from a state-run television channel in late 2005. He later took his show to an open-air stage in Bangkok's Lumpini Park on Fridays and sometimes to Thammasat University's Tha Prachan campus, located near his Manager Media Group's headquarters. He used these sessions to launch accusations, including those of corruption, human rights violations, misconduct and notably disloyalty to the monarchy, against Thaksin and his government. By fighting against Thaksin, Sondhi sought to protect the monarchy, for he believed that the revered institution was weakened by Thaksin's power and popularity. "The monarchy is the last resort for us when the country is ruled by immoral politicians. If the king becomes their rubber stamp, our nation could be sold out. We cannot rely on the constitution since it is produced by politicians. The politicians are dictated to by their parties, which are dominated by the owners of capital", Sondhi said during a session of his mobile television show in September 2005.[7] During his show, Sondhi himself, his crew and followers wore yellow shirts with the motto "*su phuea nai luang*", or "fight for the king", to convince his audience that his conflict with Thaksin was nothing personal. Previously, Sondhi and his media group had been cheerleaders for Thaksin's government, and he had obtained assistance from the billionaire politician in restoring his media business from bankruptcy in the wake of the 1997–98 Asian Financial Crisis. He has since consistently said that the decision to turn his back on Thaksin was motivated not by business conflict but rather by considerations of morality and dignity, and that he felt guilty for having told lies in defending Thaksin. While many doubted his motives at the beginning, Sondhi's discourse of fighting for the monarchy ignited widely followed debates about royal prerogative and the role of the monarchy in politics.

With the support of intellectuals, members of the business elite, opposition politicians and activists, Sondhi's yellow-shirted movement—which later called itself the People's Alliance for Democracy (PAD)—lodged petitions with the palace urging it to exercise royal prerogative to replace Thaksin with a royally appointed prime minister. Based on the ideas of members of Thailand's intellectual elite, like the prominent political scientist Chai-anand Samudavanija, Sondhi reasoned in his petition that "the people at large are the owners of the sovereign power bestowed by the crown, so they have the absolute right to call for the return of this power and to hand it over to the crown to exercise it in cooperation with the people."[8] The PAD held that the royal prerogative was embedded in Section 7 of the 1997 Constitution, empowering the monarch to change the head of government as he wished.

King Bhumibol Adulyadej rejected the idea proposed by Sondhi, saying to judges during a pair of royal audiences on 25 April 2006 that the constitution did not allow him to do whatever he wished, despite what was widely believed.[9] Section 7 simply said, "whenever no provision under this Constitution is applicable to any case, it shall be decided in accordance with the constitutional practice in the democratic regime of government with the King as Head of the State." While the PAD and its legal experts tried to employ historical analogy in noting that the monarch had had his men to run the government after the deadly political turmoil of the student uprising in October 1973, after the Thammasat University massacre in October 1976, and after the middle-class revolt of 1992 that culminated in the "Bloody May" events, it was argued that there was no such crisis in 2006. More importantly, the 1997 Constitution, then still in effect, allowed only an elected member of parliament to take the position of head of government. There was thus no room for the sovereign to intervene.

If history were a guide, then history student Sondhi knew that the palace could give him a royally appointed premier only after the charter was scrapped by military intervention. During a public assembly at the Royal Plaza on the night of 4 February 2006, Sondhi went briefly to meet with General Sonthi at the Army Headquarters, located a few hundred metres away from the protest site, to ask the military to help the people topple Thaksin.

While they shared the same ultimate goal, General Sonthi said in his interview with the author that he had no relationship with the media mogul who shared his first name.[10] "I had not known him before, and that night was the first time that I met with Khun Sondhi in person. Frankly speaking, I just listened to him but committed to nothing", General Sonthi recalled. He added that he did not at the time take Sondhi's request seriously. The media mogul might have just been invoking the revered monarchy to build up popular support for his movement, he said.[11]

Sondhi and the leaders of the PAD claimed that their street campaigning in fact had a deep connection with the palace, as their receiving a precious gift from a highly placed anonymous benefactor in

September 2006 showed. It was a pack of 300 light blue scarves with characters that read: "902, 74, 12 *singhakhom* 2549 *mae khong phaendin*". The security code for Queen Sirikit was 902 as she was the number two figure in the ninth reign of the Chakri Dynasty, while 901 was King Bhumibol's security code. And the queen marked her seventy-fourth birthday on 12 August 2006. *Singhakhom* is the Thai word for August, 2549 is a reference to 2006 in the Buddhist Era, and *mae khong phaendin* means "Mother of the Land".

Sondhi wore one of these scarves around his neck during a press conference four days before the 19 September coup. He also disclosed that he had received a handbag with 250,000 baht in cash from a noble lady, along with an encouraging message for his struggle to protect the monarchy.[12] With such backing, Sondhi told his followers that they would definitely defeat Thaksin.

However, the decisive factor precipitating the coup emerged that same month when General Sonthi received intelligence indicating that pro-Thaksin groups might incite clashes with a big protest that Sondhi was set to hold at the Royal Plaza on 20 September 2006 in a final push to get rid of Thaksin, who was then in New York to attend the United Nations General Assembly.

The general, who then held the position of Army chief, anticipated that Thaksin's government or his supporters might organize a mob to clash with the protesters to create a pretext to enforce emergency law and to instruct the Army commander to crack down on the protests or face dismissal. "Initially, I intended to take control on 20 September, but that might have been too late as people would have come out to fight each other in the streets and I could be sacked. So, I acted a day earlier to prevent such possible bloodshed", he said.[13]

Fifteen years later, Thaksin recalled from exile in Dubai that the military staged the coup against his administration because of his conflicts with senior persons in the inner circle of the royal institution. His comments shed some light onto elements of Thailand's network monarchy. Prior to the coup, "I met by chance one day the son of the owner of a media outlet and asked him why his father attatcked me so fiercely. He told me that his father had received a message from a senior people from the palace indicating that the palace did not want me anymore. I asked him which palace but he simply said 'the palace'", Thaksin said in a talk show programme via the ClubHouse social media application. Thaksin added that he did not have any personal dispute with King Bhumibol, and that, in conducting relations between the head of government and the head of state, he had served the king well. "I respected him because he was not only our king but also my boss", he said, while noting that senior officials working in the palace might view the relationship differently.

During the reign of King Bhumibol, the Office of Royal House Hold was under the authority of the prime minister, and Thaksin saw himself as the boss of royal officials. "I took office when I was 51, younger than many senior civil servants in top positions who were mostly in their late fifties. It is unacceptable in Thai society for older officials to follow instruction of a younger superior", he said.

"During my time, I labelled people who were not directly involved in administration but exploited the monarchy's cult and charisma to intervene in matters of government as 'influential people outside the constitution'. These days academics called them 'the deep state'. I don't think the monarch had anything to do with this [the coup against him]."[14]

The former premier had realized that there would be a coup to topple his government. He had therefore prepared an emergency declaration and left the signed document with his secretary Dr Prommin Lertsuridet and Deputy Prime Minister Chidchai Wannasathit before his departure for New York. But it was too late to exercise power under that declaration to prevent the coup.

Plot and Plan

The military coup of 19 September 2006 did not come out of the blue. The palace network led by Privy Council President Prem had signalled that it wanted to limit, if not eliminate, Thaksin from the time his Thai Rak Thai Party managed to complete its first term in office and win an overwhelming victory in the elections of April 2005. Those polls saw the party swallow up 375 out of 500 seats in the House of Representatives. Such a victory could make Thaksin's government the strongest elected administration in recent Thai history. As one scholar observed, "Thaksin's electoral popularity placed him in a position to mount a historical assault on the reserve domains of unelected institutions such as the palace, the military and the bureaucracy."[15]

Generally, a popular government was not considered a serious threat to the military and the establishment. But the risk was that

Thaksin wanted to grip both civilian and military power in order to consolidate his absolute authority to rule the kingdom. "To be fair, he had reason to fear a coup against his government as the Thai military has intervened in politics throughout history since 1932", General Sonthi said. "Look, we [the military] staged the first coup in 1933, only a year after the change of regime from absolute to constitutional monarchy."[16] Prior to General Sonthi's coup, there had already been eleven successful ones in the previous seven decades, not to mention several failed attempts.

Every civilian prime minister in Thailand needs military support for the survival of his or her government, but Thaksin was different. He wanted to control the military in order to secure his regime. As Duncan McCargo and Ukrist Pathamanand have argued, Thaksin therefore began the re-politicization of the Thai military, after it had been depoliticized since Bloody May 1992.[17] The problem was that the military belonged to the monarchy, not the government. The king's chief adviser, Prem, who had acted as the godfather of the military in the decades since he stepped down from the premiership in 1988, gave a much-reported special lecture to nearly 1,000 cadets at the Chulachomklao Royal Military Academy in July 2006. He used the lecture to compare the military to a race horse and the government to a jockey hired by the horse's owner. The latter was, of course, the monarchy. Jockeys come and go, but the owner of the horse stays the same, Prem said.[18] A week after this statement, Army chief General Sonthi conducted an urgent reshuffle of 129 officers at the rank of colonel who commanded the battalions necessary to have in place to seize power.[19]

Thaksin had been blamed since 2003 for bringing into power in the armed forces his favourites, close associates, cousins and notably former classmates from Class 10 of the AFAPS even though they were not senior or capable enough for the key positions they were thrust into. In the reshuffle of that year, he made his cousin General Chaiyasit Shinawatra Army chief and his close confidant, General Pornchai Kranlert, the Armed Forces Headquarters' chief of staff. However, it would be an exaggeration to say that Thaksin managed to control the entire armed forces through his connections. Prem's men in fact remained in crucial positions after the 2003 reshuffle. The reshuffle did bring about the retirement of General Surayud Chulanont, who had apparently never been on goods term with Thaksin and now became a member of the Privy Council. His last active-duty post was that of chief of defence forces,[20] a post to which he had been "elevated" from the more powerful one of Army commander. At the same time, the reshuffle saw Prem's favourites General Pongthep Thesprateep and General Pathompong Kesornsuk obtain the positions of Army chief of staff and deputy chief of staff, respectively, while Thaksin loyalist General Lertrat Ratanavanich remained in place as the other deputy chief of staff.

The 2003 reshuffle also placed several of Thaksin's outright enemies in important Army posts. Key Thai Rak Thai Party member and former Army chief General Chetta Thanajaro, who would become Thaksin's defence minister the following year, and influential Eastern Region politician Sanoh Thianthong sponsored the appointment of General Prawit Wongsuwan as assistant Army chief. Promotion to this position paved the way for Prawit's elevation to the post of Army commander in 2004. More importantly, General Anupong Paochinda, a member of Thaksin's class at the AFAPS but also a man closely connected to Prawit, was promoted to the post of commander of the 1st Infantry Division (King's Guard) in the 2003 reshuffle.

Thaksin did not have full control of the Army at the time of the 2004 military reshuffle, which saw Prawit become commander of that branch of the armed forces, as pressure from Privy Council President Prem and Prem's protégé and fellow Privy Councillor Surayud brought General Sonthi from the Special Forces Command in Lopburi to the position of assistant Army chief. Sonthi would move from that position to the Army's top position in 2005. Thaksin was nevertheless able to secure a cut of the promotions, as his AFAPS classmate Lertrat was promoted to the post of assistant Army chief, with a chance to take the top job later. Further, General Prin Suwannathat became commander of the 1st Division, replacing Anupong, who was promoted to deputy commander of the 1st Army Region.

The 2005 reshuffle was a dead end for Thaksin in the armed forces, as he failed to secure the promotion of his supporter Lertrat to the top Army job or that of General Songkitti Jaggabatara to the position of Army chief of staff to replace Prem's man Pongthep. Songkitti, a member of AFAPS Class 10 who had experience in peace keeping in strife-torn Timor Leste in 1999, was an officer who enjoyed international renown.

Prem consistently blamed Thaksin for mishandling tensions and violence in the Deep South, where insurgents increased their attacks from early 2004. The situation in the predominantly Muslim region gave Prem a good excuse to bring the Muslim officer General Sonthi to the top Army job and to kick Thaksin's favourites, Lertrat and Songkitti, over to the impotent Royal Thai Armed Forces Headquarters.[21]

General Sonthi said that he initially wanted to utilize his capacity and ability to restore peace in the restive South, but political tensions created by the Yellow Shirt group trapped him mostly in the capital, where he needed to remain prepared to confront possible emergencies. In fact, planning for a seizure of power began in February 2006, with the participation of a number of officers, including 1st Army Region commander Anupong and his deputy, General Prayut Chan-ocha.[22] "The 1st Army Region commander played a crucial role in the coup", General Sonthi said in his interview with the author. "The 1st Army Region and the 1st Division were the main units of operation in almost every coup in history. Unless the commander of the 1st Army Region were on your side, the coup would never succeed", he added.[23] It was Anupong who controlled the operation, instructing all units under his command to join with the 1st Division—which was the decisive unit in many coups in the past. Special Forces troops loyal to Generals Surayud and Sonthi were moved from Lopburi to the capital, together with troops from the 9th Infantry Regiment from Kanchanaburi and the 21st Infantry Regiment from Chonburi. All operated under Anupong's command. It was also Anupong who helped General Sonthi conduct an urgent reshuffle of colonels after Prem's July remarks on horses, jockeys and horse owners. While it was reported that as many as forty-three battalions joined the operation, General Sonthi said in the interview that "my coup was the most compact and cheapest, as I spent only 500 million baht for allowances for my troops who risked their lives to accomplish the mission."

It was widely believed that King Bhumibol's chief adviser Prem was involved in the coup plot from the beginning.[24] A few hours after securing the capital from any possible effort on Thaksin's part to strike back, Prem led the coup leaders, including Navy chief Admiral Suthiraphan Keyanont and Air Force chief Air Chief Marshal Chalit Phukpasuk, to an informal audience with King Bhumibol and Queen Sirikit at Bangkok's Chitralada Palace. While a picture of the event was widely circulated and published, Prem denied in public more than two years later that he had been behind the putsch or that had accompanied the coup makers to an audience with the king.[25] As always, the monarch gave his blessing to the successful putschists, granting permission to have Privy Council member and Prem's protégé Surayud resign to take the position of prime minister in the government to be set up by the junta. The 2006 coup shed light on the roles of the monarchy in political intervention and on its relations with the military. General Sonthi's junta changed its name from the original Council for Democratic Reform under the Constitutional Monarchy to the Administrative Reform Council and finally to the Council for National Security in an effort to avoid what it feared would be misperception of the role of the monarchy in its assumption of power.[26] But that change of names did not help, as actions had already spoken louder than words.

The Rise of the Queen's Guard and the Eastern Tigers

In his capacity as the junta's leader, General Sonthi said he did nothing more than maintain security and order during the fourteen days before the formation of the administration led by his mentor Surayud.[27] The latter spent his year in office as prime minister working to remove Thaksin's network in the bureaucracy and military and to strengthen the hold of the palace's network over them. Before stepping down as Army commander at the end of September 2007, General Sonthi demoted all of Thaksin's allies, notably members of AFAPS Class 10 save for Anupong, in order to eradicate their influence in the Army. In the mid-year reshuffle, Pornchai was further downgraded from deputy chief of staff of the Armed Forces Headquarters to the post of adviser in the Office of the Permanent Secretary of the Ministry of Defence. Prin was transferred from the post of chief of staff in the Office of the Permanent Secretary of the ministry to serve as special adviser at the Armed Forces Headquarters. Thaksin's former AFAPS classmates serving in the Navy and Air Force were also demoted. Vice Admiral Suvichai Sirisalee was transferred from the post of chief of the Thai Marine Corps to an advisory post, and Air Chief Marshal Sukampol Suwannathat was moved from the position of assistant Air Force commander to an inactive post.[28]

While there were a few candidates for the post of Army commander, Anupong's role as the key operator in the 2006 coup and his strong connections with the palace as a leading member of the Queen's Guard led General Sonthi to back him fully as his successor. A former commander of the 21st Infantry Regiment, Anupong had been groomed by Sonthi's predecessor, Prawit, the man regarded as the big brother of the Army's Eastern Tigers. In 2007, Anupong had a few more years left in service. Also, he had strong support from subordinates in his own clique—notably Prayut, who followed in his footsteps closely. Asked in his interview with the author if he had had candidates besides Anupong in mind—such as hard-line General Saprang Kalayanamitr, who had brought troops from the 3rd Army Region to back the coup, or General Montri Sankhasap, the moderate Army chief of staff—General Sonthi said that Saprang did not participate in the plot at the beginning and that he himself had said "no" to recommendations of other possible successors. "Of course, people from above suggested many other choices, but Anupong worked with me at the beginning", he said.[29] General Sonthi added that, in the absence of candidates who shared his own Special Forces background, Anupong's help in ousting Thaksin made him the only candidate for Army chief to merit his backing.[30]

One might categorize factions in the Thai military in a number of ways, depending on how their members grouped together. In the early 1990s and before, Chulachomklao Royal Military Academy class affiliations mattered. Class 7 played a leading role in launching the premiership of Prem in the 1980s, though it would soon turn on him. And General Suchinda Kraprayoon, who as Army commander led the 1991 coup to topple the elected government of Chatichai Choonhavan, was the leader of the academy's Class 5. He promoted all his classmates to prominent positions after he took power. In a departure from this earlier emphasis on Chulachomklao Royal Military Academy ties, former police officer Thaksin raised many of his classmates from Class 10 of the pre-cadet school, the AFAPS, to powerful posts during his time as premier. On the other hand, the factionalism of Prawit, Anupong and Prayut on display after the 2006 coup had yet a third basis. These men promoted officers who had worked with them in the 2nd Infantry Division. Rivalry in the Army since that time has been understood as opposing soldiers who served in different units rather than members of different academy or pre-cadet school classes. Most important was the rivalry between the 1st and 2nd Infantry Divisions.

Located in the Eastern border province of Prachinburi, the Royal Guard 2nd Infantry Division chose the tiger as its emblem, and its members called themselves the *Burapha phayak* or Eastern Tigers. Meanwhile, the 21st Infantry Regiment, a unit under that same 2nd Division, was assigned for palace duty, with Queen Sirikit as its honorary commander in 1958, when strongman Field Marshal Sarit Thanarat began the monarchization of the military.[31] Starting in the 1980s, Queen Sirikit became intensively involved with this unit. It actively participated in quelling the 1981 coup attempt against then Prime Minister Prem, and thus it become a personal passion of the queen's. She asked permission from the king to change the unit's colour and that of the uniform that its soldiers wore during parades and ceremonies from red to her favourite purple.[32] One rising star who played a crucial role in the operations to put down the 1981 coup attempt was then Lieutenant Colonel Narongdej Nandha-phothidej, who would serve as commander of the 21st Infantry Regiment between 1982 and 1984. Narongdej served as the queen's close bodyguard for a long time and trained Queen's Guard soldiers himself. He died of heart attack on 22 May 1985, while he was in the United States. To some it was unbelievable that a heart attack was the cause of his death as Narongdej was tough and strong. There was a rumour that he was murdered for some reason. "At his funeral, the queen appeared to grieve openly."[33] His statue was erected, with a memorial museum, in the barracks of the 21st Infantry Regiment.

Calling themselves *thahan suea rachini* or the queen's tigers soldiers, Prawit, Anupong and Prayut served in that regiment from the time when they were young soldiers. They always mingled and hung out together at Prawit's residence within the barracks. While Prawit had no experience in directly commanding the unit, as he had been elevated to command of the 2nd Infantry Division, Anupong and Prayut were both former top commanders of the 21st Regiment Queen's Guard. They had a deep connection with Narongdej, their superior and mentor. Prayut in fact chose 22 May as D-day for his coup to seize power in 2014 in commemoration of the death of Narongdej.[34]

The military reshuffle in 2007 made Anupong Army chief. Prayut retained the key position of commander of the strategic 1st Army Region for another year as a means of keeping the military free of Thaksin's influence during the elections of December 2007. Unfortunately, from the point of view of the departing junta, those polls brought the pro-

Thaksin People's Power Party to power, and the right-wing royalist Samak Sundaravej became prime minister.

Thaksin made veteran politician Samak his political proxy after the 2006 coup for three reasons. First, Samak was a popular and seasoned politician in the capital, where anti-Thaksin sentiment remained strong. He won a landslide victory in Bangkok in the race for governor of the capital in 2000 and held that position until 2004. Second, Samak traced a record of loyalty to the monarchy back to the 1970s, when he spearheaded a crusade against leftists that led to the massacre of students in Thammasat University in October 1976. Third, his unchanging royalist and ultra-rightist ideology was trusted among members of the Thai military elite. "Prime Minister Samak was very friendly with the military's top brass and had very good personal relations with them", said orator-cum-politician Nattawut Saikua, a former spokesman for Samak's administration.[35] Samak found himself a perfect choice to play this role. He could both fulfil his personal ambition to serve as head of government and reconcile rightist-royalists, who might still admire him and his political history, with Thaksin's camp.

Samak's record and qualifications meant nothing to Anupong. The general wanted to see his mentor Prawit take the post of defence minister in Samak's government and thus serve as the Army's political boss. After all, the Eastern Tigers' big brother Prawit had himself been Army chief during Thaksin's administration, and he had strong connections with factions in Thaksin's camp. But Samak disagreed with the idea of appointing Prawit to serve as defence minister. Instead, he went ahead with his own plan to take the position for himself in order to have direct command over the armed forces. While Thaksin wanted to restore his loyalists to power, Samak nevertheless sought an alliance with Anupong. He was friendly towards the general, took him on trips abroad, and sought the advice of the Army's top brass on security affairs. In order to please his Army chief, defence minister Samak also granted permission to the Army to purchase 96 Ukrainian-made armoured personnel carriers—a purchase that had been put on hold since Surayud's government because of questions concerning after-sale servicing.[36] General Sonthi said that the project had originally been handled by Anupong and that it had encountered numerous production and delivery problems.[37]

The 2008 Defence Act, promulgated during the transition period from Surayud to Samak, empowered the defence minister to chair a committee to decide on military reshuffles at the level of general. It also preserved the full authority of top commanders of the respective branches of the armed forces to manage the allocation of posts under their responsibility.[38] The act sought to prevent intervention in the process on the part of civilian politicians. Samak gave liberty to the commanders of the three branches, and notably to Anupong of the Army, to exercise their authority in annual military reshuffles. The 2008 mid-year reshuffle in the Army further cleared the path to power for officers of the Queen's Guard and the Eastern Tigers clique, demoting not only Thaksin loyalists but also General Sonthi's men from the Special Forces Command. It thus strengthened the connection between the crown and the military—to be more precise, between the queen and the Army—via the Queen's Guard clique.

Resistance to Civilian Control

Although his government had popular support and dominated the parliament, Samak's cabinet was relatively weak when it came to its ability to control and command the military and even manage its relations with the armed forces. Thaksin's return to Thailand from self-imposed exile in March 2008 reawakened Yellow Shirt leader Sondhi, who then enjoyed strong links to and support from the establishment—notably in the form of financial assistance to his media firm. He would soon enjoy a heroic triumph. The PAD, in its second crusade, was backed by the strength of former Bangkok governor and retired Major General Chamlong Srimuang and of the Buddhist puritan Samana Pothirak's Santi Asok sect and Dharma Army Foundation. It was also firmly allied with the Democrat Party. In the second season of its crusade, the PAD was obviously equipped with a royal-nationalist ideology. It accused Thaksin's proxy government of selling the national soul to neighbouring Cambodia because of Thailand's support for Phnom Penh's application for the listing of the Khmer Hindu temple of Preah Vihear as a UNESCO World Heritage site—a stance that in fact had been adopted by the previous government under Surayud. In this connection, PAD protesters opposed all interactions with Cambodia, including boundary demarcation and negotiations on the overlapping claims to the continental shelf in the Gulf of Thailand. With the strong support of judicial activists, they were granted legal protection for their protests, including the occupation of Government

House in August 2008, in the form of a civil court injunction. Samak's foreign minister, Noppadon Pattama, was forced to step down after the Constitutional Court ruled as unconstitutional his joint statement with Cambodian Deputy Prime Minister Sok An supporting Phnom Penh's World Heritage application.[39]

Army chief Anupong, who was then fully secure and feeling confident of his power, suggested that the elected Prime Minister Samak dissolve the House of Representatives and call for new elections. His demand was refused; instead, Samak passed the hot potato to Anupong by instructing the Army to join the police in flushing out PAD protesters out from Government House. In the meantime, the protesters spread through the capital and stormed the building housing the National Broadcasting Service of Thailand. There they attempted to have the state-run television station relay the signals from Sondhi's ASTV channel, which was broadcasting the ongoing PAD protest from the Government House live and around the clock. Anupong resisted the instruction to flush out the protesters. He simply assigned 1st Army Region Commander Prayut to have 1,000-man-strong anti-riot forces on standby awaiting a request for support from the police. With such a cold response from the Army chief, Prime Minister and Defence Minister Samak contemplated kicking Anupong upstairs to replace General Boonsrang Niumpradit, who would retire from the position of chief of defence forces at the end of September. To replace Anupong as Army chief, Samak looked for an officer who might be friendlier to his government. But Anupong disagreed with this plan, recommending instead that his AFAPS Class 10 classmate Songkitti fill the vacant post of chief of defence forces while he remained Army chief for another year. The 2008 reshuffle thus reflected Anupong's influence. He made his favourite Prayut as the Army chief of staff and promoted General Kanit Sapitak from deputy commander to commander of the 1st Army Region.

A popular mandate resulting from elections and good personal relations with the top brass meant nothing to the government's authority over the Army, as Anupong continually refused to comply with the government's instructions, according to Nattawut.[40] The Army chief refused to take any action when Samak declared a state of emergency in the opening days of September to try to control the situation. A pro-government movement clashed with the PAD in an incident that killed one person and injured a dozen others. "General

Anupong was assigned to implement the emergency law, but instead he left the government to fend for itself by shifting the responsibility to the police", said Nattawut, who also had connections with the then pro-government Red Shirt group.[41]

The emergency law empowered the commander to remove the protesters from any location by force if necessary. Anupong was quoted by the media as saying, "if we thought we could use police and soldiers to get them out with a peaceful conclusion, we would do it. But we think that would create more problems."[42]

Anupong reportedly failed in an attempt to topple Samak's government by convincing parties to withdraw from the coalition. Rather, it was the Constitutional Court that brought Samak down with a ruling that his receiving payment for hosting a cooking show on television was unconstitutional.[43] The court's decision, however, did not defuse the tension as the ruling People's Power Party picked Thaksin's brother-in-law, Somchai Wongsawat, to replace Samak, and the PAD continued its protests. Anupong maintained his stance, declining to use military force to evict protesters from Government House. This stance prevented Somchai from physically entering the prime minister's office. Finally, on 2 December 2008, the Constitutional Court dissolved three parties in the ruling coalition for election fraud, resulting in the dissolution of the government, too.

Protesters had chased Somchai everywhere that he went. Violence erupted on 7 October, when police launched an operation to clear the way for the premier to enter the parliament to announce his government's policies. Somchai had to climb over a fence to enter the parliament compound. The clash caused the deaths of two PAD protesters—one from an explosion in his own car and another, according to forensic expert Dr Pornthip Rojanasunand, from exposure to tear gas.[44] The score of injured people included policemen. Army chief Anupong reiterated his clear stance. He would neither use his troops to help the government disperse the protesters nor stage a coup to take control, as called for by PAD protesters. "But he led all the commanders of the armed forces and the police chief to appear on a TV show demanding that Somchai take responsibility by stepping down or dissolving parliament", recalled Nattawut, who added that his own phone call to offer a rebuttal on the same television programme was refused. "How weak the Somchai government was, when it allowed the military top brass to make such a demand in public", he said;

"it was a soft *coup d'état*." Then serving as government spokesman, Nattawut suggested to Somchai that he fire Anupong, but the premier rejected his advice.[45]

As the military under Anupong tried to isolate the Somchai government, the palace rather openly took the side of the PAD protesters, with Queen Sirikit showing her support for their battle. She presided over the cremation ceremony of 28-year-old protester Angkana Radappanyawuthi on 13 October 2008 and donated a million baht to treat injured protesters.[46] Princess Chulabhorn, several members of the Privy Council and Anupong accompanied the queen to the cremation. The queen announced that the young demonstrator had died in a noble cause, trying to protect the royal institution. She also had a private conversation with PAD leader Sondhi, during which she expressed her support, before leaving the ceremony.[47]

A Government Formed in Military Barracks

As the court did its part to dissolve the People's Power Party, the Chart Thai Party and the Matchima Party for election fraud, thus ending Somchai's government, Anupong and Prayut carried on with the task of forming a new, anti-Thaksin coalition government led by the Democrat Party. Retired General Prawit came onto the scene as he had good connections with politicians. The top brass of the Queen's Guard invited politicians to a meeting at a military residence in the 1st Infantry Regiment compound to convince them to defect to the anti-Thaksin camp. The key figure was Newin Chidchob from the Northeastern province of Buriram, who had a strong connection with Prawit. Formerly a Thaksin loyalist, Newin had had a bad experience with the military at the time of the 2006 coup. He was humiliated while in detention and banned from politics after the dissolution of the Thai Rak Thai Party. Nevertheless, he had no difficulty in switching camps just two years later. He led thirty politicians who called themselves the "friends of Newin" to join the newly established Phumjaithai Party and thus made a new, military-sponsored government possible. The new administration, with young Oxford-educated Democrat Party leader Abhisit Vejjajiva as premier, was formed in mid-December 2008 in military barracks and under the influence of Queen's Guard men.[48] Big Brother Prawit took the position of defence minister and had both full legal authority over and great personal influence in military affairs.

Deputy Prime Minister Suthep Thaugsuban a veteran politician known as the government's manager, was assigned to oversee security matters. But he appears in fact to have played the role of coordinator between the government and the armed forces, if not as executor of the top military brass's wishes. Like many other civilian politicians, Suthep kept the top brass happy for the sake of the government's security and stability. The seasoned politician from Surat Thani Province in Southern Thailand now became an additional part of the dominant military triumvirate—comprising Defence Minister Prawit, Army chief Anupong and Army chief of staff Prayut—as he was seen to stick with them all the time.

The triumvirate founded Abhisit's government as its pet project and thus felt obliged to protect it at all costs. With the support of six parties in the new ruling coalition, Abhisit's government was secure in parliament. It survived a no-confidence vote in March 2009. The top brass also needed to make sure that no faction of the military would topple the government. In the April 2009 mid-year reshuffle, it thus further purged Thaksin loyalists such as Generals Manas Paorik and Prin Suwannathat. The top brass moved the two men to inactive posts in the offices of the defence ministry's permanent secretary and of the defence minister, respectively. In the meantime, the triumvirs shored up the positions of their Eastern Tigers and Queen's Guard fellows by placing them in strategic posts. General Weewalit Chornsamrit was elevated from deputy commander of the 2nd Army Region to commander of the 2nd Army Corps, and General Thongchai Theparak was promoted from commander of the 33rd Military Circle to deputy commander of the 3rd Army Region.

Full consolidation of the military triumvirate's power was seen in the annual reshuffle carried out in September 2009. Anupong retained his position as Army chief, and Prayut was promoted to the position of Army deputy commander. Anupong's close associates Generals Wit Thephasadin Na Ayutthaya and Theerawat Boonyapradap were promoted to Army assistant commanders, and another close associate, General Piroon Paewpolsong, was promoted to Army chief of staff. Anupong's classmate Weewalit, who had received a promotion in April, was elevated another step to the post of commander of the 2nd Army Region.

Meanwhile, Prayut saw to the insertion of his own close associates and favourites into key positions. General Daopong Rattanasuwan became deputy chief of staff of the Army, and General Surasak Kanchanarat assistant chief of staff for civil affairs. The strategic position of commander of the 1st Army Region landed on the shoulders of the Eastern Tigers' Kanit Sapitak, a former commander of the 2nd Infantry Division.

Other Eastern Tigers officers were also promoted. General Theerachai Nakwanich moved from the post of deputy commander of the 1st Army Corps to that of deputy commander of the 1st Army Region. General Udomdej Sitabutr received a particularly big piece of pie when he went from being commander of the 9th Infantry Regiment in Kanchanaburi Province to becoming deputy commander of the 1st Army Region. Nepotism in favour of close relatives was evident in the reshuffle. Anupong's brother, General Thanadol Paochinda, received a promotion from deputy commander to commander of the Territorial Defence Command, while Prayut's brother, General Preecha Chanocha, was elevated from 3rd Army Corps chief of staff to become the 3rd Army Region's chief of staff. The reshuffle affected offices who were not members of the Queen's Guard/Eastern Tigers faction as well. General Kampanat Ruddit was elevated from the position of commander of the 15th Military Circle to become commander of the 1st Infantry Division King's Guard, replacing General Paiboon Kumchaya. The latter was promoted to deputy commander of the 1st Army Region.

In the Navy, Admiral Kamthorn Phumhiran retained his position as the Navy chief and moved his classmate Admiral Niphon Chaksudul from assistant to deputy Navy commander in the September 2009 reshuffle. Meanwhile, Air Force chief Air Chief Marshal Itthaporn Subhawong promoted Air Chief Marshal Anawin Piromrat to the post of his deputy, and Air Chief Marshal Prajin Juntong was elevated from Air Force deputy chief of staff to chief of staff.

Cracking Down on the Red Shirts

A major challenge for the military, and for the government that it installed after the September 2006 coup, was the street battles waged by a pro-poor movement, which stood up against the establishment from shortly before the coup. The movement took the name United Front for Democracy against Dictatorship (UDD) after the coup. Its emergence posed real challenges to the stability of the government and, in some sense, to the security of the monarchy as well. The UDD's leaders included veteran politician Veerakan Musikapong, former student activist-turned-politician Jatuporn Prompan and the silver-tongued Nattawut Saikua.

A precursor to this lower middle-class movement against established elites was originally mobilized by the Thai Rak Thai Party when Newin Chidchob supported rallies of villagers from the Northeast in the capital under the name Caravan of the Poor. These rallies were not only held in support of Thaksin but also intended to counter the royalist PAD. Their presence in Bangkok in early 2006 was an excuse for the military to stage the coup to ease tensions between the opposing groups and to prevent violence in case of clashes between them. The pro-poor and anti-elite nature of the demonstrations was highlighted at the beginning since the demonstrators were originally from the low-income Northeastern region—known in Thailand as Isan and a stronghold of the succession of pro-Thaksin political parties. Northeasterners benefited from Thaksin's populist policies and were loyal in voting for Thaksin's allies in every election since 2005.

The demonstrations were not originally against the royal institution. On the contrary, the participants tried to play the role of loyal subjects protecting the reputation of the crown. Hundreds of them blocked the headquarters of the Nation Multimedia Group in Bang Na to protest against the publication in the group's Thai-language newspaper *Khom chat luek* of an interview with PAD leader Sondhi. In that interview Sondhi referred to his protests as a fight for the king, thus dragging the revered institution down into street protests. The UDD demonstrators accused Sondhi of insulting the monarchy with those comments.[49]

The group decided to protest against established elites after the 2006 coup when they realized that Privy Council President Prem was the mastermind of the successful military intervention to topple Thaksin. Their struggle had a sense of not only class difference but also identity politics. One of the key leaders, Nattawut, declared a war against *amattayathippatai* (aristocracy) because the king's chief adviser was in effect a modern-day aristocrat who intervened in and dominated politics. Nattawut led the protesters to a blockade of Prem's residence at Sisao Theves on 22 July 2007, demanding that the former premier step down from his position as head of the Privy Council. He was jailed for the first time after the protest, to be followed by many other jail terms for his role in the struggles since then. Nattawut adopted the term *phrai* to describe himself and the members of his movement in order to capture their position as people of low class in a hierarchical society. A term originally used for those who owed corvée labour to the crown or to influential patrons, *phrai* could more broadly mean peasant, servant, person of low status, commoner, subject, folk or citizen.

While Sondhi and members of the PAD wore yellow shirts to associate themselves with the monarchy, as yellow represented the royal institution and the day of the week on which King Bhumibol was born, Nattawut said that his group was inspired by social activist Sombat Bunngamanong, who suggested that the colour red was hot and that, like a traffic signal, it symbolized "stop" or "halt". It was therefore a fitting colour for the UDD's campaign for rejection of the military-sponsored charter in the referendum of August 2007. Coincidentally, leftist movements around the globe mostly preferred red for use in their political campaigns. "It is an irony; we had no idea about colour code, even wearing yellow like the PAD at the beginning", Nattawut said in his interview with the author. He could not be regarded as an anti-monarchist, and he was very cautious when spoke about the monarchy. "I make it clear that we fight for democracy with the monarch as the head of state", he stressed, "nothing else".[50]

The Red Shirts' struggle was disturbing for many Bangkokians, but it remained relatively peaceful in 2007 and 2008. It became tense, tough and bloody in April 2009, however. This was a time known among Red Shirts as *songkran lueat* or Bloody Songkran—in a reference to the Thai water festival held in that month—because of the military's heavy-handedness in confronting protests against Abhisit's government.[51] A series of violent events erupted after protesters stormed the facilities hosting the ASEAN and East Asia Summits in Pattaya on 11 April following a clash outside the meeting venue with the pro-government "blue shirt" group organized by Newin. The next day, after the declaration of a state of emergency, Red Shirt protesters attacked Prime Minister Abhisit's car, severely injuring his secretary, Niphon Promphan, in the compound of the Ministry of Interior in Bangkok. The military took fierce action in the early hours of Songkran Day, 13 April, with troops from the 2nd Infantry Division Eastern Tigers dispersing protesters in the Din Daeng quarter of Bangkok. They turned weapons of war with live ammunition directly on the desperate protesters. The shooting caused many casualties and resulted in the end of the protest, but not of the crusade. The Red Shirt movement retreated and took a break for several months before launching another major battle the following year.

It is important to note here that on 17 April 2009 Yellow Shirt leader Sondhi was seriously injured in an attack featuring weapons of war on Samsen Road—a few kilometres from his office in Bang Lamphu. While the investigation offered no clues to enable prosecution of any culprits, Sondhi openly blamed influential figures in the military, rather than his enemy Thaksin or the Red Shirts, for this assassination attempt.[52]

The second episode in the Red Shirts' battle kicked off at the beginning of 2010, after the court ruled Thaksin guilty of malfeasance and confiscated 46 billion baht of his assets in February. While Thaksin's role and support from Phuea Thai—the third incarnation of the Thai Rak Thai Party—could not be ruled out, the struggle had nothing directly to do with the former prime minister's legal cases. Instead, throughout two months of demonstrations, the protesters demanded the dissolution of parliament and the holding of fresh elections. They clearly tried to distance themselves from Thaksin and the party and to stand firmly on their own feet, rejecting the government's allegation that Thaksin had hired them.

In March 2010, Red Shirt protesters launched marches in the capital, visiting the defence ministry, Army headquarters and notably the 11th Infantry Regiment, where the government's officials and the top brass had their war room. The protesters came from various parts of the country, though mostly from Northern and Northeastern provinces. They occupied two major locations: first Ratchadamnoen Road at the Phan Fa Bridge and later the business district of Ratchaprasong. These locations became battle grounds for urban guerrilla warfare until a series of major crackdowns completely dispersed protesters remaining at the second site on 19 May 2010; the Red Shirts had moved away from the first site in late April.

On the government side, Deputy Prime Minister Suthep was in charge, commanding the operation with the clear intention of removing Red Shirt protesters by all possible means. Army chief Anupong and his deputy Prayut oversaw the removal, with troops drawn mostly from units under the command of members of the Eastern Tigers clique. The mid-year—and mid-struggle—reshuffle at the beginning of April saw General Thanin Ketthat demoted from the post of Army deputy chief of staff responsible for logistics because of his reluctance to fight the Red Shirts. Prayut's close friend, General Chatchai Salikanya, was elevated from deputy comptroller general to replace Thanin as the deputy chief of staff to oversee the task.

As the situation was tense, Prime Minister Abhisit declared a state of emergency in Bangkok on 7 April, empowering the military to use force to remove the protesters. A brief clash took place on 9 April. After the signal for broadcasts from the protest sites was cut off, protesters put pressure on the operators of the Thaicom satellite to allow them to resume uploading that signal. General Apirat Kongsompong—then commander of the 11th Infantry Regiment, a unit under the 1st Division King's Guard—was assigned to take charge at the station. He failed as he was barricaded inside the Thaicom earth station by angry protesters for the whole night. "I did not want to embarrass the future army chief. I then did not know who the commander there was. I just wanted to have our television on air", said Nattawut, who went to the scene later to ease the standoff.[53]

The most dramatic incident during the operation to quash the 2010 protests took place on the evening of 10 April when troops from the 2nd Infantry Division in Prachinburi—home of the Eastern Tigers clique—under the command of General Walit Rojanapakdi, together with the unit's deputy chief of staff, Colonel Romklao Thuvatham, were attacked with M67 and M79 grenades in front of Satriwitthaya School on Ratchadamnoen Road. Four soldiers, including Romklao, died instantly, and Walit was seriously injured. The government blamed well-trained "men in black" for the deadly attack, but an investigation and a subsequent trial indicated that there was no solid evidence to pinpoint the identity of the attackers. The military suspected that either Thaksin loyalists or military rivals of the Eastern Tigers may have been behind the attack. Major General Khattiya Sawasdipol, an Army officer serving in an inactive post as one with "special qualifications", was a prime suspect; the authorities believed that he trained Red Shirt security guards and had placed men with expertise in launching M79 grenades at the protest. There was no proof for this theory, but Khattiya—better known as Se Daeng or "Staff Officer Red"—was shot dead on 13 May, apparently by a sniper, at Bangkok's Sala Daeng Intersection a week before the final crackdown on the Red Shirts.

Romklao was posthumously granted the rank of four-star general. Queen Sirikit presided over his royal bathing rite on 12 April 2010, and then Crown Prince Vajiralongkorn as well as senior officials of the military and government accompanied her to that ceremony at Wat Thepsirintharawat. As a senior military officer, Khattiya was eligible for a royally sponsored cremation at Wat Sommanat Rajavaravihara, but his rites saw no special treatment from the palace. Those in attendance at his funeral were mostly Red Shirt protesters and leaders, rather than officials from the government or the military.

"I just simply knew that troops from Prachinburi were assigned to disperse us from Ratchadamnoen Road on that day, but I had no idea who their commanders were or which factions of the military they were from", Nattawut recalled. "It was Korbsak Sabhavasu, who was then secretary to Prime Minister Abhisit, who called me saying that the future Army chief was shot dead. I replied to him that I did not know that but, for our part, a number of unarmed protesters died. I just begged the military to stop the operation."[54]

Nattawut did not regard Khattiya as part of the Red Shirt leadership. The maverick general did not train Red Shirt security guards for armed struggle. During the protests, he always appeared in his combat uniform, walking around the protest site, greeting protesters, giving them moral support and having meals with them sometimes, according to Nattawut. "He was not involved in any security arrangement, which was mostly managed by protesters from Isan. Some of them might have been ex-soldiers, but not professional ones in service."[55]

Khattiya told a few journalists, including this author, over a private dinner a week or so before his death that he sided with the Red Shirt because he wanted to lead the "people's army" to fight against the government. He obviously disagreed with the Red Shirt leaders, as he said that their leadership was too weak for times of war. He urged them to step down so that he and other aggressive figures could take control.

Nattawut said that he had obtained inside information from military officers whom he called *thahan taengmo*—"watermelon soldiers", a metaphor for those who look green outside but are red on the inside—that enabled him to know the military's movements. But he had not obtained any military assistance for the protesters in their armed struggle with the government.

Nattawut's wife, Sirisakul Saikua, has strong connections with Suthep, as her father was a committed supporter of the Democrats in Surat Thani, and more importantly with Anupong, who was her classmate at the National Institute of Development Administration. "But such connections meant nothing for the political protests. Suthep had my father-in-law call me to tell me to dissolve the protests, but I refused. And I told my wife when I was jailed after the crackdown not to ask for any favours or assistance from Anupong", Nattawut said.[56]

It is worth highlighting that Army chief Anupong chose to respond to the Yellow and Red Shirt protests differently and that his sense of respect for the monarchy accounted for the difference. He was reluctant to take any actions against the royalist Yellow Shirt protest during Samak's and Somchai's premierships in 2008. But the Army under his leadership did not hesitate in 2009–10 to launch a brutal crackdown on Red Shirt protesters, who were believed to be anti-monarchist. Under the authority of the same emergency law that Anupong had been instructed to implement in 2008, the 2009–10 crackdown on the Red Shirts killed nearly 100 people, including security officials, and injured more than 2,000. The war-like operations took place in the heart of the Thai capital and even at the Buddhist sanctuary of Wat Pathumwanaram—where six people, including volunteer nurses Kamonket Akkhahad and Akkharadet Khankaew, were shot dead while working to save the lives of protesters.

Reports prepared by the courts, government officials, participants in so-called independent inquiries, and international and domestic human rights defenders indicated that weapons of war, apparently fired by soldiers in the areas concerned, killed most of those who lost their lives in the events of April and May 2010. But no military officers took responsibility for these casualties. The government-sponsored Truth for Reconciliation Commission of Thailand, chaired by the eminent law professor and former attorney general Kanit Na Nakorn, reported that the Red Shirt protests had been relatively peaceful until 10 April 2010. On that evening, men in black attacked government troops, and protesters bent on provocation were likely to have resorted to violence while resisting efforts to flush them out. Violence committed between April and May 2010 caused 92 deaths and more than 1,500 injuries, according to the commission's report.[57] The governments of Abhisit and Yingluck Shinawatra allocated 32 and 45 million baht in August 2010 and December 2011, respectively, to the commission in support of its mission to find out the truth about those events. But the commission failed to arrive at credible conclusions, let alone to determine who was responsible for what had happened. In contrast, a fact-finding report on the crackdowns of April–May 2010 compiled by the People's Information Centre indicated that Prime Minister Abhisit's military-backed government used excessive force against the relatively peaceful Red Shirt protesters. It had ordered a total of 50,000 troops to the capital and used over 100,000 bullets, of which 2,000 were fired by marksmen in tactics resembling ambushes. These tactics resulted in 94 deaths, including those of 10 government officials, 76 ordinary citizens, 6 first aid volunteers and 2 journalists.[58] The protesters themselves were unarmed, or as video footage from local and international media showed, carried only slingshots, firecrackers, large fireworks, bottle bombs made from energy drink bottles, and pieces of wood. "No weapons were found anywhere near the corpses of the protesters and until now [2017], no trace of gunpowder has been found on the hands of any protesters."[59]

From the military's point of view, the crackdown on the Red Shirts was not a normal anti-riot operation but rather a war against "terrorists" who were a threat to the monarchy, the key pillar of national security. Red Shirt leaders and their sympathizers were accused of plotting a conspiracy to overthrow the crown. In April 2010, the Centre for Resolution of Emergency Situation (CRES), which oversaw the operation against the protesters, released a chart showing the connections among a vast number of people working to *lom chao* or topple the monarchy. It purported to reveal a network of people including former Prime Minister Thaksin; Red Shirt leaders like Nattawut; billionaire activist Thanathorn Juangroongruangkit, who would almost a decade later found the Future Forward Party; the eminent historian Somsak Jeamteerasakul, who would go into exile after the 2014 coup; and the revered scholar Sutthachai Yimprasert, who would pass away when Thailand was again under military rule in 2017. Later, CRES spokesman Lieutenant General Sansern Kaewkamnerd told the court after being sued for defamation by Sutthachai that CRES had released the chart to prove the existence of a movement to overthrow the monarchy. The Red Shirts had accused Queen Sirikit's secretary, Thanphuying Jarungjit Thikara, of making phone calls to give instructions to the CRES. This suggested the role of monarchy in the crackdown. In retaliation, Sansern made up the chart, and it was released in order to turn the tables—by incriminating as members of a movement seeking to topple the monarchy those who had spread the rumour about Jarungjit's activities.[60]

There was indeed ultimately no proof of the accuracy of the chart or of its allegation of a wide-ranging conspiracy, as the two sides agreed to settle the case out of court. Sansern backed off that allegation, refusing to confirm whether the persons in question had committed any actions to undermine the royal institution. Sansern thus not only confirmed the Red Shirt discourse that the military had used the smear of *lom chao* to legitimize its crackdown but also indicated some extent of palace involvement in the battle. Queen Sirikit's presence at the funeral of the Yellow Shirt protester killed in 2008 and of the Queen's Guard colonel killed in 2010 had told the story. Red Shirt leader Jatuporn said in April 2011, during a gathering to mark the first anniversary of the crackdown, that using soldiers from King's Guard and Queen's Guard units to kill protesting Red Shirts was equivalent to "granting royal bullets" to the people. "It's really painful for us; we the Red Shirts are just normal *phrai* who did nothing against the nation's parents [the monarchy]. It happened only in this country, killing children to protect the parents", he said on the stage in front of thousands of Red Shirts. Two days later, the military filed a lawsuit against Jatuporn, but the case was dropped a year later, after a Phuea Thai Party government came to power.[61]

Mission Accomplished

The defeat of Red Shirt protesters in the urban battles of 2010 was a tremendous victory for the military, one that paved the rosy way for the Eastern Tigers/Queen's Guard clique to fully dominate the army. Anupong left office in October of that year, having his favourite, Prayut, replace him as Army chief. Daopong Rattanasuwan, a key man in the May crackdown, became Army chief of staff. The promotion of Daopong was regarded as an act of reconciliation between military factions. He had been a close friend of Prayut's since they were AFAPS Class 12 classmates, but he was also a member of the competing *Wongthewan* clique as he had served in the 1st Division when he began his career. Prayut was secure in the top position of the Army; his close friend would not pose any threat to him. In addition, other politically influential posts went to Eastern Tigers. Udomdej Sitabutr became the commander of the 1st Army Region, replacing Kanit; the latter was demoted to the post of Army special adviser for his hesitation in dispersing the Red Shirt protest. Theerachai Nakwanich became the commander of the 1st Army Corps, and General Vilas Arunsri an assistant to the Army chief of staff. Another Queen's Guard officer, General Thanasak Patimapakorn, received a promotion from chief adviser to the Armed Forces Headquarters to the chief of staff of the Thai Armed Forces. He was a unique queen's man, as he served her outside the 21st Infantry Regiment but was close to his AFAPS classmate Prayut. Nepotism also was in play this time around, with Prayut's younger brother, Preecha, being promoted from the post of 3rd Army Corps chief of staff to deputy commander of the 3rd Army Region.

Prayut spent his first six months as Army commander moving to inactive positions hundreds of troops or watermelon soldiers who expressed obvious sympathy for the Red Shirts. He also announced the dissolution of factions in the Army for the sake of unity. The 2011 mid-year military reshuffle saw Kanit being kicked out of the Army to become a specially qualified officer in the Office of the Permanent Secretary of the Ministry of Defence. The shake-up also rewarded Walit, elevating him from the post of commander of the 2nd Infantry Division Eastern Tiger to that of deputy commander of the 1st Army Region. He was supposed to have received this promotion sooner, but it was delayed because of the severe injuries that he had suffered during the clash at Satriwitthaya School more than a year earlier. Walit was replaced by General Pisit Sitthisan, who had previously been the deputy commander of the 1st Division King's Guard. The latter promotion indicated the seriousness of Prayut's intention to end the rift between the two rival factions in the Thai Army so that soldiers could serve in any unit that their bosses deemed appropriate and necessary. Just as Queen's Guard officers can command King's Guard units, so those who considered themselves born to be King's Guard can also lead Queen's Guard/Eastern Tigers units.

While it was not clear who the so-called watermelon soldiers in the Army were exactly and whether such tactics to unite the armed forces would really work, Prayut's position and hold on power appeared secure and firm. The victory of the hard-to-defeat Phuea Thai Party in the general elections of 3 July 2011 presented the Army commander with a big challenge. The polls resulted in Thaksin's sister Yingluck

Shinawatra becoming Prayut's notional boss in her capacity as prime minister and later also minister of defence.

While attractive populist policies, a strong political base and skilful electoral management figured importantly in Phuea Thai's and Yingluck's success, the brutal 2010 crackdown on the Red Shirt protest was a major political mistake for the Democrat Party. It helped cause the party's failure in the 2011 polls, notably on the home turf of the Red Shirts in the North and Northeast.

The main theme in Yingluck's election campaign was *kaekhai mai kaekhaen*, or "to solve, not to take revenge". But, once in office, the new premier faced a dilemma: how to reconcile with the men in green while seeking justice and compensation for those who had lost their lives and sustained injuries in the April–May 2010 crackdown? On top of this, her brother Thaksin wanted to return home from self-imposed exile with the honour of a winner—a wish that could ignite fierce resistance from the establishment.

It was not easy for a female politician to take charge in a patriarchal society like Thailand's. Commanding the military, which apparently stood on the side opposing Yingluck's government in the country's great political divide, presented a particular difficulty. The new prime minister's educational background and previous business career would not be of much help. She had earned a bachelor's degree in political science and public administration from Chiangmai University and a master's degree in management information systems from Kentucky State University before beginning a business career in companies in which her family held major stakes. Being one of Thaksin's sisters was a handicap for her in her dealings with the military, whose leadership was comprised mostly of foes and not friends of her brother.

During the first year of her administration, two retired military officers, General Yutthasak Sasiprapa and Air Chief Marshal Sukampol Suwannathat, served the female premier as minister of defence. Yutthasak was a former *Wongthewan* officer and permanent secretary of defence during General Chavalit Yongchaiyudh's government in the late 1990s. He was in the ministerial position for six months, from August 2011 to January 2012, with the clear mission of helping Yingluck cope with military resistance. But he failed to restore Thaksin's connections in the military. Two factors contributed to his failure. First, the 2008 Defence Administration Act tied the hands of civilian governments by preventing them from intervening in military reshuffles. Second,

Thaksin loyalists were all in inactive posts, sitting in waiting for their retirement in a year's time. The 2011 reshuffle was in the hands of incumbent commanders who had relative freedom to pick their own men. It saw Queen's Guard Thanasak become the chief of defence forces, Daopong being elevated from Army chief of staff to Army deputy commander, Chatchai being moved from assistant chief of staff to deputy chief of staff of the Army, and Theerachai being promoted from commander of the 1st Army Corps to become an assistant chief of staff of the Army.

Sukampol served as defence minister from January 2012 to June 2013. He was unable to do any better than Yutthasak, given that he was Thaksin's AFAPS Class 10 classmate and a relative of the former premier's close friend Prin, who was then serving as the defence minister's chief of staff. While Sukampol did his best to please the top brass in the armed forces, a 2012 reshuffle within his office at the defence ministry backfired for him. It saw a disagreement between the minister and incumbent permanent secretary General Sathien Permthongin over the choice of the latter's successor. Sathien favoured his deputy, General Chatree Thatti; Sukampol preferred General Thanongsak Apirakyothin, who had been serving as an assistant to the Army chief. The minister managed to install his preferred candidate and to move Sathien to an inactive post within the ministry. But Sathien and Chatree fought back by lodging a petition with Privy Council President Prem and with the Administrative Court—a judicial branch authorized to rule on contentious issues and complaints against state agencies. They accused Sukampol of intervening in the reshuffle and of unfair treatment. The court ruled in favour of the minister in the case of Sathien, but it blocked Chatree's transfer to an inactive post.

This dispute between the minister and the permanent secretary did not affect other aspects of the shake-up in the armed forces, most notably in the Army. Prayut reinforced his secure position as Army chief and saw to the elevation of his favourites. Udomdej moved from 1st Army Region commander to Army chief of staff, Theerachai from Army assistant chief of staff to deputy chief of staff, Walit from deputy commander of the 1st Army Region to Army assistant chief of staff, and Prayut's brother Preecha from 3rd Army Region deputy commander to 3rd Army Corps commander.

After two years in office, Yingluck felt more confident in her ability and political support. She made herself defence minister in a cabinet reshuffle in June 2013 and formed her own team for security and military affairs. She made Yutthasak, himself previously the minister, her deputy minister to help screen routine work and to mentor her in security matters as he was senior to and more welcoming than Sukampol or many other Thaksin loyalists. While Prin's brother, Lieutenant General Phanluek Suwannathat, had been assigned as the prime minister's close aide in 2012, Yingluck kept her distance from the influence of AFAPS Class 10 and Thaksin's network. She picked the former commander of the 4th Army Region, General Kwanchart Klahan, a member of AFAPS Class 8, as the defence minister's secretary. Her advisers were former commanders of the 3rd and 4th Army Regions, respectively, Generals Jiradej Kotcharat and Pisarn Wattawongkiri. Both were members of AFAPS Class 9.

Like Samak, Yingluck employed a human touch in strengthening her personal ties to and winning support from the military's top brass. She demonstrated publicly that she highly respected Queen's Guard man Thanasak and apparently made Prayut her *de facto* adviser on security matters and military affairs. The prime minister and the Army commander were regularly seen in public together from the time of the major flooding in Central Thailand in 2011—which occurred soon after Yingluck took office—onward. She gave the commanders of the different branches of the armed forces a free hand in picking men to fill key positions. But the selection of General Nipat Thonglek, a Queen's Guard man, as permanent secretary of the Ministry of Defence in 2013 was Yingluck's own decision. It had been reported that outgoing permanent secretary Thanongsak and Army commander Prayut wanted General Jiradej Mookkasamit, an assistant to the latter, to take the position. He had only one remaining year in service, while Nipat was three years from retirement. But Yingluck, who also needed to convince her brother Thaksin, argued that Nipat was young and skilful and that he had a remarkable record in security affairs.[62] She prevailed, and in return Prayut secured the appointments of his favourite Eastern Tiger Udomdej as his deputy and of his close friend Chatchai as assistant to the Army chief. He also secured the promotion of Eastern Tiger Theerachai from Army deputy chief of staff to 1st Army Region commander.

Yingluck agreed to other appointments suggested by the incumbent commanders in 2013. She approved Admiral Narong Pipatthanasai as the Navy chief following the suggestion of Admiral Surasak Runroenrom, and Air Chief Marshal Pajin Juntong retained his position as the Air Force chief for another year.

With such arrangements in place, Yingluck believed that she had the full support of the military. In Nipat, she had another trusted man who was accepted by all senior commanders of the armed forces. Privy Council President and military godfather Prem was not obviously opposed to the humble Yingluck. He allowed her to lead all the top brass of the armed forces to his Sisao Theves residence to offer him birthday wishes in 2013 and accepted her invitations to many events.

With strong support from Nipat, Yingluck was confident in her capacity as prime minister and defence minister. She made the crucial decision in November 2013 to restructure the Royal Security Command and the King's Close Body Guard Command, moving them from the Armed Forces Headquarters to the jurisdiction of the Defence Ministry. To the military officers concerned, these were special units. One was an office with the military call code 904, and the other a combat-ready unit under the direct command of Crown Prince Vajiralongkorn as part of the Royal Security Command.[63] It was the duty of the 1st Infantry Division King's Guard to have its troops rotating to serve in the latter unit, to provide security for members of the monarchy. More importantly, the 1st Division had been the source of manpower for almost every successful military *coup d'état* in Thai history. Yingluck's decision could be interpreted in various ways. It could mean that she wanted to be able to control such a key unit. It could be understood to indicate that the palace had become close to her government and wanted to send a signal to the rest of the military. Or it could have been a straightforward bureaucratic adjustment relating to the allocation of budgetary resources. Nevertheless, such a restructuring would never happen without the consent of the palace and the entire armed forces. They would not have allowed Yingluck to implement this decision unless they were confident that real power and authority over the troops remained in their hands.[64]

Relations between the premier and the men in green meant nothing to the stability of the government. The military brass could turn on the politicians anytime they had an excuse to say that the crown was in danger. A series of street protests were ignited by Democrat Party deputy leader Suthep against an amnesty bill intended ultimately to bring Thaksin back home. While calling for street protests, the opposition Democrat Party boycotted the vote on the bill in the House of Representatives, resulting in the passing of the bill by 310 votes to none on the last day of October 2013. In response to Suthep's call, a huge number of people wearing whistles on ribbons in the colours of the national flag came out to demonstrate. When Yingluck had second thoughts and decided to drop the bill in the face of growing protests and of Suthep's determination to topple her government, it was too late.

Prayut did his part, asking permission from Defence Minister Yingluck in November to have thousands of troops provide security for the protesters. In the meantime, those protesters fanned out across the capital amid scenes of violence as unknown forces launched M-79 grenades at them. The Army chief moved armoured vehicles from the 2nd Infantry Regiment Eastern Tigers in Prachinburi to Bangkok on the pretext of planning to hold a parade on Military Day, 18 January, but he kept this hardware at the 11th Infantry Regiment in the capital for months afterwards. He weighed the pros and cons, and considered the legal consequences, of enforcing of martial law. He was also in contact with Suthep, who announced that he was leaving the Democrat Party and formed the People's Democratic Reform Committee (PDRC) in order to be able to coordinate the protests more effectively. Prayut and Suthep met from time to time at Prawit's residence within the compound of the 1st Infantry Regiment on Vipavadi Road in Bangkok. As the big brother of the Eastern Tigers, Prawit still lived in a residence on base—despite having retired and owning a home in Bangkok's Lat Phrao area. Officially, that residence was designated as the office of the *Munlanithi pa roito ha changwat*, or the Five Provinces Junction Forest Foundation. Former Army chief Anupong, who also had a residence on the same base, joined these meetings for situation assessments and planning.[65] Suthep and the triumvirate of officers were not strangers. They had worked as a dream team during Abhisit's 2008–11 administration. Their reunion in 2013 was meant to ensure that Thaksin was kept at bay when the kingdom was about to enter the critical transition period to a new reign: King Bhumibol was ageing, weak and ill.

Prior to his final decision to seize power, Prayut pretended to help all stakeholders to seek peaceful and lawful solutions to the crisis precipitated by the government's amnesty bill and the protests that it provoked. He invited his boss, Yingluck, to meet with protest leader Suthep on 1 December 2013 at the 1st Infantry Regiment

Headquarters. The meeting included Navy commander Narong and Air Force commander Pajin. These talks failed to reach an agreement as Suthep insisted on the transfer of power to his protest movement and to the establishment of a "people's assembly" to run the government.

The dissolution of the lower house of parliament on 9 December and the scheduling of snap elections for 2 February 2014 failed to stop the protest against Yingluck's government. The Democrats boycotted the elections, and protesters disrupted polling. The elections were later ruled by the court to be invalid, creating a political vacuum that enabled easy military intervention. "As the dissolution of parliament could not solve the dispute, experience told us that a military coup was inevitable", recalled Nattawut, a member of Yingluck's cabinet.[66]

As the drums of war were beaten in early May 2014, judicial activists on the Constitutional Court handed down a verdict against now caretaker Prime Minister Yingluck and nine members of her caretaker cabinet for having improperly removed Thawil Pliensri from the position of secretary general of the National Security Council three years earlier. This verdict forced Yingluck and the ministers to step down. But that was not the end of her legal ordeal, as an anti-graft body lodged a number of accusations against her, including corruption in her government's rice pledging scheme.

The caretaker government was then weaker than a lame duck, and Prayut assessed that the situation was ripe enough for a takeover. The Army chief imposed martial law in the early hours of 20 May 2014, pretentiously inviting all stakeholders—including government representatives and supporters as well as representatives of the opposition and of the protesters—to meet to seek solutions to the political impasse. Prayut announced the coup on 22 May, when representatives of the caretaker government refused to resign. Leading figures on both sides of the political divide were detained in military camps in the capital and in nearby provinces. While Suthep and his crew were happy with this turn of events, their opponents were held in detention for "attitude adjustment". Those summoned to report for such adjustment included members of Yingluck's government and Red Shirt leaders, as well as progressive intellectuals and activists. Dissidents were prosecuted in military courts.

Unlike General Sonthi in 2006, Prayut and the other leaders of the 2014 coup did not seek an immediate audience with King Bhumibol. They did not want to send the message that the palace connived in the putsch. The king and the queen had been staying at Klai Kangwon summer palace in Hua Hin, nearly 200 kilometres south of Bangkok, since King Bhumibol's discharge from Siriraj Hospital in August 2013. While Prayut tried to portray his action as one taken independently of the palace, his first statement to justify military intervention nevertheless needed to mention that the coup makers remained loyal to, vowed to glorify, and would protect the royal institution. "The monarchy stays above all conflicts", the new junta's first statement, dated 22 May 2014, stated. In fact, Prayut treated his coup like a routine procedure, notifying the palace in writing after the seizure of power. The king in return gave him his blessing on 26 May, formally appointing then Army chief Prayut as the chairman of the National Council for Peace and Order (NCPO) with full authority to rule the country. Prayut was granted an audience with the king two months later, when the monarch endorsed the junta's interim charter on 22 July 2014. Article 44 of the charter gave Prayut absolute power to issue orders. It also authorized him to perform, or refrain from performing, any act, regardless of whether the effect of such an act was legislative, executive or judicial. In this regard, all acts and actions in compliance with such orders of his were to be deemed lawful and constitutional. Prayut told an audience of 1,500 when he kicked off his reform roadmap on 9 August 2014 at the Army Convention Hall that it was the tradition that the sovereign authorized those who seized power to run the country, regardless of whether the monarch agreed or disagreed with such action. "I know I did the wrong thing, but I asked for and finally obtained royal forgiveness", he said, "but it does not mean that the monarch ordered me to do such a thing. The king knows better. How many years has he already been on the throne? He knows what a king should do and how. Otherwise, he cannot have been the king for such a long time. Please do not bring him down [to politics]."[67]

Prayut had his men and the military's top brass sit on the NCPO junta, in the cabinet, in the National Legislative Assembly and in important agencies. Eastern Tiger big brother Prawit was rewarded with the post of defence minister, with Udomdej as his deputy minister. Number two brother Anupong took the powerful interior ministry to oversee civilian administration throughout the country. Thanasak became deputy prime minister and foreign minister, Prajin transport minister, Chatchai commerce minister, Narong education minister,

Paiboon justice minister, Daopong natural resource and environment minister, Surasak labour minister, and former National Police chief Police General Adul Saengsingkaew minister of social development and human security.

The 2014 military reshuffle was a straightforward matter for Prayut, as there were no civilian politicians involved. The NCPO head demoted Nipat from the post of defence ministry permanent secretary to an inactive post as an adviser to the ministry, while at least having the mercy to select him as a member of the National Legislative Assembly. Army chief of staff General Sirichai Ditthakul replaced Nipat as permanent secretary. General Woraphong Sanganetr was elevated to replace Thanasak as the chief of defence forces. Justice Minister Paiboon retained his military position as deputy chief of the defence forces. Deputy Defence Minister Udomdej took the Army's top job as Prayut retired upon reaching the age of sixty. Udomdej also served as the secretary of the NCPO junta. Commerce minister Chatchai became Army deputy chief. Theerachai was promoted from commander of the 1st Army Region to an assistant Army chief. Prayut's brother, Preecha, was also elevated from the post of 3rd Army Region commander to become an assistant Army chief. Like Theerachai, the holder of that position could become a candidate for Army commander-in-chief in the future. Apirat stepped up from 1st Division commander to become deputy commander of the 1st Army Region. Admiral Kraison Chansuwanit was promoted to Navy chief from the position of assistant chief. Air Chief Marshal Treetod Sonjang was elevated from the post of Air Force chief of staff to that of Air Force commander-in-chief.[68]

The first Prayut government, one marked by extreme intolerance towards criticism from its opponents, remained in power for five years after the coup. Prayut and many of those close to him retained power after Thailand's March 2019 elections. His government steered Thailand through a transition period, as King Bhumibol passed away on 13 October 2016 and Prem served as regent until the Crown Prince Vajiralongkorn ascended the throne to become Rama X on 1 December 2016.

The NCPO and organs of its creation—including the National Legislative Assembly, the Charter Drafting Committee, the Reform Committee and Prayut's government—used all means to construct a system of governance to empower the crown and uphold royal supremacy. The palace apparently intervened in the process, making changes in sections of the military-sponsored 2017 Constitution concerning royal prerogatives even after it had already been approved by referendum. Of 50 million eligible voters, 16.8 million voted to accept the constitution on 7 August 2016, after the 2014 coup scrapped the previous supreme law of the land. Prior to the promulgation of the new charter, it was reported that the palace had indicated some reservations and asked the government to make changes to the document accordingly. Thais realized that various sections of the constitution on which they had expressed their will had been changed only when it was published in the *Royal Gazette* after its royal endorsement on 6 April 2017.[69] Key changes were evident in Sections 5, 16, 17, 18 and 182; these changes gave the monarchy more liberty in palace administration and the freedom to engage in political manoeuvring.

Section 5 was particularly controversial as it was widely believed that the drafters of the charter wanted to empower the heads of the Constitutional Court, the Supreme Court, the Supreme Administrative Court, the Senate, and the House of Representatives along with the prime minister, the leaders of the opposition and the heads of independent agencies to make decisions in joint meetings for crisis management in cases where no provision of the charter could be applied. The palace asked that the section be revised to match the text of Section 7 of the 1997 Constitution, which pro-Yellow Shirt and royalist intellectuals had interpreted during the 2005–6 protests against Thaksin as enshrining a royal prerogative to intervene in politics.

As a result of its amendment in accordance with the king's request, Section 5 of the 2017 charter read, "whenever no provision under this Constitution is applicable to any case, it shall be decided in accordance with the constitutional convention in the democratic regime of government with the King as Head of State." Such ambiguity could be useful for the monarchy in the future if the political situation allowed intervention.

Sections 16, 17 and 18 concerned the king's freedom to decide whether or not to appoint a regent when he was absent from the kingdom or unable to perform his functions. The version of the charter on which Thais voted in the 2016 referendum made clear that the king must appoint a regent to perform his duties whenever he was absent or unable to perform those duties. After revision, however, that provision was removed.

Some clauses of Section 182 of the version of the charter approved in the referendum were also cut so that the charter now read, "all laws, royal rescripts and royal commands relating to the state affairs must be countersigned by a minister unless otherwise provided in the Constitution." In practice, many royal commands, particularly those concerning palace administration or royal personnel, issued during the new reign required no countersignature from any government official.

The amendment of the constitution after the referendum violated both the people's will and the principle of constitutional monarchy. Thai constitutional convention, as established since the 1932 revolution, did not authorize the monarch to amend or order an amendment of a constitution or a drafted charter. Legally speaking, such amendment was even a violation of the junta's own provisional charter of 2014, which authorized the king merely to endorse or not to endorse the drafted permanent charter. But Prayut's government amended its own provisional constitution to legitimize the king's move. The fourth amendment of the 2014 charter was announced on 15 January 2017—nearly five months after the 7 August 2016 referendum. Section 4 of this amendment rewrote Section 39/1 of the 2014 charter to say that, if the king stated any reservations with the text of the drafted constitution within 90 days after its submission, the premier must amend the draft accordingly and resubmit it for royal endorsement within 30 days.[70] In other words, the military-backed government elevated the monarchy to sovereign above, not under, the constitution.

****

In conclusion, while the 2006 coup launched by General Sonthi might not have been able to sustain the resultant junta in power for a long time, that intervention did secure military power. It also revealed the role of the royal institution in Thailand's ongoing political conflict and the ties between the royal and military institutions. The monarchy stepped to the front in the battle against any movement that could be regarded as anti-monarchist or looked like threats to the royal institution, even without any proof.

After the 2006 coup, the military fell under the control of the clique known as the Eastern Tigers, which apparently had personal links with members of the royal family. That clique managed to dominate the Army and to manipulate politics. It did so by all means, including the use of violence in 2009–10 to prevent their opponents from gaining access to power—perhaps not only during the transition period of royal succession, but also in the long run.

Developments between 2008 and 2014 made clear in both the public and political spheres that the Thai military belonged, as the late Prem Tinsulanonda said in 2006, to the monarchy, and not to any elected government that came to power with the people's mandate. The military chose to stand with governments or political movements that it deemed loyal to the revered royal institution. The military protected the Yellow Shirt movement as its members claimed they fought for the monarchy and proved that they had close connections with the palace. The armed forces hesitated to flush out Yellow Shirt protesters when ordered to do so by a government that the country's military leadership disliked. But they were not reluctant to turn their guns on the Red Shirts, as they believed the movement was not favoured by the palace. At the same time, the military took the side of the conservative Democrat Party, both when it was in office and when it organized street protests against the Yingluck government, because the military and the party shared enmity towards Thaksin and the Red Shirts.

For the establishment elite, the 2014 coup was inevitable. It served to secure and to nurture royal supremacy and a hierarchical regime. Prayut therefore sought to stay in office without elections for as long as possible after May 2014. The NCPO junta used almost five years to design and install a regime to weaken egalitarian forces while at the same time empowering the royal institution.

NOTES

1. Interview with General Sonthi Boonyaratglin, former Army chief and leader of the September 2006 coup, Bangkok, 18 December 2019.
2. Prime Ministerial Order 66/2523, issued in 1980 just months after General Prem assumed the premiership, changed the policy to defeat the Communist Party of Thailand to one centred on political means rather on military force alone. Communist insurgents consequently began to feel comfortable laying down their arms. But they lived in fear of punishment until 1989, when Prime Minister Chatichai Choonhavan granted them amnesty. See "Phraratchabanyat nirathotsakam kae phukrathamkan anpen khwamphit to khwammankhong khong rat phainai ratcha-ananachak tam pramuankotmai

aya lae khwamphit tam kotmai waduai kanpongkan kankratham anpen khommionit pho so 2532" [The 1989 amnesty law on national security offenders in accordance with the Penal Code and Anti-Communist Law], *Royal Gazette*, vol. 106, Section 142, Special Edition, 30 August 1989 http://www.ratchakitcha.soc.go.th/DATA/PDF/2532/A/142/4.PDF (accessed 22 June 2020).

3. Interview with General Sonthi.
4. Ibid.
5. Ibid.
6. Ibid.
7. Khamnoon Sitthisamarn, *Prakottakan Sondhi chak suea lueang thueng pha phan kho si fa* [The Sondhi phenomenon: From yellow shirt to blue scarf] (Bangkok: Ban Phra Athit Publishing, 2006), pp. 54–55.
8. Ibid, p. 236.
9. "Banthuekwai pen prawattisat nai luang ratchakan thi kao naeothang kae wikrit kanmueang chat" [The historical record of Rama IX's resolution of national crises], *Matichon sutsapda*, 16 October 2016.
10. As spelled in Thai, the given names of Sonthi Boonyaratglin and Sondhi Limthongkul are identical.
11. Interview with General Sonthi.
12. Khamnoon, *Prakottakan Sondhi*, pp. 275–81.
13. Interview with General Sonthi.
14. "'Thoni' chae ro bo ho pi 49 sue ang wali 'wang mai ao'-phoei phaen su Sonthi-rap phlat nirathot thukchong yuet amnat samsong" ["Tony" discloses 2006 coup details, media told "palace doesn't want him", unveils a plan to fight back against Sonthi, admits mistake on the amnesty bill, used for second coup], *Voice Online*, 14 September 2021, https://www.voicetv.co.th/read/qd0c-b0wz?fbclid=IwAR2hhtkUWpTnOxI06_MiOdwNal6thQ_-X8KpW6GTRyuq7ZBfB5gKq0IhLv4 (accessed 24 September 2021). "Tony Woodsome" is the name that Thaksin uses on ClubHouse.
15. Federico Ferrara, "Unfinished Business: The Contagion of Conflict over a Century of Thai Political Development", in *Good Coup Gone Bad: Thailand's Political Development since Thaksin's Downfall*, edited by Pavin Chachavalpongpun (Singapore: Institute of Southeast Asian Studies, 2014), p. 32.
16. Interview with General Sonthi.
17. Duncan McCargo and Ukrist Pathmanand, *The Thaksinization of Thailand* (Copenhagen: NIAS Press, 2005), pp. 121–65.
18. Paul Chambers, "A Short History of Military Influence in Thailand", in *Knights of the Realm: Thailand's Military and Politics, Then and Now*, edited by Paul Chambers (Bangkok: White Lotus, 2013), p. 267.

19. Thanapol Eawsakul, "Kae roi phanthamit prachachon phuea prachathippatai phu ok batchoen hai khanaratthprahan" [Tracing the People's Alliance for Democracy, the folks who extended an invitation to the coup makers], in *Ratthaprahan 19 kanyayon* [The 19 September coup], edited by Thanapol Eawsakul (Bangkok: Fadiaokan, 2007), p. 313.

20. In Thai, that post is *phubanchakan thahan sungsut*, formerly translated as "Supreme Commander".

21. Chambers, "A Short History of Military Influence in Thailand", pp. 262–63.

22. Ibid, p. 275.

23. Interview with General Sonthi, on which the rest of this paragraph also draws.

24. Laura Southgate "The Enduring Influence of Prem Tinsulanonda", *Global Risk Insights*, 1 February 2017, https://globalriskinsights.com/2017/02/asian-power-broker-series-the-enduring-influence-of-prem-tinsulanonda/ (accessed 24 September 2021), and Grant Peck, "Former Thai Prime Minister Prem Tinsulanonda Dies at 98", *Associated Press*, 27 May 2019, https://apnews.com/article/4e5193aa780e4b32ae34966f647f2fc5 (accessed 24 September 2021).

25. "Prem pat bueanglang patiwat-mai dai nam 'pho o Sonthi' khaofao" [Prem brushes off being behind the 2019 coup, never lead General Sonthi to see the king], *Prachatai*, 30 March 2009, https://prachatai.com/journal/2009/03/20540 (accessed 24 September 2021).

26. Sulak Sivaraksa, "Sathaban kasat kap ratthathammanun" [The royal institution and constitutions], in *Ratthaprahan 19 kanyayon* [The 19 September coup], edited by Thanapol Eawsakul (Bangkok: Fadiaokan, 2007), p. 20.

27. Interview with General Sonthi.

28. Chambers, "A Short History of Military Influence in Thailand", p. 290.

29. Interview with General Sonthi.

30. Ibid.

31. Thak Chaloemtiarana, *Thailand: The Politics of Despotic Paternalism*, 2nd ed. (Ithaca, New York: Cornell Southeast Asia Program Publications, 2007), p. 210. While Thak indicates that the queen took the honorary position in 1952, sources such as Chambers, cited above, say that the queen became the honorary commander of the 21st Infantry Regiment in 1958. Chambers is probably correct, as Sarit assumed the premiership in 1958.

32. Wassana Nanuam, *Senthang phayak Prayut Chan-ocha* [A Tiger's Path: Prayut Chan-ocha] (Bangkok: Matichon Books, 2014), p. 71.

33. Chambers, "A Short History of Military Influence in Thailand", p. 215.

34. Wassana, *Senthang phayak*, p. 93.

35. Interview with Nattawut Saikua, Bangkok, 17 December 2019.

36. "Rough Road for Thailand's BRT-3 APC Purchase", *Defence Industry Daily*, 17 October 2007,(https://www.defenseindustrydaily.com/rough-road-for-thailands-btr-3-apc-purchase-04028/ (accessed 21 February 2020).

37. Interview with General Sonthi.

38. "Phraratchabanyat chat rabiap krasuang kalahom pho so 2551" [Defence Ministry Administration Act 2008], *Royal Gazette*, vol. 125, Section 26 *ko*, 1 February 2008, http://www.ratchakitcha.soc.go.th/DATA/PDF/2551/A/026/35.PDF (accessed 13 January 2020).

39. Puangthong R. Pawakapan, *State and Uncivil Society in Thailand at the Temple of Preah Vihear* (Singapore: Institute of Southeast Asian Studies, 2013), p. 63.

40. Interview with Nattawut.

41. Ibid.

42. Ian MacKinnon, "Thailand: State of Emergency Declared in Bangkok", *The Guardian*, 3 September 2008, https://www.theguardian.com/world/2008/sep/03/thailand (accessed 13 January 2020).

43. Chambers, "A Short History of Military Intervention in Thailand", p. 307.

44. "Khunying Pornthip fan thong san RDX prakop raboet kha nong Bo" [Khunying Pornthip confirms RDX substance killed Nong Bo], *Manager Online*, 13 October 2008, https://mgronline.com/crime/detail/9510000121393 (accessed 29 January 2020).

45. Interview with Nattawut.

46. Chalathip Thirasoonthrakul, "Thai Queen Attends Funeral of Anti-Govt Protester", Reuters, 13 October 2008, https://uk.reuters.com/article/thailand-protest/upadte-1-thai-queen-attends-funeral-of-anti-govt-protester-idUKBKK40018720081013 (accessed 13 January 2020).

47. "Rachini sadet ngansop nong Bo songchom dek di rak sathaban kasat" [Queen attends Nong Bo's funeral, praising her as a good girl who loved the monarchy], *Manager Online*, 13 October 2008, https://mgronline.com/daily/detail/9510000121836?fbclid=IwAR3mlIwvduav5C60e-oiXM3uNohPS-Nw1MWs3VMouV5FwHu6Lw-HwOUS4H0 (accessed 13 January 2020).

48. Wassana Nanuam, *Lap luang phrang phak sam kongthap tangsi suek sailueat cho po ro* [Secrets, deceit, camouflage part 3: armies of different colours and conflict among Chulachomklao royal military academy lineages], 10th ed. (Bangkok: Matichon Books, 2010), p. 292. It was widely believed among members of the Thai press corps that Suthep Thaugsuban rather than prospective Prime Minister Abhisit himself represented the Democrat Party at this meeting.

49. "Khuk song pi! Kaennam kharawan khon chon-liulo maeo thuean pitlom nechan [Two years in prison! For leaders of caravan of the poorThaksin lackeys for blockading *The Nation*], *Manager Online*, 30 November 2009, https://mgronline.com/crime/detail/9520000145332 (accessed 24 February 2020).

50. Interview with Nattawut.

51. On the events of April 2009, see Michael J. Montesano, "Four Thai Pathologies, Late 2009", in *Legitimacy Crisis in Thailand* [King Prajadhipok's Institute Year Book No. 5 (2008/09)], edited by Marc Askew (Chiang Mai: Silkworm Books, 2010), pp. 273–302.

52. "Ha wan lopsanghan 'Sondhi' mue puen loi nuan—phon ek chua rap ngan kha" [Five days after Sondhi assassination attempt, gunmen have made clean getaway—dirty general took on the job of murder], *Manager Online*, 22 April 2009, https://mgronline.com/crime/detail/9520000044877 (accessed 29 January 2020).

53. Interview with Nattawut.

54. Ibid.

55. Ibid.

56. Ibid.

57. "Raignan chapap sombun khanakammakan itsara truatsop lae khon ha khwamching phuea kanpgrongdong haeng chat karakadakhom 2553-karakadakhom 2555" [Complete report of the National Truth for Reconciliation Commission of Thailand, July 2010–July 2012], September 2012, p. 73, http://www.thaipublica.org/wp-content/uploads/2012/09/Final-Report-TRCT_17-9-12_2.pdf (accessed 4 January 2021).

58. Puangthong R Pawakapan, "Voice of the Victims: Truth for Justice", in *Truth for Justice: A Fact-Finding Report on the April–May 2010 Crackdowns in Thailand,* edited by Kwanravee Wangudom, 17 May 2017, pp. 5–6, http://www.pic2010.org/en-report/ (accessed 4 January 2021).

59. Ibid.

60. "Khosok so o cho yomrap taeng phang lomc hao phuea topto kansairai thanphuying Jarungjit" [CRESs spokesman admits fabrication of anti-monarchist chart to respond to allegations against Lady Jarungjit], *Prachatai*, 26 May 2011, https://prachatai.com/journal/2011/05/34974 (accessed 20 January 2020).

61. "'Khangkhok Tu' phon khadi min sathaban tham chai 'Bik Tu' yom dai rue mai" ["Toad Tu" *lèse majesté* case dismissed, is this acceptable to "Big Tu"?], *Manager Online*, 11 May 2012, https://mgronline.com/politics/detail/9550000058387 (accessed 20 January 2020).

62. "Yingluck khlia Thaksin, lueak Nipat nang palat kalahom" [Yingluck clears with Thaksin, chooses Nipat as defence ministry permanent secretary], *Thai rat*, 30 August 2013, https://www.thairath.co.th/content/366852 (accessed 22 January 2020).

63. "Pharatchabanyat chat rabiap ratchakan krasuang kalahom chabap thi song pho so 2556" [Ministry of Defence Organisation Act of 2013], *Royal Gazette*, vol. 130, Section 109 ko, 20 November 2013, p. 2, http://www.ratchakitcha.soc.go.th/DATA/PDF/2556/A/109/1.PDF (accessed 5 February 2020), p. 2.

64. Chapter 3 returns to this matter.
65. Wassana Nanuam, *Awasan Yingluck* [The end of Yingluck] (Bangkok: Matichon Books, 2014), pp. 272–75.
66. Interview with Nattawut.
67. "'Prayut' mop naeothang patirup prathet thai" ["Prayut" lays out reform guidelines for Thailand], *Krungthep thurakit*, 9 August 2014, (https://www.bangkokbiznews.com/news/detail/598041 (accessed 23 January 2020).
68. "Prakat samnak nayokratthamontri hai nai thahan rap ratchakan" [Announcement of prime minister's office on military reshuffle], *Royal Gazette*, vol. 131, Special Section 176 *ngo*, 8 September 2014, http://www.ratchakitcha.soc.go.th/DATA/PDF/2557/E/176/1.PDF (accessed 28 January 2020).
69. "Six Changes in Constitution", *Bangkok Post*, 6 April 2017, https://www.bangkokpost.com/thailand/general/1228183/six-sections-changed-in-constitution (accessed 4 February 2020).
70. "Ratthathammanun haengratcha-anachak thai chabap chuakhrao phuthasakkarat 2557 kaekhai phoemtoem chabap thi 4 (2560)" [Fourth amendment to the 2014 provisional constitution of the Kingdom of Thailand], *Royal Gazette*, vol. 134, Section 6 ko, 15 January 2017, http://www.ratchakitcha.soc.go.th/DATA/PDF/2560/A/006/1.PDF (accessed 4 January 2021).

3

A SOLDIER KING

The public image of Rama X of the Chakri Dynasty, who reigns as *Phrabat Somdet Maha Vajiralongkorn Phravajiraklaochaoyuhua*, has been projected as that of a career military man, a brave soldier and, later, a skilled jet fighter pilot. When King Vajiralongkorn ascended the throne on 1 December 2016, local media depicted the new sovereign as a military monarch, suggesting that the position he held under the constitution was not simply that of a ceremonial top commander but rather that of the "actual head of the Thai armed forces with resonances of the US President as Commander-in-Chief."[1]

On the occasion of the king's birthday in 2019, the year of his formal coronation, Thailand's sole national English-language newspaper, the *Bangkok Post*, presented the new monarch's military profile in its headline, "Head of State with the Heart of Gold; His Majesty the King has an Illustrious Military Background":

> When His Majesty King Maha Vajiralongkorn Phra Vajiraklaochaoyuhua ascended the throne, he became the head of state and the head of Royal Thai Armed Forces, as per the Constitution. Therefore, His Majesty the King gives precedence to royal missions which benefit Thailand and its people. He also gives various recommendations for the improvement and development of Thai troops.[2]

One of the king's trusted warlords, Army Commander-in-Chief General Apirat Kongsompong emphasized during a high-profile public lecture on 11 October 2019 that the monarchy had led the military in wars and battles throughout the nation's history to protect the kingdom. King Vajiralongkorn had, when he was the crown prince, fought shoulder to shoulder with brave soldiers on the battlefield, the general said.[3]

"The monarchy, military and people are inseparable. In the past, the king was on an elephant, surrounded by soldiers. Not only soldiers but also the people, men and women who volunteered and sacrificed in battle alongside the king to protect the land of the Thais", Apirat said during the rare public lecture. This speech explained the role of the monarchy and its asymmetrical relations with the military. While he did refer to the people, the general defined them as self-sacrificing, loyal subjects under the military, which played the role of protector in the hierarchical polity.

In the twenty-first century, Thailand has a modern military. The king does not need to mount an elephant to lead soldiers and peasants into battle anymore, but every constitution in the post-1932 era with the exception of the first, provisional one has specified the role of the monarch as the head of the armed forces. The 1949 Constitution, which first established the concept of a "democratic regime with the king as the head of state" even specifically mentioned that the king was also the commander in chief of all Thai soldiers. King Vajiralongkorn is in fact a trained soldier. He completed his secondary education at Millfield School in Somerset, England. In 1970, he attended a military training course at the King's School in Sydney, Australia. Two years later, he enrolled at the Royal Military College–Duntroon, in Canberra, Australia. Information about his education there differs a bit in various publicly available sources. Thai media reported that the curriculum of the college was divided into two parts: a military training course designed by the Australian armed forces and a bachelor's degree course under supervision of the University of New South Wales.[4] An unofficial biography published in Thailand in 2018 states that the king graduated with a bachelor of liberal arts degree in military studies from the University of New South Wales in 1976.[5] A work published to commemorate the 100th anniversary of the Chulachomklao Royal Military Academy simply mentioned that the then crown prince had graduated with an excellent performance from the Duntroon military college before bringing his educational success back to Thailand.[6]

Whatever the case, it is said that the king certainly received military training before returning to the country in 1976.

During his subsequent military career, the king also attended courses at Thailand's Command and General Staff College in 1977–78 and the National Defence College of Thailand in 1990. His military training was enhanced with participation in programmes in conventional warfare in the United States, the United Kingdom and Australia.[7] The commemorative publication on the military academy highlights the fact that the then crown prince undertook the year-long course at the Command and General Staff College, a serious and tough training programme, to prepare to become the future leader of the armed forces and a master of the modern science of war. "With his diligence and talent, His Royal Highness was ranked second in his class in the final examination for graduation from the college", according to the book, which did not mention who received the top score in the class.[8]

It is pointless to try to find out whether the king in fact did well at school or whether he graduated from an institution of higher education and completed a tough training course. The reality must be stated. Nobody needs a degree to apply for the position of monarch. Having become king, he can, regardless of the means, also make his offspring and loyal subjects anything that he wishes them to be. It was not abnormal in the Kingdom of Siam for princes or princesses to be soldiers, but many of their military roles were ceremonial as they neither functioned in service nor commanded any units. King Vajiralongkorn was initially made a military officer for the sake of his pride, when his father King Bhumibol granted him the rank of sub-lieutenant in 1965. He was then 13 years old, an age at which he could have been deemed a child soldier, according to the Protocol to the United Nations Convention on the Rights of the Child on the involvement of children in armed conflict. He was named special officer in the 1st Infantry Regiment Royal Guard, the Royal Thai Navy and the Air Force Academy. He was promoted to the rank of first lieutenant in the Army, lieutenant junior grade in the Navy, and flying officer in the Air Force in 1971. However, these ranks were granted in order to fulfil and give honour to the crown prince and heir apparent to the throne, a title bestowed on him on 28 December 1972.

King Vajiralongkorn actually performed his dual roles as crown prince and active-duty military officer upon returning from his education overseas. He served as an officer in the Royal Thai Armed Forces

Headquarters, then known as the Directorate of Intelligence of the Supreme Command, in 1976. He was posted as deputy commander of the *kong thahan mahatlek*, or royal guard contingent, of the Bangkok-based 1st Infantry Regiment in 1978, before moving up to serve as the commander of the unit two years later. He assumed command of the Royal Guard Regiment in 1984, of the Royal Guard Command in 1988 and of the Royal Security Command, a unit then under the Supreme Command, in 1992. In June 1991, the crown prince—by then a lieutenant general—was commissioned as a special officer in the 2nd, 12th, 21st and 31st Infantry Regiments, the 4th Cavalry Squadron, 1st Artillery Regiment and 1st Engineering Battalion.[9] While holding the rank of colonel, he had already been named a special commander of the 1st Special Regiment of the 1st Special Forces Division of the Lopburi-based Special Forces Command in 1986.[10] A retired military officer said on condition of anonymity that the then crown prince held an actual command position only in the Royal Guard Command, while the positions of special officer or special commander were honorary.[11]

The Prince in Action

King Vajiralongkorn gained experience on the battlefield in November 1976, during Thailand's anti-communist war. This experience was highlighted occasionally by the military for propaganda purposes when the king was still crown prince. Army chief Apirat and media publications also highlighted it when he was crowned king. The Communist Party of Thailand (CPT) took up weapons against Thai authorities in early August 1965, but 1976 was the peak year of the armed conflict between the party and the Thai state. A rightist political offensive and the military's crackdown on and massacre of students in Thammasat University on 6 October 1976 forced thousands of leftist and radical students to join the guerrillas in the jungle. The palace considered the communist insurgency the most dangerous threat to national survival. With US support, the monarchy played a significant role in the anti-communist war. King Bhumibol, Queen Sirikit and other members of the royal family visited remote areas in red zones—areas intensively infiltrated by the insurgents—to give moral support to the soldiers and villagers. Such visits were considered a component of psychological warfare to win the hearts and minds of local people likely to be sympathetic towards and supportive of the CPT.

Crown Prince Vajiralongkorn regularly accompanied his parents to perform such duties in the anti-communist war; sometimes, too, he went alone. The incident that gave him a real sense of military action took place in Dan Sai District of the Northeastern province of Loei in late October 1976, when a series of heavy communist attacks killed at least eight government troops.[12]

An episode that came to palace attention took place on 29 October 1976, a few weeks after the massacre of students at Thammasat University. Some 100 insurgents attacked a security outpost in Ban Makkhaeng, Tambon Kok Sathon in Dan Sai District of Loei Province. This attack killed one Border Patrol Police officer and injured another. A helicopter dispatched to rescue them was shot down in the jungle nearby.[13] As the rescue team from that chopper failed to gain access to the site because of fierce resistance from the insurgents, a patrol was dispatched to go through the jungle to the site on foot. But the rescue team encountered an ambush that killed two soldiers and wounded another three.

The Army's three-volume work commemorating the 100th anniversary of the Chulachomklao Royal Military Academy relates that King Bhumibol assigned the crown prince to visit soldiers, police and security volunteers who had had encounters with communist insurgents in order to give moral support both to those personnel and to local people in war zones.[14] Crown Prince Vajiralongkorn landed at Ban Huai Mun outpost in Loei's Dan Sai District on 5 November 1976 and received a briefing from ground commanders about ongoing military clashes between government troops and communist insurgents. According to the book's account, the crown prince, who then held the rank of captain, surprised then Third Army Region Commander Lieutenant General Somsak Panjamanont, by saying that he had to go immediately to fix the problem on the ground by himself. "No time to wait, we have to fix it up by today, (move) now", the crown prince was quoted as saying to the commander, who strongly objected to the prince's intention out of fear for his safety.[15] In fact, a reinforcement and rescue team had been dispatched to the site three days earlier, but its slow pace in moving through the jungle meant that it managed to arrive at the site of the clash only ten minutes before the helicopter carrying the crown prince landed. Those also on board the helicopter included Somsak and then Colonel Pijit Kullawanit. The latter would later become a member of King Bhumibol's Privy Council.

The royal helicopter came under small-fire attack as it landed at the site, according to the commemorative book. "As the helicopter was about to touch down in the landing zone, the Crown Prince jumped off to take cover before commanding ground troops to fight back", it said. "His Royal Highness bravely returned gun fire at the insurgents during the battle."[16] From this point, the crown prince took command of the ground operation. He ordered artillery fire on the insurgents' base nearby, made recommendations on tactics and deployments for the troops, and led a patrol into the surrounding area to assess the situation and plant anti-personnel landmines. The book clearly mentions that the Third Army Region commander raised an objection to these actions out of fear for the safety of the heir to the throne. But the military chain of command did not work in this situation as Captain Crown Prince Vajiralongkorn acted as the ground commander of the operation. He stayed overnight, ate and slept on the earthen floor of the bunker with the ground troops.

"With courage, decisiveness and love of military life, His Royal Highness intended to do what other persons could not. He went into such a dangerous area without fear", the book went on. "There is no other country where the Heir to the Throne takes up weapons to fight shoulder to shoulder with soldiers against national enemies. It was an historical movement which might not happen again in the future."[17]

Media archives do not mention the details of the crown prince's combat role in this episode. But they indicate that he did pay a visit to the frontlines and met with soldiers wounded in the Dan Sai clash who had been hospitalized in Phetchabun Province, where he stayed overnight. Print media including the *Bangkok Post, The Nation, Thai rat* and *Ban mueang* presented the mission in different ways. The *Bangkok Post, Thai rat* and *Ban mueang* mentioned the Dan Sai incident during late October and early November 1976. *Ban mueang* and the *Bangkok Post* reported on the clash, while *Thai rat* published coverage of the deceased soldiers, with columns honouring them.[18] However, only the coverage in *Thai rat* included a photograph of the crown prince on the mission. The newspaper reproduced pictures distributed by the palace showing the prince at the hospital visiting injured soldiers.[19] More importantly, it also carried a picture showing him at the scene of the fighting in combat uniform, holding an M-16 assault rifle in his right hand and receiving a military salute. The caption read, "His Royal Highness the Crown Prince visited military and police at Ban Huai

Mun outpost amid cold weather and danger of communist insurgents during 5–6 November."[20] More than four decades later, during Apirat's high-profile October 2019 lecture, the general would present and highlight a picture showing the crown prince running with an M-16 assault rifle in his hand and apparently jumping off the chopper, to prove that he really encountered the insurgents.[21] As Peter Jackson puts it, "while the Cold War ended and the CPT ceased activities over two decades ago, images of anti-communist operations from the 1970s still have political valence, reflecting the continuing role of anti-insurgency thinking against often-unnamed 'enemies' of the nation in the military's approach to politics to this day."[22]

Public images of King Vajiralongkorn in the years before his accession to the throne also showed him as a pilot involved in both military and civilian aviation and as a fighter captain. The king was trained in military aviation for the first time during a ten-month course in Australia in 1976. He enrolled in a special training course on flying helicopters in Thailand in 1979. As a participant in a US assistance programme, he attended a military air transport course at Fort Bragg, North Carolina, in 1980. He was trained to operate the UN-1N Bell Helicopter, before shifting to propeller airplanes, jet aircraft and fighter planes in 1981–82. He began flying jet fighters with the Vietnam-War-era T-33, before beginning to fly the more sophisticated F5-E/F. He attended a training course on flying the F5-E/F in combat at Williams Air Force Base, Arizona, in 1982. Since 1994, when the then crown prince was an officer in the Army, he has served as an F-5E/F trainer for the Air Force.

The Royal Thai Air Force has seldom experienced any air battles in its history. Air strikes during the anti-communist war were mostly conducted by Army helicopter gunships. One well-known operation involving jet fighters was the border clash over a territorial dispute with Laos at Ban Romklao in late 1987 and early 1988, but there was no report that the crown prince participated in air combat during that battle. He had, however, accumulated 2,000 flying hours, as certified by the manufacturer of the F-5E/F, Northrop Corporation, in May 1997.

King Vajiralonglorn switched to flying wide-body commercial aircraft as the co-pilot of Boeing 737-400s jumbo jets in 1999. He obtained certification from Thailand's Civil Aviation Institute in 2004 and was upgraded to full captain by the state-run national carrier, Thai Airways International, in 2006. It was reported that he sometimes flew the jumbo jet for the national carrier and his own Boeing 737 when he travelled overseas.[23] The palace highlighted the high-profile charity flights that he operated to raise funds from high society in the kingdom in 2007, 2010 and 2012. The first of these flights led him to have a romantic moment with flight attendant Suthida Tidjai, who later became the queen of Thailand.[24]

Militarized Queen, Princesses and Consorts

King Vajiralongkorn seems to want people around him to become soldiers, like himself. He requires military training for the members of his inner circle—particularly his daughters, queen and royal consorts. They were trained, given military ranks and assigned to royal guard units. The king had his two daughters become military officers. His eldest daughter, Princess Bajrakitiyabha Narendiradebyavati, assumed the rank of Army captain years ago. She was promoted to major general in March 2018 and assigned to serve as the king's special bodyguard and a special officer in the Royal Guard Command.[25] His younger daughter, Princess Sirivannavari Nariratana Rajakanya, who obviously preferred fashion design and equestrian activities to military pursuits, was given the rank of colonel and assigned to a teaching post at the Cavalry School of the Royal Thai Army Cavalry Centre.[26] She won a silver medal competing in dressage with the Thai equestrian team at the 2017 Southeast Asian Games in Malaysia. The two princesses were seen in military uniforms at the parade marking the king's coronation ceremony in May 2019. While Princess Bajrakitiyabha walked with other bodyguards to the king, Princess Sirivannavari rode on horseback with other troops from the cavalry division to honour her father.

Queen Suthida was married to King Vajiralongkorn on 1 May 2019, the same day that she was granted the title of queen and a few days before the royal coronation ceremony that brought her investiture as Her Majesty Queen Suthida Bajrasudhabimalalakshana.[27] Born as a commoner on 3 June 1978 into a Southern Thai family in Hat Yai District of Songkhla Province, the queen was then known as Suthida Tidjai. The palace has only released a brief version of her biography, one without mention of her parents, and the mainstream Thai media have followed suit. The English version of Wikipedia gives the name of a person called Kham Tidjai as her father and that of an ethnic Chinese woman called Jangheang Tidjai as her mother. Jangheang was granted the Most Illustrious Order of Chulachomklao decoration on 3 January 2018,[28] suggesting palace recognition more than a year before the royal marriage. However, as of 21 July 2020, the Thai version of Wikipedia offered different names for the queen's parents; it stated that her father's name was Suthep Tidjai and her mother's name Chitta Tidjai.

The queen obtained a bachelor's degree in communication arts from the School of Communication Arts of Assumption University in Bangkok before entering the aviation industry as a flight attendant for JALways—formerly Japan Air Charter Co. Ltd—from 2000 until 2003. She later moved to Thai Airways International, where she met then Crown Prince Vajiralongkorn when he captained a charity flight on which she was working. She served with the national flag carrier until 2008, before being trained as a soldier and pilot upon the crown prince's command.

On 14 May 2010, the queen was given the rank of Army second lieutenant, as Suthida Vajiralongkorn—with the new surname indicating special relations with the crown prince.[29] She rose in military rank very quickly: she was promoted to Army first lieutenant on 14 November 2010 and climbed the ladder from captain in 2011 to colonel in 2012.[30] Such fast-track promotion is seen only in the case of persons who have special relations with the Thai military elite. Suthida was promoted to the rank of two-star general on 11 November 2013 and full general on 6 December 2016.[31] The timeline on the queen's CV-style biography, as released by the palace and reproduced by media in Thailand, makes clear that she moved on a fast track in her military career. (See Table 3.1.)

Prior to her official wedding, the queen was often seen wearing a military uniform and beside the king in a position that led the public to notice that she was not an ordinary bodyguard to the monarch. She joined the royal guard parades both during funeral ceremonies for King Bhumibol in 2017 and, when she had already been bestowed the title of queen, during the royal coronation ceremony of King Vajiralongkorn in 2019.[32] The palace justified her military career with the release of a number of pictures in 2019 demonstrating that Queen Suthida had undergone intensive military and pilot training courses. Local media picked up the release of these photographs to raise the profile of the new queen as a tough military officer. "Her Majesty completed physically demanding field training and military programmes alongside male personnel. These programmes ranged from flight training to the

TABLE 3.1
Queen Suthida's Official Positions and Ranks

Year	Position
2010	• Acting Operations Staff Officer, Operations Section, Royal Guard Unit, Royal Guard Regiment, Royal Security Command.
2012	• Deputy Battalion Commander, Royal Guard Unit, Royal Guard Regiment, Royal Security Command. • Commanding Officer of the Training Battalion of the Royal Guard, Training Unit of the Royal Guard, King's Guard School, Royal Guard Unit, Royal Security Command.
2013	• Deputy Commanding Officer of King's Guard School and Commanding Officer of Training Unit of the Royal Guard, Royal Guard Unit, Royal Security Command. • Special Operations Officer, Office of the Crown Prince's Special Operations Officer, Royal Security Command. • Commanding Officer of King's Guard School, Royal Guard Unit, Royal Security Command.
2014	• Chief of Staff of the Royal Guard Unit, Royal Security Command.
2016	• Special Operations Officer, Office of the Crown Prince's Special Operations Officer, Royal Security Command. • Deputy Commander of the Royal Security Command, with the rank of general.
2017	• Deputy Chief Aide-de-Camp to the King, Royal Aide-de-Camp Department, with the rank of special general. • Deputy Commander of the Royal Security Command, with the rank of special general.

Note: Public Relations Department, Thailand, "Royal Biography of H. M. Queen Suthida Bajrasudhabimalalakshana", n.d., https://thailand.prd.go.th/ewt_news.php?nid=8035&filename=index (accessed 29 October 2019).

navy's marine programme, as well as a night-time parachuting course in Sattahip, Chon Buri. Her Majesty is the first female officer to have trained in the course", wrote the *Bangkok Post*.[33] "The air training programme was organized by the Special Warfare School under the Special Warfare Command in Lopburi. Her Majesty performed the parachuting tasks five times and shot firearms in various categories. She also participated in hostage rescue drills and close-quarters combat training", the newspaper went on to report, displaying photographs handed out by the palace. The palace and the government's Public Relations Department made pictures of the queen taken during the training course available online for download.

The Royal Thai Air Force trained the queen as a pilot qualified to fly Cessna T-41 military aircraft in 2010. She took an additional pilot's course in Germany in 2012. The palace has said in her biography that she was qualified for a European Union pilot's licence to fly Cessna 712, Mooney M20 and Piper PA-34 Seneca by aviation authorities in Germany and that she has a commercial pilot's licence for the Boeing 737. She has been a co-pilot on the jumbo jet, according to the biography released by the palace.[34] Other than the images distributed by the palace, there is no independent report of the pilot queen flying any aircraft for the purpose of civilian transportation.

It is an open secret that since the time when he was crown prince King Vajiralongkorn has brought a number of young women into military service for unclear purposes, but not necessarily to serve as royal guards. The public knew that these young women had special relationships and deep connections with the crown prince, as he granted them new surnames—either his own name or similar names. These surnames included Vajiralongkorn Na Ayutthaya, which Queen Suthida took when she first entered military service; Wongvajirapakdi, which Noble Consort Sineenat uses; and Sirivajirapakdi, which was granted to a number of other women.

All these surnames signified loyalty to Vajiralongkorn. In 2016–17, the *Royal Gazette* announced military ranks for a number of women with the Sirivajirapakdi surname. These included Krongthong, made a first lieutenant on 2 November 2016;[35] Anusara, given the same rank on 22 June 2016;[36] and Nattha, who became a major on 18 December 2017.[37] Waraporn, Pornthip and Pathriya attained the rank of second lieutenant on 27 March 2016.[38] All of these women served in Royal Guard units under the Royal Security Command. But, in contrast to the later announcements of their demotions, the announcements of their promotions in rank did not refer clearly to their positions or functions. Chayuta, for example, attained the rank of first lieutenant on 2 November 2016, with the position of platoon leader in an unspecified Royal Guard company, but she was demoted to sergeant for incompetence and sent for retraining on 21 November 2017.[39]

The promotion and demotion of these women were not transparent, let alone made with any apparent reference to fairness. For example, Sutthattaphakdi Yuwarajborirak's name came to the attention of the public in a *Royal Gazette* announcement in November 2013. The announcement stated that the female Lieutenant Commander Sutthattaphakdi, an officer in the Office of the Crown Prince, had received a royal decoration making her a Commander Third Class of the Most Exalted Order of the White Elephant.[40] A further announcement indicated that she had become a Knight Commander Second Class of the Most Exalted Order of the White Elephant in April 2014, with a new position as an executive officer attached to the Office of the Crown Prince.[41] In February 2016, she was fired and stripped of her naval rank for having a negative attitude towards the royal institution, lacking discipline, and *kanpraphruet chua yangrairaeng* or cross misconduct.[42] However, an announcement four years later noted the transfer of a female civil servant named Sutthattaphakdi Borirakphumin from the position of officer attached to the royal household to that of active military officer, along with a promotion from major to colonel in the infantry of the Royal Thai Army.[43] The announcement said nothing about the background of this officer, and it was impossible to confirm whether she was the same Sutthattaphakdi who had been dismissed and stripped of her military rank earlier. The change in surname from Yuwarajborirak and Borirakphumin revealed nothing about her identity, as each was an unusual surname apparently related to the crown. "Yuwarajborirak" literally means "guardian of the crown prince", while "Borirakphumin" refers to a guardian of the king. The same January 2020 announcement in the *Royal Gazette* also noted the unusually rapid promotion of Naruemon Samphat from major to major general and her new position as a special operative officer attached to the Office of King's Guard Command.[44] The palace did not give any information about her background. Social media floated unconfirmed information that she, known by the nickname of Nut, was a former nurse who had cared for Prince Dhipankara Rasmijoti, a son of the king.

Several military officers, interviewed in January and February 2020 with promises of anonymity, expressed mixed reactions to the appointment, promotion and demotion of these female royal officials.

A naval officer said such moves were nonsense but that they had no implication for the armed forces since the female officers in question were few in number and confined only to the jurisdiction of the palace-run Royal Security Guard Command. An Army officer, however, was furious about the practice, as granting ranks and positions to unqualified persons could cause moral hazard in the military. Only war heroes who sacrificed their lives to protect the country or the throne merited great leaps in rank such as that from major to major general, he said.

The Rise and Fall of a Royal Consort

Service in the inner circle of King Vajiralongkorn meant that one's life and career could be uncertain. One could be promoted, demoted or fiercely punished in accordance with the king's wishes. A young woman named Niramon Ounprom, who went by the nickname "Koi" and came from Tha Wang Pha District in the northern province of Nan, become one of the most controversial topics in the recent history of the Siamese royal court after she took the name Sineenat Wongvajirapakdi in 2014. The dream of a Cinderella from the countryside became true five years later, in July 2019, when at the age of thirty-four she received the title of Royal Noble Consort or *chao khun phra*. But she fell from the heavens very quickly, some three months later, and obviously because of jealousy. Unbelievably, however, she would return to the same exalted rank, position and status in the royal hierarchy, second only to the queen of Thailand in less than a year. On 28 August 2020, the king issued a royal command stating that Miss Sineenat Wongvajirapakdi was "flawless" and reinstating her as *Chao khun phra* Sineenat Bilaskalayani with the same military rank of major general, same position as deputy commander of the palace guard regiment, and same royal decorations that had been bestowed upon her—all as if she had never been stripped of that rank, that position, or those decorations.[45]

Sineenat's disappearance from public view in late October 2019 was accompanied by a royal command declaring that she had been stripped of her status, position, royal decorations and military rank because she had made several attempts to stop the installation of General Suthida Vajiralongkorn as queen the previous May. It was allegedly her wish to be crowned instead. "However, things did not turn out the way she had wished for. After the royal ceremony, with aspiration and ambition, she tried to find ways to get herself bestowed the title", according to the *Royal Gazette*, whose detailed account of problems and controversies in the palace was rare, if not unprecedented.[46] The sensational story was published because the king, who had revived Siamese court polygamy in the twenty-first century, had also tried to ease the resultant tensions and prevent "inappropriate actions against the monarchy and the nation" by bestowing upon Sineenat the title of Royal Noble Consort on his birthday, 28 July 2019. The position known in Thai as *chao khun phra* had last been used more than a century earlier during the reign of Rama V to honour the king's wives.

In the view of the king and members of the royal family, commoners must be satisfied with what people on high grant them. Ambition and greed are not acceptable. The palace said in its statement that Sineenat was ungrateful and that she behaved in a way unbecoming of the holder of the royal title bestowed upon her. She had sought by all means to rise to the level of the queen. She had exploited her title by giving orders and claiming that the monarch had told her to do so on his behalf. "Therefore, the king commanded all of her positions, ranks and decorations to be stripped away."[47]

When the title of Royal Noble Consort was bestowed on Sineenat, the palace released her profile with pictures of her private life with King Vajiralongkorn and her activities during military training. Interest in this release reportedly caused the website of the Royal Office to crash.[48] The official profile said that the new royal consort had performed military service as a royal bodyguard from the time the king was still crown prince.

Born on 26 January 1985, Sineenat graduated from the Royal Thai Army Nursing College at the age of twenty-three before beginning nursing service at Phramongkutklao military hospital in Bangkok in 2008. Then still known as Niramon Ounprom, she received the rank of first lieutenant on 1 November 2010,[49] two weeks before Queen Suthida was given the same rank in the Army. Sineenat underwent military training between 2014 and 2018, starting with the course for members of the Royal Guard and including training as an aide-de-camp. She graduated from a course in jungle warfare in 2015 and completed a course offered by the Army's Command and General Staff College in 2017. Sineenat also completed the Army Special Warfare School's airborne training programme in 2015 and then the Thai Marine Corps School's airborne programme in 2017. She graduated from the Royal Thai Air Force's Flight Training School and also joined a programme for those seeking private pilots' licences at the Jesenwang flying school in the German state of Bavaria. She held key positions in the aide-de-camp unit under the Royal Guard Command starting in 2016 and served as bodyguard to the king starting in 2017. In that latter capacity, Sineenat appeared in public as a commander in royal parades during the funeral rites for the late King Bhumibol and the coronation of King Vajiralongkorn.

After her demotion, social media and a German news website reported in October 2019 that Sineenat had been sentenced by a military court to two years' imprisonment.[50] The sentence could not be confirmed. There was no report to indicate whether she had obtained fair treatment as the accusation against her was made quietly and on the king's instructions. It would be difficult to apply regular laws and regulations in considering prosecution and punishment within the palace, not least because the charges levelled sometimes related to norms and traditions. Sineenat's case saw the application of ancient rules known as *ratchasawat* and written up in the form of poetry by King Vajiravudh. The rules indicate behavioural norms for royal officials including consorts, aides-de-camp and royal bodyguards. The ten rules include a prohibition on hiding anything from the king; serving with courage; working with care, honesty and humility; harbouring no ambition; not sitting in the same chair as the king; staying relevant; and refraining from acts of adultery, notably with consorts and members of royalty.[51] The rules were applied again a few weeks after Sineenat's demotion, when a number of military officers were sacked from their positions in the Royal Guard units.[52] These officers included an aide-de-camp who guarded the royal bedrooms and was accused of misconduct, malfeasance and adultery.[53] It is not possible to say whether those cases had any connection with Sineenat's demotion. Furthermore, two of the officers involved, Captain Pithakronnachai Sukwattanamai and First Lieutenant Kanyanat Sappanthakul, were reinstated in early November 2019.[54]

Royal Noble Consort Sineenat was often seen in public—sometimes, but only sometimes, with the king and the queen—making merit at Buddhist temples or mingling and taking selfies with loyal subjects. These appearances took place starting in October 2020, after youthful protesters demanding reform of the monarchy began to criticize the royal institution. Her earlier disappearance and re-emergence raised questions about the king's private life, about practices of gender equality, and, more importantly, about whether the king's reign was subject to the law. For the palace was never transparent about the reward and punishment of royal persons. In the view of some observers, the king treated his servants like his belongings, with which he could do as he wished.

Shake-Up, Sack and Purge

In 2015, early in the transition period from the reign of the former Thai monarch to that of King Vajiralongkorn, the latter, then still crown prince, purged senior police officers who had worked closely with or had close connections to him. Accusations of misconduct, misbehaviour, corruption, conflicts of interest, exploiting the monarchy's good name for their own interests and insulting the monarchy justified these purges. The most controversial cases related to the former chief of Central Investigation Bureau, Pongpat Chayapan, and the former deputy national police chief and grand chamberlain, Jumpol Manmai.

In January 2015, Pongpat, who was stripped of the rank of police general rank when the controversy exploded, was sentenced along with five other police officers to twelve years in prison. However, these men's sentences were commuted by half because they confessed to charges of *lèse majesté* and involvement in other illegal activities. It was alleged that these former officers had used the name of his royal highness to solicit bribes. They were also charged with malfeasance and many other crimes and sentenced to a total of thirty-six years and four months of imprisonment after three years of court trials that started in 2014.[55]

Lèse majesté charges under Article 112 of the Penal Code were pressed against the officers because Pongpat and his men "put the Royal Crest pin on their shoulders and put a badge bearing the portrait of Prince Dhipankara Rasmijoti, the son of then Crown Prince Vajiralongkorn and his former consort Srirasm, on their left pockets at all times to indicate that they had the palace's backing."[56] Pongpat's case mattered to the palace because he was an uncle of Srirasm, whom the crown prince divorced and who stepped down from the position of royal highness and princess in December 2014.[57]

Jumpol was one of the former king's closest aides. He was sacked when King Vajiralongkorn ascended the throne. He was also stripped of the rank of police general during the course of the legal battles that he soon faced. Jumpol had been appointed as the lord chamberlain after retirement from police service in 2011. He was promoted to deputy secretary general of the Royal Household, with responsibility for security matters and special affairs, in 2016.[58]

Jumpol had long been seen as a rising star. He was a classmate of former Prime Minister Thaksin Shinawatra at the Police Academy, and he had assumed the position of director general of the Special Branch during Thaksin's administration. He was transferred to head the National Intelligence Agency after the 2006 coup. With his strong connections with the palace, Jumpol was a strong candidate for the top job in the National Police Office during the government of Prime Minister Abhisit Vejjajiva. However, a stalemate over that appointment ensued in 2010 as Abhisit insisted on picking his own favourite candidate, Police General Pathep Tanprasert. Jumpol then retired as deputy national police chief before taking an important position in the palace in 2011.

Jumpol was sacked from his position as grand chamberlain in February 2017. He faced accusations of gross misconduct, conflict of interest and political partisanship.[59] The palace did not disclose the specific alleged wrongdoing or its connection to Jumpol's official position, but in March 2017 the grand chamberlain, his wife and five associates were arrested and charged with encroaching on the Tablan National Park in Wang Nam Khiao District of Nakhon Ratchasima Province.[60] Jumpol was sentenced to six years in prison, but the sentence was commuted to half that length because he confessed his guilt.[61]

The fall of Jumpol took place around the same time that the stock of his schoolmate from the prestigious Suan Kularb School, Thailand's oldest all-boys secondary school, Air Chief Marshal Sathitphong Sukwimon, rose. Sathitphong was a close aide to King Vajiralongkorn, whom he had served since his appointment as a royal guard in October 1999, when the latter was still crown prince.[62] Sathitphong was originally a civilian who obtained a bachelor's degree in mass communications from Chiangmai University in 1972. But he became an Air Force officer as an alumnus of the Kamphaengsaen aviation training school who underwent training courses at the Air Command and Staff College and the Air War College. He won quick promotion to the rank of Air Chief Marshal in 2001, when he was appointed as deputy aide-de-camp to the crown prince.[63] Sathitphong was one of the most trusted members of the inner circle of King Vajiralongkorn. In 2017, he was named chairman of the board of the Crown Property Bureau (CPB), which oversees the king's fortune.[64] The next year, he became the CPB's director general and secretary general of the palace.[65] As of January 2021, Sathitphong held six positions in the service of the king, including chief of royal officials, secretary general of the palace, private secretary to the king, chairman of the CPB's board, and manager of the king's personal property. It was unusual for the monarch to allow a single official to hold various positions and functions in his palace.

There were sometimes no clear explanations for reshuffles, rewards and punishment within the palace. General Jakkraphob Bhuridej, the chief of the king's Close Body Guard Command, and Colonel Naraporn Saenthi, acting commander of the palace guard unit, were removed from their respective positions for negligence on 21 April 2019.[66] They were re-installed in the same positions within two weeks, on 2 May 2019.[67] Jakkraphob, who was said to be one of the most trusted close bodyguards, had served the king since 2010, starting as head of the then crown prince's own guard squad with the rank of group captain—a rank reflective of the fact that he was originally an Air Force officer.[68] His case must remain a matter of speculation, but it certainly does reflect the unsystematic and unclear procedures for reward and punishment in the Royal Security Command. The king took swift action to fire officers and close aides in that command who were allegedly guilty of gross misconduct, described in Thai with the strong words *kanpraphruet chua yangrairaeng*. On 22–23 October 2019, six officers serving in the inner circle of the palace security, including Grand Chamberlain Police Lieutenant General Sakolkhet Chantra, were sacked on such charges.[69] Sakolkhet, previously seen in public serving as the king's representative at many social activities, was also charged with abuse of power for exploiting his position to ask for personal favours.

Another case, involving Tharinee Rodson, came to the attention of the public when she was sacked and reinstated within a few weeks. The former lecturer was transferred from the Communication Arts Department in the Faculty of the Humanities at Kasetsart University to serve in internal affairs with the Office of the Crown Prince in December 2005.[70] She received a promotion to the post of special official, a position equivalent to Assistant Secretary of the Royal Household, in July 2008.[71] She was granted military ranks, beginning with second lieutenant on 12 March 2016, followed by promotion to first lieutenant less than 20 days later, on 31 March 2016.[72] After the crown prince ascended the throne, Tharinee received a fast-track promotion from lieutenant colonel in January 2017 to major general in April of the same year.[73] She was at the time the director of palace affairs in the office of the chief of staff of the King's Guard Command. She was sacked and, like many others, stripped of her rank and royal decoration in October 2019 on accusations of gross misconduct and abuse of power.[74] However, she was reinstated in the same position and restored to the same rank in November without any clear explanation.[75]

The Royal Security Command

King Vajiralongkorn has taken military affairs more seriously than ceremonial parades. He has not only made people around him, such as his queen, daughters, consorts and close aides into soldiers and assigned them security functions but also restructured security arrangements in the palace and relations with the armed forces as a whole. A number of laws have been promulgated and amended to justify the restructuring of those arrangements and to empower the monarch. The palace administration, previously under the government, is now subject to the direct control of the monarch. It is important to note that many of the changes in question were prepared and even quietly effected in the years before the king's accession to the throne.

The new arrangements relate to the structure and duties of the Privy Council and the Royal Household. As this volume is concerned with ties between the monarchy and the military, this chapter considers only arrangements governing the Royal Security Command. Bestowed the status of the key royal security or guard unit by King Bhumibol in November 1992, when Chuan Leekpai was prime minister, the agency was at the time under the authority of the Royal Thai Armed Forces Headquarters, formerly the Supreme Command.[76] In 2013, during the premiership of Yingluck Shinawatra, the Royal Security Command was transformed into a juristic entity under the direct command of the Ministry of Defence.[77] King Vajiralongkorn, then crown prince, had commanded this agency. Another royal decree further clarified its structure in April 2014. The decree cited the command's four departments: the command office, the crown prince's special force's office, the office of the crown prince's chief of staff, and the King's Guard *mahatlek rajawallop raksa phra-ong* unit.[78] The crown prince's special forces unit, commonly known by the name Rajawallop 904,[79] had grown to 5,000 troops selected from the armed forces. Its members came mostly from the 1st Division and the 2nd Infantry Regiment and had capabilities for rapid deployment and riot suppression under the prince's direct command.[80]

King Vajiralongkorn officially and drastically restructured the palace administration in April 2017, four months after ascending the throne. That month saw the National Legislative Assembly, the rubber stamp of the National Council for Peace and Order (NCPO) junta, pass the Royal Service Administration Act to transfer all agencies concerned with palace affairs, including asset and security management, to the direct command of the monarch.[81]

Against the norms of constitutional monarchies, which tend to limit monarchs' powers, Section 4 of the 2017 act states clearly that the management and administration of agencies under the law are subject to the king's wishes. Unless specified in other laws, agencies under the jurisdiction of the palace are not deemed "government agencies'" under the law on national government administration, and they are not state entities under any other law. If any of those agencies is required to remain a "juristic person", that fact has to be mentioned in decrees or laws enacted for that particular purpose. Section 5 says that the cabinet must allocate budgetary resources to the palace accordingly. If any agencies under the palace administration generate income, such revenue will not go to the national treasury. Section 7 authorizes transferring the Royal Aide-de-Camp Department, Royal Security Command and Royal Police Guard from the Royal Thai Armed Forces Headquarters, the Ministry of Defence and the National Police Office, respectively, to palace jurisdiction.

Interestingly, attached to the act was a statement to explain its promulgation. The Office of the King's Principal Private Secretary, the Bureau of the Royal Household, the Royal Aide-de-Camp Department, and the Royal Security Command under the Ministry of Defence were government agencies with duties concerning royal service and the functions of the monarch and members of the royal household, it said. As they were thus required to provide services in line with ancient royal traditions and the royal pleasure, their governmental activities were different from those of government agencies in the executive branch. "Accordingly", the explanatory statement read, "it is appropriate to newly determine the status of the said governmental agencies as royal agencies which carry out governmental activities and are directly subject to the monarch, with specific administrative organization and personnel administration in compliance with the royal pleasure, so that the administration of the royal service would become suitable and compatible with the missions of the royal service and harmonious with the provisions of the constitution."[82]

To that end, the government issued another royal decree on 10 May 2017 detailing the transformation and organization of governmental affairs and administration for royal service.[83] Section 3 of the decree states that royal agencies under the jurisdiction of the palace and subject directly to the king comprise the Bureau of Royal Household, the Office of Privy Council and the Royal Security Command. "The royal agencies under this clause shall have juristic personality, shall have the objective of performing missions relating to royal service for the monarch and members of the royal household at the royal pleasure, and shall be directly subject to the monarch."

Section 8 of the decree says that the Royal Security Command has the duty to plan, direct, coordinate, command, control, supervise and perform work related to guarding and honouring the king, the queen, the heir to the throne, members of the royal household, and other persons as may be designated by the monarch. This work includes ceremonial duties as may be assigned to the command, the maintenance of peace and order within the royal precincts, and duties under the laws concerning the safeguarding of the king, the queen, the heir to the throne, members of the royal household, royal representatives and royal visitors.

"The Royal Security Command shall adopt a system of command that is directly subject to the monarch", the decree said.[84] King Vajiralongkorn conferred the *chaichaloemphon* flag on the unit in December 2019 so that the troops could show allegiance to the monarchy—a military tradition to show loyalty practised since the 1957–63 premiership of Field Marshal Sarit Thanarat.[85]

Figure 3.1 presents the structure of the Royal Security Command as designed by the king. The principal duty of the Office of the Commander is to command, control and direct royal security operations for the king, the queen, the heir to the throne, the regent, members of the royal family, royal representatives and royal visitors.

The Office of the Royal Duty Officers implements the directives of the commander of the Royal Security Command as well as carrying out work for the king.

FIGURE 3.1
The Structure and Duties of the Royal Security Command

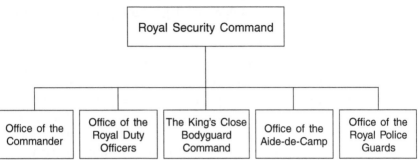

Source: Royal Office Website, https://www.royaloffice.th/en/about-royal-office/royal-security/ (accessed 31 October 2019).

The Office of the Aide-de-Camp is responsible for planning, ordering, coordinating, directing and managing royal activities to ensure order and success.

The King's Close Bodyguard Command provides honour and security to the crown, follows royal orders, maintains security within the palace compound and performs other duties as assigned. These include provision of security for members of the royal family, the regent, royal representatives and royal visitors.

The Office of the Royal Police Guards provides security details and honour to the king, the queen, the heir, the regent, members of the royal family, royal representatives, royal visitors and others as assigned by the king. It manages other affairs as instructed by the king, and according to tradition. It is important to note the existence of another police unit, the *Tamruat mahatlek rajawallop raksa phra-ong* 904 or Royal Police Guard 904, which is under the jurisdiction of the Central Investigation Bureau of the Office of National Police rather than that of the palace. The unit, originally known as the Royal Security and Special Task Division, changed its name in January 2019 in accordance with its main function. The unit was commissioned to perform ten duties including providing safety to members of royalty and royal guests; detecting, investigating, and suppressing crimes against the monarchy; and supporting, and functioning as a normal police unit under, the commander of the Central Investigation Bureau.[86] The unit has participated in many operations to suppress major criminal cases such as a notorious gold robbery and murder in Lopburi in January 2020, a mass shooting in Nakhon Ratchasima province in February 2020, and even a case involving an illegal surrogate birth operation in February 2020.[87]

A cabinet resolution of 14 July 2020 changed the name of the Royal Police Guard 904 to *Kong Kongbangkhapkan patibatkan phiset* or Special Operations Command, with additional tasks including countering terrorists and acts of sabotage, operations in emergency situations, and anti-riot and crowd control activities that may occur and affect royal security in the vicinity of the palace. "In order to conduct operations to provide security to the crown in accordance with royal wishes and royal traditions as well as to coordinate with other agencies speedily and effectively for maximum security, it is necessary to give additional duties to the unit and appropriate to change its name accordingly", said the announcement of the cabinet resolution.[88]

There were some difficulties in recruiting police officers to royal service in August 2019. The *Prachatai* news website reported that a number of police officers resisted transfers to the Royal Police Guard. They had concerns relating to ambiguous orders, the structure of the new unit and their career paths after the completion of training for the unit. The Office of National Police issued an order to select 873 outstanding commissioned and non-commissioned police officers, ranking from police lance corporal up to police colonel, to participate in a six-month training course running from 1 October 2019 to 31 March 2020 in preparation for royal service. The criteria for selection were such personal characteristics as having straight legs, not being emaciated or having sloping shoulders, not wearing spectacles, being of the appropriate weight, having a strong physique, being between 1.7 and 1.8 metres tall, and demonstrating loyalty, a good attitude and preparedness in all aspects. The selection process may not in fact have been conducted with all the officers' consent or knowledge: while eligibility required having signed an application for royal duty, a number of "selected" officers chose to resign from police service rather accept this transfer and others refused to apply for a transfer to the royal guard unit. "The latter group was 'disciplined' for a nine-month period, part of which must be spent in the three southernmost provinces", *Prachathai* reported, noting the mass resignation of a total of 993 officers ranking from police senior sergeant major to police colonel in the 2020 fiscal year.[89]

The Rajawallop King's Close Bodyguard

(mahatlek rajawallop raksa phra-ong)

Among all units in the Thai military, that closest to the king has been the royal pages bodyguard, originally created during the reign of King Chulalongkorn, when he adapted his father King Mongkut's "Scarecrow Corps" to create the first royal guard unit.

In 1859, King Mongkut directed that twelve children from royal and aristocratic families be trained as modern military officers. He assigned them to help scare the crows away as the birds disturbed him when he was offering morning alms to Buddhist monks. Dubbed as *mahatlek lai ka* or "crow-scaring aides-de-camp", the group of twelve performed this duty every morning. When King Chulalongkorn ascended the throne in 1868, he took the matter more seriously. He designated twenty-four youths as a royal guard unit, calling them *mahatlek song lo* or "two dozen aides-de-camp" and armed them with Snider-Enfield rifles. They served as his personal bodyguards, basically attached to his bedroom.[90] By 1870, the king had commissioned Phraya Surasakmontri (Saeng Chuto) to recruit young men from noble families and to set up a king's guard unit to provide security for the monarch in the palace and whenever he travelled outside the capital. There were altogether seventy-two recruits initially before the unit's expansion to include commoners—mostly the offspring of elite families. As the numbers were growing, Rama V upgraded the king's guard unit to the King's Guard Aides-de-Camp (*Mahatlek raksa phra-ong*) under his direct command. In 1872, he reorganized the regiment and renamed it the Rajawallop King's Guard (*Krom thahan mahatlek rajawallop raksa phra-ong*). King Chulalongkorn commanded the regiment himself until 1873, when he appointed Lieutenant General Chao Phraya Phasakornwongse as its first military commander. The Bangkok-based 1st Infantry Regiment King's Guard of today claims roots dating back to these origins a century and a half ago.

Rajawallop literally meant "the king's favourite", *mahatlek* meant "pages", "aide-de-camp" indicated close aides, and *raksa phra-ong* referred to royal bodyguards or sometimes specifically to the king's own bodyguards. When he was crown prince, King Vajiralongkorn created a unit under his direct command known as the *Thahan mahatlek rajawallop raksa phra-ong nai somdet phraboromorasathirat* or the Crown Prince's Rajawallop Guard. Now that he is on the throne, the *Thahan mahatlek rajawallop raksa phra-ong* are the king's bodyguard, although he has also assigned them to help provide security for other members of royalty. There have been other royal guard units outside the jurisdiction of the palace that are called simply *raksa phra-ong*. Their commanders, senior officers or some selected troops were required to perform duty as royal guards, but mostly in ceremonial roles to honour kings, queens or key members of the royal family. These soldiers could, however, serve dual purposes. One purpose is the personal safety of the king, the queen and members of the crown, while the other is the security of the crown as an institution.

Initially, selected soldiers rotated from the armed forces to perform duty in the Crown Prince's Rajawallop Guard. Later on, young male and female civilians were recruited to the unit. It is unclear when such recruitment took place for the first time, but the first public announcement for it appeared in 2015 and was circulated via networks of the Ministry of Interior and other government agencies throughout the country.[91] The announcement said that the unit wanted to recruit males between 20 and 28 years old. Those with experience of military service must have lower-secondary-school educations, and those who lacked such experience upper-secondary-school educations. It also sought females between 18 and 26 years old. Those interested in joining the unit must apply in person at the King's Guard School, located in Dhaveevatthana Palace, which an observer said was not an ordinary residence of the king.[92]

Applicants to the Crown Prince's Rajawallop Guard who responded to this 2015 announcement had to pass a military examination and a physical examination before undergoing five months of military training between October and April. Men were to serve as privates in the Crown Prince's Guard for at least ten consecutive years without the right to quit or be transferred to other units. Female applicants must be single. Male soldiers would receive salaries of 9,000 baht a month, and female soldiers would receive an additional 2,800 baht a month for accepting special positions as the crown prince's servants. A lack of clarity surrounded the nature of these special positions.

The unit issued similar recruiting announcements every year until 2019, but it stopped accepting applications from females in 2017 for reasons that are unclear. Further, there were no public announcements identifying those who had passed the examinations and had been recruited into the unit. The number of troops in this unit is therefore unknown to the public.

Recruitment of high-ranking officers into service for the royal guard or the king's bodyguard also happened occasionally, with the palace announcing in the *Royal Gazette* the names of military and police officers appointed to provide security for the monarch and members of royal family. Numbers recruited varied from only one to more than 500 officers.[93]

Qualified officers at the rank of colonel or general and in positions as commander to commander-in-chief were also listed among those serving as royal guards. Former Army chief General Theerachai Nakwanich and Prime Minister Prayut Chan-ocha's younger brother, General Preecha Chan-ocha, for example, were appointed to serve as king's guards in 2016.[94] Former Army chief General Chalermchai Sitthisart and his successor General Apirat Kongsompong, who was then commander of the 1st Army Region with the rank of lieutenant general, were appointed to serve as the king's guards in July 2017.[95]

Former Army chief General Sonthi Boonyaratglin explained that the procedures relating to service as royal guards differed during the reigns of King Bhumibol and King Vajiralongkorn. During King Bhumibol's reign, the commanders and deputy commanders of units designated as royal guards automatically performed their duties to the sovereign, on a rotating basis. In contrast, King Vajiralongkorn would selectively pick senior officers to serve as royal guards according to his own considerations. "The senior officials who were appointed as *thahan ratcha-ongkharak* would really be called to perform the duty upon request, while the regular shifts were basically filled by soldiers already attached to the palace", he said.[96]

Prototype Soldiers

Since the time he was crown prince, King Vajiralongkorn has been praised by the military as "the great military mentor" for his role in mentoring and training troops in royal guard units under his command and in the King's Guard School.[97] The king's bodyguard has now come to have more influence over the armed forces, and notably the Army, as the king wants members of his bodyguard to serve as prototype soldiers.

A training handbook distributed to military and police units and to service academies indicates that the crown prince has set the guidelines, philosophy and doctrines for them to use as their fundamental principles of practice. "Providing safety for the crown concerns performing according to the norms of royal ceremonies, royal traditions and royal doctrines. In addition to strong and magnificent conduct, [troops] must show the highest honour [to the monarchy]", according to the book's preface.[98] The king's five philosophies for the royal guard are "commanding of aide-de-camp, simmer, standard, SIKU toy car and grassroots."

The book goes on to explain that commanders and trainers of royal guard troops must know the philosophy of command, staff and objectives. They had to know how to set objectives and to aim high. On training, the book introduced a philosophy of simmering, an analogy with cooking *khai phalo* or boiled eggs in sweet brown sauce. The king told his guards that the art of training soldiers was similar to cooking this dish. The cook had to boil eggs in the sauce at the proper temperature—below the boiling but higher than the poaching point—and for the proper period of time, until the egg absorbed the sweet brown sauce. The king also wanted the royal guard unit to set a high standard for other units in the armed forces. "Like a high-end brand product, it [the royal guard unit] had to attain its own outstanding quality", the book said.[99] The philosophy of SIKU was adapted from the brand of the toys with which the king played when he was a boy. The toy car branded SIKU, produced by the German company Sieper Lüdenscheid Gmb H & Co, was tested hundreds of times by the future king to ensure its quality. "The king played with them, fixed them when they broke and tested them again and again until the toy cars meet the standard", according to the training handbook.[100] The king also trained his royal guard in the same way that he tested the SIKU toy cars. The fifth philosophy for the royal guard was looking at the grassroots, which meant paying attention to all levels and details. "His Majesty the King climbed in his military career from below. Therefore, when he was at the top, he had to look down to the grassroots level", the handbook said, suggesting that commanders and supervisors in royal guard units had to do the same.[101]

The King's Guard School was commissioned to play a key role in education and training in accordance with the new guideline set by the king. It was enlarged and upgraded. Pichit Onintra assumed leadership of the school in July 2014, when he held the rank of colonel and the school was then under the supervision of the crown prince.[102] Four years later, when the new king ascended the throne, Pichit was promoted to the position of commandant, with the rank of lieutenant general, as the school became a model of military education and training.[103] The commandant had two deputies holding the rank of major general, one of whom oversaw the school's training centre.[104]

In 2017, King Vajiralongkorn picked fifteen senior officers, including then assistant Army chief Apirat, to attend a special course for three months. He subsequently commissioned them as members of the King's Guard Task Force 904, grooming them to be the real loyalists to the monarchy. Apirat was the head of the task force, a position that he also held when he became the Army chief. The group was known as *thahan kho daeng*, red-neck or red-rim soldiers, for wearing t-shirts with a red stripe at the collar beneath their uniforms. This elite squad, which later played a crucial role as the king's men in the Army, was assigned to produce prototype soldiers for the Thai armed forces.[105] One of them, Air Chief Marshal Phumjai Chaiyaphan, a former commander of the Air Force Security Command and special-qualification officer of the Air Force, was granted the Army rank of four-star general and attached to the office of King's Bodyguard Command under the Royal Security Command in September 2019.[106] Promoted to head of the Office of the Commander of Aides-de-Camp in April 2020,[107] he has been a close aide, serving as secretary to the crown prince and now king, since then.[108]

Task Force 904 later selected 600 commissioned officers from 30 battalions of royal guard units across the country, 1,500 non-commissioned officers and 1,500 privates to participate in the royally bestowed training course at the King's Guard School in Daveevatthana Palace for three months. The course mostly focused on physical training, manners and a new style of military salute to make the soldiers look strong and disciplined. The first batch of 150 troops finished their training course in August 2017.[109] In 2019, the task force dispatched its first 100 prototype soldiers to offer demonstrations and provide on-site training to other soldiers in their barracks across the country.[110] After assuming the Army's top post in 2018, Apirat employed parts of the king's guidelines in his campaign to make soldiers strong and disciplined.

A style of military salute and form of courtesy conceived by King Vajiralongkorn when he was the crown prince became well known to the public during the funeral ceremonies for King Bhumibol in 2017 and the new king's own coronation in 2019. It was called *yok ok uep*—a style of salute in which soldiers must raise their chests to salute senior officers. The new military salute was practised within royal guard units and later put into the curriculum for all soldiers in the armed forces. Privates drafted to military service in the year 2019 were the first group trained under the new royally bestowed curriculum, including the new style of salute.[111]

The King's Private Army

Concerned that the Rajawallop King's Guard, which provided security for the monarchy during previous reigns, may not be enough to secure the throne during the new reign, King Vajiralongkorn issued a royal decree, countersigned by Prime Minister Prayut on 19 September 2019, to transfer the 1st and 11th Infantry Regiments from the jurisdiction of the Army to that of the Royal Security Command—a unit subject to the direct authority of the king.[112] In practice, the regiments' budgets and personnel would be under the management of the palace. The government noted that the main duties of the Royal Security Command were to plan, direct, coordinate, command and control operations to provide safety for the king, the queen, the heir to the throne, the regent, and members of the royal family as well as royal guests. "In order to do so effectively for the optimal security of the royal circle, it was rational to transfer the personnel and budgets of the 1st and 11th Infantry Regiments to be under the Royal Security Command."[113] The two combat-ready regiments, with six battalions, were powerful units with a combined strength of some 3,000 soldiers, one stationed in Bangkok's Samsen District and the other in the capital's Bang Khen District.[114] The two units were strongholds of the *Wongthewan* or King's Guard faction of the Army, the arch rival of the *Burapha phayak* or Eastern Tigers faction. As discussed in the previous chapter, the latter clique dominated the Army during the period of transition to the new king's accession to the throne.

This transfer of troops became a contentious issue in the Thai parliament. Thailand's 2017 Constitution authorizes the executive branch to issue royal decrees for "emergencies of necessity and urgency which is unavoidable", but such decrees need approval from the parliament as soon as possible after they go into effect.

When the Prayut administration did submit the decree for the parliament's endorsement in October 2019, opposition politicians accused the government of having bypassed the legislature's authority in choosing to exercise executive power and issuing a royal decree for the transfer. The opposition Future Forward Party's secretary general Piyabutr Saengkanokkul was the sole member of the House of Representatives who called for debate. The transfer was not an urgent or emergency matter that justified the exercise of executive power to issue a royal decree; many other laws concerning the monarchy, such as the Royal Service Administration Act of 2017, had been promulgated by the National Legislative Assembly rather than the executive branch, said the legal expert Piyabutr. Nevertheless, the lower house eventually passed the decree with 374 votes in favour, 70 votes against, and two abstentions.[115] Among the seven opposition parties in the lower house of parliament, all 70 votes against the decree were cast by members of the Future Forward Party. The party's stance, however, became a source of internal conflict. The party later grilled a few members who had voted against the party line. Sinual Boonlue, a member of parliament for Chiang Mai, said she had to vote in support of the decree because of her loyalty to the monarchy and not because she was betraying the party's stance.[116]

The main opposition Phuea Thai Party voted to support the decree as party adviser Paradorn Patthanathabutr, a former secretary general of the National Security Council, said, "it's hard to refuse."[117] Nobody in Thailand could raise critical questions about the transfer of the two Army units, whether it was appropriate from a legal point of view or could have any implications for the military, the monarchy or the political system.

The Future Forward Party, which exercised its constitutional right to debate the decree in the parliament, was questioned by conservative and royalist senators during the debate in the upper house. Senator Somchai Sawaengkarn accused the party of stirring conflict in the country. He defended the urgency of the decree, saying it was a matter of national security. The senator called for an end to what he described as the Future Forward's "anti-monarchist stance", saying it could lead to a crisis in the country.[118] Future Forward deputy leader and member of parliament Lieutenant General Pongsakorn Rodchompoo said in an interview that his party did not oppose the transfer of the two infantry regiments to the jurisdiction of the palace but that it had voted against the government's proposal because it was unnecessary to pass such a decree in so hasty a manner. Members of the House of Representatives should have the right to participate in the process, rather than serving as rubber stamps for such an important decision, he said. According to Pongsakorn, the party had a master plan for military reform to create modern, compact and efficient armed forces with the clear objective of properly positioning the military in politics. [119] The plan was shelved as the Future Forward Party was dissolved in February 2020 for taking illegal donations. Pongsakorn and a dozen party executives were banned from electoral politics for ten years.

The royal decree transferring the two regiments eventually received parliament's endorsement and became regular law on 20 October 2019. [120] The central government thus effectively lost its authority to command the two elite units of the armed forces stationed in the capital.

The transfer of two powerful, well-armed and combat-ready regiments to palace command ignited questioning and criticism from international observers. These observers said that the concentration of too much power in the king's hands might risk the alienation of segments of the military. "This is yet another intervention by the king that secures the army and budget to his person", Kevin Hewison, a veteran specialist on Thailand, said in an e-mail message to the Associated Press wire service. "His efforts to aggregate power and wealth appear to have been accepted by the current regime, which needs the king's ongoing support, but does the king (and the regime) risk alienating factions within the military by these actions?" [121]

Neither retired nor serving military officers were willing to offer analysis of the negative implications for the armed forces or for Thai politics of developments such as the transfer of the two regiments to royal control. Pongsakorn said in an interview with the author that the transfer would have no significant impact on the armed forces as a whole because the two units had in fact had the function of protecting the monarchy since the beginning. "Now it is their honour to be under the direct command of His Majesty the King", he said, "It is our pride as soldiers to serve the monarchy. It's our mission. There is no question about that". And there would be no major impact on the rest of the armed forces since ample manpower and resources remained available to serve the core purpose of the military concerning national defence, he said. [122]

For his part, General Sonthi said that protecting the monarchy was one of the main missions of the Thai military. The only difference now, after the transfer of the regiments, involved just the line of command. The regiments were under the direct command of the palace, while the rest of the armed forces performed the same duty under their own superiors or the government. "What the military has to do is to adjust the line of command accordingly", he said.[123]

Pongsakorn, in fact, foresaw political benefits resulting from the transfer of the regiments since the military would see less opportunity to stage a coup to topple governments that it disliked. The 1st and 11th Regiments had been primary actors in coups for a long time as they were stationed in the heart of the capital, close to the seats of political power in the country, he said. Thailand's most recent two coups were plotted and planned within the barracks of the King Guard's units. As General Sonthi explained, in remarks quoted in the previous chapter, his coup in 2006 was driven mainly by troops in those regiments. Pongsakorn suggested that it would be difficult from now on for any commander who wanted to use force to topple a government to move troops to surround and seize Government House. Units in Bangkok were now all under the king's command. The military also planned to relocate non-royal guard units such as artillery and cavalry elements to the provinces, he said. The unnoticed movement of troops from outside the capital would not be easy, the retired general added.[124]

In the final analysis, it might be difficult to predict whether arrangements like the new one would prevent military coups in the future since history has already indicated that *coups d'état* never succeed without the consent of the palace. Still, the king's creation of a personal army would create rifts and alienation within the armed forces, between those who were the monarch's favourites and those who were not. A military coup could possibly be attempted by soldiers in the latter group. Whether carried out by a unified military or not, whether with or without the palace's consent, and whether successful or not, a coup against a government would have implications for Thailand's political stability.

A Big Challenge

The nexus of monarchy and military and the new arrangements discussed above came under serious challenge on 10 August 2020, when Thammasat

University undergraduate Panusaya Sithijirawattanakul took the stage at the university's Rangsit campus to shock the nation with ten demands for reform of the monarchy. The aim of the proposed reforms was to position the royal institution within the Thai system of government and to rearrange its relations with the armed forces—all in accordance with the principles of constitutional monarchy. Panusaya won praise from the BBC as one of 100 inspiring and influential women in the world.[125] Her group, called the United Front of Thammasat and Demonstration (UFTD), and students and young activists from across the country called a series of rallies to express their pent-up grievances, which first burst to the surface after the dissolution of the Future Forward Party in February 2020. The March 2019 elections had seen many first-time voters cast their ballots for the progressive new party, in the hope of a brighter future. They saw politics clearly enough to understand that the Future Forward, which had begun to use the parliament to call for examination of transfers of troops to royal control, was disbanded by the establishment in order to maintain the status quo and the privileges of the elite in a hierarchical society.

The youthful protesters were of the same generation as Panusaya and had formed their political ideas after the 2014 coup. They perceived the roles of the monarchy and the military differently from members of their parents' generation and wanted to see the monarchy positioned under the constitution and operating according to constitutional conventions. Among the ten demands listed by the UFTD, one called for the monarchy not to endorse future military *coups d'état*. The youthful protesters also called for abolition of the Royal Office. They contended that units with clear duties, such as the Royal Security Command, should be transferred and placed under other agencies and no longer be under the direct control of the king. Agencies unnecessary for administration, such as the Privy Council, should be disbanded, they said.[126]

Many in the Thai population regarded themselves as loyal subjects rather than citizens on an equal footing with the head of state. It was thus very rare to see a segment of that population openly criticizing the monarchy and expressing the will to place the royal institution in a proper place within the polity. The students' demands represented a flash-back to the revolution of 1932, when the People's Party or *Khana ratsadon* replaced Siam's absolute monarchy with a constitutional regime, marking the first milestone of Thai democracy. The UFTD's statement made the group's view of political development clear.

Since the People's Party fomented a revolutionary transformation, the people have hoped that our country would be a democracy with the king as head of state who is truly above politics. But it has not been as such as the king has exercised power to intervene in politics from above. For example, whenever a coup topples a government that has arisen from a real democratic process, the king has signed to appoint the head of the junta. This constitutes the endorsement of each and every coup as legal.

Moreover, the king has moved troops and also transferred a significant amount of the national budget to belong to himself personally. He has exercised extralegal royal authority to amend the [2017] constitution, which had already passed a referendum, to allow him to reside outside the kingdom without having to appoint a regent.

This could be done because the dictatorship government bowed down under the shadow of the king and continues to claim the monarchy for its own benefit. It can be seen that they mutually benefit. Such a situation constitutes an enemy to the principles of a democracy with the king as head of state. There is no democratic country in which such actions take place.

The people ought to know that the king of our country is not above politics. This has consistently been the root of political problems ....[127]

The students demanded Prayut's resignation from the premiership and the adoption of a new charter that actually the monarchy under the rule of law. They wanted to revoke Section 6 of the military-sponsored 2017 Constitution, which grants the monarch immunity from being sued. They held that the country's new constitution should allow parliament, which holds an electoral mandate from the people, to examine the king's wrongdoing, as was stipulated in the constitution promulgated by the People's Party in 1932. The protesters employed several tactics in their street protests, including flash mobs—assemble quickly, demonstrate briefly, and then disperse rapidly. They used social media to call for attention from the palace and to pressure the authorities to respond to their demands. The protesters, who later called themselves the *Khana ratsadon* 2563 or the People's Party of 2020 in order to carry on the spirit of the revolutionaries of 1932, submitted their demands in writing through the king's advisory body, the Privy Council, in September.

On the afternoon of 14 October, a royal motorcade carrying Queen Suthida and Prince Dipangkorn Rasmijoti encountered marching demonstrators, who flashed three-finger salutes—a rebellious symbol famously borrowed from the *Hunger Games* films and used to protest against the establishment since the 2014 military coup. A month later, on 14 November, the protesters used the salute to express their defiance, sang the national anthem—rather than the royal anthem—and turned their backs to the royal motorcade of King Vajiralongkorn and Queen Suthida, while yellow-clad royalists sat, and some prostrated themselves, on sidewalks chanting "Long Live the King and the Queen".[128] On 29 November, thousands of protesters gathered in front of the 11th Infantry Regiment headquarters in Bang Khen District, home of the King's Guard unit, which had become royal property after the transfer in 2019. Thammasat University student Parit "Penguin" Chiwarak read a statement demanding the return of the combat-ready unit to the Army's jurisdiction.[129]

King Vajiralongkorn, Prayut's government and the military indicated they were not interested in negotiating with the youthful protesters, and the authorities began again to enforce the draconian *lèse majesté* law—which Prayut had said in June 2020 the king was averse to using—against the protesters. The government pursued charges of *lèse majesté* under Section 112 of the Penal Code against thirty-nine students and young activists, including a sixteen-year-old high school student, between 24 November 2020 and 6 January 2021.[130] Well-known student activists and young protesters—such as Jatupat Boonpattararaksa, who was the first victim of the *lèse majesté* law under the new king's reign; Panusaya; Parit; and lawyer Anon Nampa—faced multiple charges under the same accusation of insulting the monarchy as they spoke out to offer the same message in different places and at different times. They were repeatedly summoned to acknowledge the charges against them and detained before being freed on bail, but such actions were unlikely able to stop them from fanning the winds of change.

In the meantime, pro-establishment activists mobilized royalists into groups with different names—such as *Thai phakdi* or Thai Loyalists under the leadership of right-wing politician Dr Warong Dechgitvigrom, who had actively protested against Prime Minister Yingluck's government before the 2014 coup. These royalist groups staged shows of force in a bid to support and protect the monarchy. The king, the queen and members of the royal family themselves took a softer approach, appearing in public more often, starting with a huge pro-palace demonstration in October 2020. Their goal was to show a human touch and to reach out to the people by mingling and taking selfies with loyal subjects. King Vajiralongkorn even gave a rare door-step interview with foreign journalist Jonathan Miller, correspondent for Channel 4 News in the United Kingdom and for CNN, on 31 October. The king told the reporter that he had no comment on the protesters' demands for reform of the monarchy but that he "love[d] them all the same".[131]

****

Since ascending the throne, King Vajiralongkorn has consolidated his *de jure* and *de facto* power, restoring in some sense an "absolute monarchy", at least in areas under palace jurisdiction. Legally, Thai constitutions position the sovereign as the head of the armed forces. And the NCPO junta introduced a number of legal instruments to allow the transfer of military units to the jurisdiction of the palace, subject directly to the king's command. Under this arrangement, the monarch would be able to exercise power as he wishes. While the king has his own wealth, it remains the duty of the government to allocate a budget from tax revenues to support the Royal Security Command. The king also has full authority to reward and punish personnel, including troops, under his command. There is no clear rule or law on the prosecution of such people, though in some cases the palace has referred to norms and traditions as its legal basis.

The transfer of soldiers and police to palace jurisdiction has generally proceeded smoothly, although there were certain difficulties as some police officers resisted the move and massive resignations from the force were reported. However, there was no report of a similar reaction from military units; the Thai military had been intensively monarchized for a long time.

The monarch has projected himself as a career military officer since the time he was crown prince. King Vajiralongkorn was educated and trained as a military officer, he practised professionally as a military officer, and he participated in military action on the battlefield in the 1970s, during the anti-communist war. The king has not only commanded military units and trained them himself, but he has also made people in his inner circle into military officers and positioned them to function as royal bodyguards. The monarch apparently wants to inculcate his military style in the armed forces and to intensify the monarchism of those forces.

It remains unclear how many forces are under the Royal Security Command today. Military experts have estimated that its strength could be thousands of armed personnel from various services, combined under the king's command. This strength exceeds the basic requirements for providing security to members of the crown, although it may not offer absolute safety to the monarchy. With well-organized, disciplined and fully equipped military units, the monarch could use this personal army for many purposes beyond just security, given that the two infantry regiments that he now controls have historically been sources of manpower for military coups.

NOTES

1. Peter A. Jackson, "A Grateful Son, a Military King: Thai Media Accounts of the Accession of Rama X to the Throne", *ISEAS Perspective* 2017/26, 26 April 2017, p. 4, https://www.iseas.edu.sg/wp-content/uploads/pdfs/ISEAS_Perspective_2017_26.pdf (accessed 13 July 2019).
2. "Head of State with Heart of Gold: His Majesty the King Has an Illustrious Military Background", *Bangkok Post*, 28 July 2019, https://www.bangkokpost.com/thailand/general/1720331/head-of-state-with-heart-of-gold (accessed 30 October 2019).
3. "Kham to kham: chat thai lae phai khwammankhong nai khwamnuekkhi tkhong phon ek Apirat Kongsompong" [Word by word: The Thai nation and security threats in the thinking of General Apirat Kongsompong], *Prachatai*, 12 October 2019, https://prachatai.com/journal/2019/10/84718 (accessed 5 June 2020). This is a report on the Army commander's special lecture titled "Our Land in Security Perspective", given at Army Headquarters in Bangkok in front of an audience of 500 people, including senior military officers, business leaders, scholars, students and media representatives. The lecture pictured new threats, with a rhetorical backdrop suggesting the need to be wary of the menace of communism.
4. "Long Live the King: Military Education", *Bangkok Post*, 1 December 2016, https://www.bangkokpost.com/life/social-and-lifestyle/1148940/military-education (accessed 3 February 2020).
5. Sataporn Books, *Somdet phrachaoyuhua Maha Vajiralongkorn Bodindradebayavarangkun phraphu pen saengsawang klang chai thai* [King Vajiralongkorn: A light in the Thai mind] (Bangkok: Sataporn Books, 2018). Besides royal news releases and articles in the mainstream media, the private publisher Sataporn Books was the first outlet to release a biography of Rama X, but the publisher declined to give further information when asked via

e-mail on 30 October 2019 about the sources of information and whether the publication occurred with royal permission or acknowledgement. The publisher said that these matters concerned internal working processes. However, the Royal Household basically required all private publishers to ask for permission before releasing publications about the current monarch. Sataporn Books was previously known for books such as novels and comics for the younger generation.

6. Royal Thai Army, *Nueng roi pi rongrian nairoi phrachulachomklao* [100 Years of Chulachomklao Royal Military Academy] (Bangkok: Royal Thai Army, 1987), vol. 2, p. 56. It is interesting to note that this work cites Prayut Sitthipan, *Chao fa* [Prince] (Bangkok: Ruamkanphim, n.d.), p. 825, rather than referring to official records.

7. "Long Live the King: Military Education", *op. cit.*

8. Royal Thai Army, *Nueng roi pi rongrian nairoi phrachulachomklao*, vol. 2, p. 58.

9. "Prakat samnak nayokratthamontri rueang taengtang nai thahan phiset" [Announcement of the Prime Minister's Office on appointment of special military officer], *Royal Gazette* vol. 108, section 104, 13 June 1991, http://www.ratchakitcha.soc.go.th/DATA/PDF/2534/D/104/5555.PDF (accessed 10 October 2019).

10. "Prakat samnak nayokratthamontri rueang taengtang phubangkhapkan phiset" [Announcement of the Prime Minister's Office on appointment of special commander], *Royal Gazette* vol. 103, section 64 (special issue), 21 April 1986, http://www.ratchakitcha.soc.go.th/DATA/PDF/2529/D/064/1.PDF (accessed 10 October 2019).

11. Interview with a retired Thai Army general, Bangkok, 18 December 2019.

12. "Battle Rages as Reds Attack Loei Outpost", *Bangkok Post*, 31 October 1976, p. 1.

13. "Pho ko ko buk nak ying helikhoptoe ruang rongphukamkap sahat" [Insurgents shoot helicopter down, gravely injure deputy superintendent], *Ban mueang*, 30 October 1976, pp. 1, 16.

14. Royal Thai Army, *Nueng roi pi rongrian nairoi phrachulachomklao*, vol. 2, pp. 280–82.

15. Ibid., vol. 2, p. 281.

16. Ibid.

17. Ibid.

18. "Battle Rages as Reds Attack Loei Outpost"; "Sala chip phuea chat" [They sacrificed their lives for the nation], *Thai rat*, 6 November 1976, p. 3; Romfa, "Sangkhom phak klang" [Central Thai society], *Thai rat*, 6 November 1976, p. 6; and "Supsip" [Gossip], *Thai rat*, 7 November 1976, p. 7.

19. Taifun, "Bukkhon nai khao" [People in the news], *Thai rat*, 9 November 1976, p. 4.
20. "Sadet naeo na" [Royal visit to the front lines], *Thai rat*, 8 November 1976, p. 1.
21. "Army Chief Lashes Communists", *Bangkok Post*, 12 October 2019, https://www.bangkokpost.com/thailand/politics/1770189/army-chief-lashes-communists (accessed 3 February 2020). The online version of this article includes a photograph showing the then crown prince on the battlefield in Loei.
22. Jackson, "A Grateful Son, a Military King", p. 5.
23. "Thailand's King Rama X—From Pilot Prince to Powerful Monarch", Reuters, 2 May 2019, https://www.reuters.com/article/us-thailand-king-vajiralongkorn-profile/thailands-king-rama-x-from-pilot-prince-to-powerful-monarch-idUSKCN1S8114 (accessed 29 October 2019).
24. "Cabin Crew, Body Guard, Thai Queen: Suthida's Meteoric Rise", *New Straits Times*, 4 May 2019, https://www.nst.com.my/world/2019/05/485564/cabin-crew-bodyguard-thai-queen-suthidas-meteoric-rise (accessed 29 October 2019).
25. "Prakat rueang phraratchathan yot thahan" [Announcement of royal bestowal of military rank], *Royal Gazette*, vol. 138, section 8 *ko*, 5 March 2018, http://www.ratchakitcha.soc.go.th/DATA/PDF/2561/B/008/1. PDF (accessed 8 November 2019); and "Prakat taengtang thahan ratcha-ongkharak phiset" [Announcement of appointment of special royal guard], *Royal Gazette*, vol. 135, section 48 *ngo*, 5 March 2018, http://www.ratchakitcha.soc.go.th/DATA/PDF/2561/E/048/1.PDF (accessed 8 November 2019).
26. "Prakat phraratchathan yot thahan" [Announcement of royal bestowal of military rank], *Royal Gazette*, vol. 135, section 25 *kho*, 24 July 2018, http://www.ratchakitcha.soc.go.th/DATA/PDF/2561/B/025/T1.PDF (accessed 8 November 2019).
27. "Prakat rueang sathapana somdet phranangchao Sutthida Bajrasud-habimalalakshana" [Announcement of installation of Queen Sutthida], *Royal Gazette*, vol. 136, section 14 *kho*, 4 May 2019, http://www.ratchakitcha.soc.go.th/DATA/PDF/2562/B/014/T_0002.PDF (accessed 29 October 2019).
28. "Prakat rueang phraratchathan khrueangrat itsiriyaphon chulachomkhlao" [Announcement of bestowal of Chulachomklaoroyal decoration], *Royal Gazette*, vol. 135, section 1 *kho*, 4 January 2018, http://www.ratchakitcha.soc.go.th/DATA/PDF/2561/B/001/1.PDF (accessed 29 October 2019).
29. "Prakat samnak nayokratthamontri rueang phraratchathan yot thahan tam kwa chan naiphon" [Announcement of Prime Minister' Office on

royal bestowal of military rank below general], *Royal Gazette*, vol. 130, section 3 *kho*, 25 January 2013, http://www.ratchakitcha.soc.go.th/DATA/PDF/2556/B/003/1.PDF (accessed 29 October 2019).

30. The announcement of her military ranks appeared some years after she had assumed those ranks, and her assumption of the rank of sub-lieutenant rank was announced more than a year after the announcement of her assumption of the rank of lieutenant. "Prakat samnak nayokratthamontri rueang phraratchathan yot thahan tam kwa chan naiphon" [Announcement of Prime Minister's Office on royal bestowal of military rank below general], *Royal Gazette*, vol. 129, section 15 *kho*, 27 April 2012, http://www.ratchakitcha.soc.go.th/DATA/PDF/2555/B/015/1.PDF (accessed 29 October 2019); "Prakat samnak nayokratthamontri rueang phraratchathan yot thahan tam kwa chan naiphon" [Announcement of Prime Minister's Office on royal bestowal of military rank below general], *Royal Gazette*, vol. 129, section 15 *kho*, 27 April 2012, http://www.ratchakitcha.soc.go.th/DATA/PDF/2555/B/015/1.PDF (accessed 29 October 2019); and "Prakat samnak nayokratthamontr irueang phraratchathan yot thahan tam kwa chan naiphon" [Announcement of Prime Minister's Office on royal bestowal of military rank below general], *Royal Gazette*, vol. 130, section 14 *kho*, 17 June 2013, http://www.ratchakitcha.soc.go.th/DATA/PDF/2556/B/014/1.PDF (accessed 29 October 2019). The last of these announcements stated that her rank of colonel had been effective since 1 October 2012.

31. "Prakat samnak nayokratthamontri rueang phraratchathan yot thahan chan naiphon" [Announcement of Prime Minister's Office on royal bestowal of military rank of general], *Royal Gazette*, vol. 130, section 27 *kho*, 11 November 2013, http://www.ratchakitcha.soc.go.th/DATA/PDF/2556/B/027/1.PDF (accessed 29 October 2019); and "Prakat samnak nayokratthamontri rueang phraratchathan yot thahan chan naiphon" [Announcement of Prime Minister's Office on royal bestowal of military rank of general], *Royal Gazette*, vol. 133, section 44 *kho*, 10 December 2016, http://www.ratchakitcha.soc.go.th/DATA/PDF/2559/B/044/1.PDF (accessed 29 October 2019).

32. "'Ro10' sadetliap phranakhon ngotngamyingyaisomphrakiatsaesong songphracharoen kuekkong" [Rama X circles Phranakhon to emphatic cries of "Long live the king!"], *Thai rat*, 6 May 2019, https://www.thairath.co.th/news/royal/1561088 (accessed 29 October 2019).

33. "Queen Exudes Military Prowess", *Bangkok Post*, 3 June 2019, https://www.bangkokpost.com/thailand/general/1688500/queen-exudes-military-prowess (accessed 29 October 2019).

34. Ministry of Education, Thailand, "Royal Biography of Her Majesty Queen Suthida Bajrasudhabimalalakshana", n.d., http://www.en.moe.go.th/

enMoe2017/index.php/articles/387-royal-biography-of-her-majesty-queen-suthida-bajrasudhabimalalakshana (accessed 29 October 2019).

35. "Prakat samnak nayokratthamontri rueang phraratchathan yot thahan tam kwa chan naiphon" [Announcement of Prime Minister's Office on royal bestowal of military rank below general], *Royal Gazette*, vol. 134, section 29 *kho*, 23 June 2017, http://www.ratchakitcha.soc.go.th/DATA/PDF/2560/B/029/1.PDF (accessed 30 October 2019).

36. "Prakat samnak nayokratthamontri rueang phraratchathan yot thahan tam kwa chan naiphon" [Announcement of Prime Minister's Office on royal bestowal of military rank below general], *Royal Gazette*, vol. 134, section 29 *kho*, 23 June 2017, http://www.ratchakitcha.soc.go.th/DATA/PDF/2560/B/029/3.PDF (accessed 30 October 2019).

37. "Prakat samnak nayok ratthamontri rueang phraratchathan yot thahan tam kwa chan naiphon" [Announcement of Prime Minister's Office on royal bestowal of military rank below general], *Royal Gazette*, vol. 135, section 21 *kho*, 25 June 2018, http://www.ratchakitcha.soc.go.th/DATA/PDF/2561/B/021/1.PDF (accessed 30 October 2019).

38. "Prakat samnak nayokratthamontri rueang phraratchathan yot thahan tam kwa chan naiphon" [Announcement of Prime Minister's Office on royal bestowal of military rank below general], *Royal Gazette*, vol. 134, section 16 *kho*, 22 March 2017, http://www.ratchakitcha.soc.go.th/DATA/PDF/2560/B/014/1.PDF (accessed 30 October 2019).

39. "Prakat samnak nayokratthamontri rueang phraratchathan yot thahan tam kwa chan naiphon" [Announcement of Prime Minister's Office on royal bestowal of military rank below general], *Royal Gazette*, vol. 134, section 29 *kho*, 23 June 2017, http://www.ratchakitcha.soc.go.th/DATA/PDF/2560/B/029/2.PDF (accessed 30 October 2019); and "Hai naithahan sanyabat ok chak yot thahan" [Stripping commissioned officer of military rank], *Royal Gazette*, vol. 134, section 61 *kho*, 24 November 2017, http://www.ratchakitcha.soc.go.th/DATA/PDF/2560/B/061/1.PDF (accessed 30 October 2019).

40. "Prakat samnak nayokratthamontri rueang phraratchathan khrueangrat itsiriyaphon pen korani phiset" [Announcement of Prime Minister's Office on special bestowal of royal decoration], *Royal Gazette*, vol. 130, section 28 *kho*, 13 November 2013, http://www.ratchakitcha.soc.go.th/DATA/PDF/2556/B/028/1.PDF (accessed 4 February 2020).

41. "Prakat samnak nayokratthamontri rueang phraratchathan khrueangrat itsiriyaphon pen korani phiset" [Announcement of Prime Minister's Office on special bestowal of royal decoration], *Royal Gazette*, vol. 131, section 10 *kho*, 6 May 2014, http://www.ratchakitcha.soc.go.th/DATA/PDF/2557/B/010/3.PDF (accessed 4 February 2020); and "Prakat samnak

nayokratthamontri rueang taengtang kharatchakan phonlaruean nai phra-
ong" [Announcement of Prime Minister's Office on appointment of civilian
official in royal service], *Royal Gazette*, vol. 131, special section 59 *ngo*,
4 April 2014, http://www.ratchakitcha.soc.go.th/DATA/PDF/2557/
E/059/1.PDF (accessed 4 February 2020).

42. "Prakat samnak nayokratthamontri rueang phraratchathan phraborom-
    marachanuyat hai thot yot thahan" [Announcement of Prime Minister's
    Office on royal permission to strip military rank], *Royal Gazette*, vol. 133,
    section 3 *kho*, 2 February 2016, (http://www.ratchakitcha.soc.go.th/DATA/
    PDF/2559/B/003/8.PDF (accessed 4 February 2020).

43. "Prakat hai on kharatchakan fai phonlaruean nai phra-ong pen kharatchakan
    nai phra-ong fai thahan lae phraratchathan yot thahan" [Announcement
    converting civilian official in royal service into military officer in royal
    service and on royal bestowal of military rank], *Royal Gazette*, vol. 137,
    special section 21 *ngo*, 28 January 2020, http://www.ratchakitcha.soc.go.th/
    DATA/PDF/2563/E/021/T_0002.PDF (accessed 4 February 2020).

44. "Prakat hai on kharatchakan fai phonlaruean nai phra-ong pen kharatchakan
    nai phra-ong fai thahan lae phraratchathan yot thahan" [Announcement
    converting civilian official in royal service into military officer in royal
    service and on bestowal of military rank], *Royal Gazette*, vol. 137, special
    section 21 *ngo*, 28 January 2020, http://www.ratchakitcha.soc.go.th/DATA/
    PDF/2563/E/021/T_0001.PDF (accessed 4 February 2020).

45. "Prakat rueang taengtang hai damrong thanandonsak lae phraratchathan
    khrueangrat itsiriyaphon thuk chantra" [Announcement on appointment
    to royal status and award of decorations of all classes], *Royal Gazette*,
    vol. 137, section 23 *kho*, 29 August 2020, http://www.ratchakitcha.soc.
    go.th/DATA/PDF/2563/B/023/T_0020.PDF (accessed 5 January 2021).

46. "Prakat hai kharatchakan nai phra-ong fai thahan phon chak tamnaeng
    thot thanandonsak lae yot thahan talotchon riakkhuen khrueangrat
    itsiriyaphon thuk chantra" [Announcement of removal of military
    officer in royal service from position, stripping royal status and military
    rank and status, and revocation of all royal decorations], *Royal Gazette*,
    vol. 136, section 55 *kho*, 21 October 2019, http://www.ratchakitcha.soc.
    go.th/DATA/PDF/2562/B/055/T_0001.PDF (accessed 22 October 2019).

47. Ibid.

48. "Photos of the Thai Consort Shooting a Rifle and Flying a Jet May Have
    Crashed a Royal Website", *Washington Post*, 27 August 2019, https://www.
    washingtonpost.com/world/2019/08/27/photos-thai-consort-shooting-rifle-
    flying-jet-may-have-crashed-royal-website/ (accessed 30 October 2019).

49. "Prakat samnak nayokratthamontri rueang phraratchanthan yott hahan
    tam kwa chan naiphon" [Announcement of Prime Minister's Office on
    royal bestowal of military rank below general], *Royal Gazette*, vol. 129,

section 15 *kho*, 27 April 2012, http://www.ratchakitcha.soc.go.th/DATA/PDF/2555/B/015/1.PDF (accessed 29 October 2019).

50. "Thai-Geliebteim Horrorknast" [Thai sweet-heart in prison of horror], *Bild*, 30 October 2019, https://www.bild.de/unterhaltung/royals/royals/koenig-rama-x-zeigt-sich-gnadenlos-thai-geliebte-im-horrorknast-65708342.bild.html (accessed 1 November 2019).

51. The *ratchasawat* rules were mentioned in many official documents, including an undated report prepared for the Constitutional College of the Constitutional Court by former royal official and close aide to the late King Bhumibol, Dr Disathorn Vajarodaya. The report, titled "Lak nititham nai nayobai kankamkap dulae ongkon thi di" (Rules of law for palace administration), is available at http://www.constitutionalcourt.or.th/occ_web/ewt_dl_link.php?nid=8773 (accessed 13 February 2020). Disathorn was himself dismissed from the position of grand chamberlain in November 2016 for disciplinary violations and severe immoral acts. He was charged by police a year later with abuse of power.

52. "Prakat hai plot naithahan chan sanyabat ok chak ratchakan lae thot yot thahan phrom riakkhuen khruengrat itsiriyaphon" [Announcement on removal of military officers from service, on stripping of rank and on revocation of royal decorations], *Royal Gazette*, vol. 136, section 57 *kho*, 29 October 2019, http://www.ratchakitcha.soc.go.th/DATA/PDF/2562/B/057/T_0002.PDF (accessed 30 October 2019). A male captain and a female first lieutenant were sacked for faults with their work.

53. "Prakat hai lai kharatchakan phonlaruean nai phra-ong ok chak ratchankan lae thot yot thahan phrom riakkhuen khrueangrat itsiriyaphon" [Announcement on removal from service of civilian officials in royal service, on stripping of military ranks and on revocation of royal decorations], *Royal Gazette*, vol. 136, section 57 *kho*, 29 October 2019, http://www.ratchakitcha.soc.go.th/DATA/PDF/2562/B/057/T_0001.PDF (accessed 30 October 2019). Two lieutenant colonels in the aide-de-camp unit guarding the royal bedrooms were fired for disciplinary violations and adultery.

54. "Prakat songphrakarunaplotklaoplotkramom hai klap khao rap ratchakan phraratchathan yot naithahan chan sanyabat phraratchathan khuen khrueangrat itsiriyaphon thuk chantra hai kharatchakan nai phra-ong" [Announcement on reinstatement, on royal bestowal of military rank and on restoration of all royal decorations to an official in royal service], *Royal Gazette*, vol. 136, section 59 *kho*, 11 November 2019, http://www.ratchakitcha.soc.go.th/DATA/PDF/2562/B/059/T_0001.PDF (accessed 12 November 2019).

55. "Chamkhuk nueng duean Pongpat Chayaphan khadi thi paet yuen banchi sapsin thet" [Pongpat Chayaphan sentenced to one month in jail in eighth

case of false asset declaration], *BBC Thai*, 27 February 2018, https://www.bbc.com/thai/thailand-43207247 (accessed 6 November 2019).

56. "Pongpat Sent to Prison for 6 Years in First Case", *Bangkok Post*, 30 January 2015, https://www.bangkokpost.com/thailand/general/462642/pongpat-gets-reduced-6-years-in-first-case (accessed 6 November 2019).

57. "Prakat rueang la-ok chak thanandonsak" [Announcement on stepping down from royal status], *Royal Gazette*, vol. 131, section 29 *kho*, 12 December 2014, http://www.ratchakitcha.soc.go.th/DATA/PDF/2557/B/029/1.PDF (accessed 6 November 2019).

58. "Prakat samnak nayokratthamontri hai banchu lae taengtang kharatchakan phonlaruean nai phra-ong" [Announcement of Prime Minister's Office on appointment of official in royal service], *Royal Gazette*, vol. 128, special section 72 *ngo*, 28 June 2011, http://www.ratchakitcha.soc.go.th/DATA/PDF/2554/E/072/10.PDF (accessed 6 November 2019); and "Jumpol Manmai khue khrai?" [Who is Jumpol Manmai?], *BBC Thai*, 1 March 2017, https://www.bbc.com/thai/thailand-39119559 (accessed 6 November 2019).

59. "Prakat samnak nayokratthamontri hai thot yot tamruat" [Announcement of Prime Minister's Office on stripping of police rank], *Royal Gazette*, vol. 134, section 10 *kho*, 10 March 2017, http://www.ratchakitcha.soc.go.th/DATA/PDF/2560/B/010/1.PDF (accessed 6 November 2019).

60. "Phanraya phon to o Jumpol Manmai khao rap 5 khoha ruk pa thaplan phoei si na khrengkhriat to ro hai prakan wongngoen 2 saen" [Wife of Pol General Jumpol Manmai acknowledges five charges of forest encroachment, released on 200,000 baht bail], *Matichon*, 3 March 2017, https://www.matichon.co.th/local/crime/news_483466 (accessed 6 November 2019).

61. "San chamkhuk Jumpol Manmai hok pi saraphap lot luea sam thot yot chak phon tamruat ek pen nai" [Court sentences Jimpol Manmaito to six years, reduced to three after confession, reduced in rank from general to private], *Thai rat*, 10 March 2017, https://www.thairath.co.th/news/880615 (accessed 6 November 2019).

62. "Prakat samnak nayokratthamontri hai naithahan rap ratchakan" [Announcement of Prime Minister's Office on the appointment of military officer to government service], *Royal Gazette*, vol. 116, section 92 *ngo*, 18 November 1999, http://www.ratchakitcha.soc.go.th/DATA/PDF/2542/D/092/51.PDF (accessed 7 January 2021).

63. "Prakat samnak nayokratthamontri hai naithahan rap ratchakan" [Announcement of Prime Minister's Office on appointment of military officer to government service], *Royal Gazette*, vol. 117, section 76 *ngo*, 20 September 2001, http://www.ratchakitcha.soc.go.th/DATA/PDF/2544/D/076/2.PDF (accessed 7 January 2021).

64. "Prakat taengtang khanakammakan sapsin suanphramahakasat" [Announcement on the appointment of board of Crown Property Bureau], *Royal Gazette*, vol. 134, special section 183 *ngo*, 17 July 2017, http://www. ratchakitcha.soc.go.th/DATA/PDF/2560/E/183/3.PDF (accessed 7 January 2021).

65. "Prakat taengtang lekhathikan phraratchawang lae phu-amnuaykan samnakngan sapsin suanphramahakasat" [Announcement of appointment of secretary general of the palace and director of Crown Property Bureau], *Royal Gazette*, vol. 135, special section 55 *ngo*, 16 March 2018, http://www. ratchakitcha.soc.go.th/DATA/PDF/2561/E/055/2.PDF (accessed 7 January 2021).

66. "Prakat hai kharatchaboriphan phon wara ratcha-ongkharak nai phra-ong" [Announcement of the end of royal official's term in royal service], *Royal Gazette*, vol., 136 special section 11 *ngo*, 23 April 2019, http://www. ratchakitcha.soc.go.th/DATA/PDF/2562/E/101/T_0001.PDF (accessed 7 November 2019).

67. "Prakat hai kharatchaboriphan taengtang pen ratcha-ongkharak nai phra-ong" [Announcement of appointment of royal official as royal bodyguard], *Royal Gazette*, vol. 136, special section 111 *ngo*, 3 May 2019, http://www. ratchakitcha.soc.go.th/DATA/PDF/2562/E/111/T_0001.PDF (accessed 7 November 2019).

68. "Prakat samnak nayokratthamontri hai naithahan rap ratchakan" [Announcement of Prime Minister's Office on appointment of military officer to government service], *Royal Gazette*, vol. 127, section 44 *ngo*, 7 April 2010, http://www.ratchakitcha.soc.go.th/DATA/PDF/2553/E/044/27.PDF (accessed 7 November 2019).

69. "Prakat hai plot ok lae lai ok thot yot naithahan chan sanyabat phrom riakkhuen khrueangrat itsiriyaphon" [Announcement of removal, dismissal, stripping of military rank and revocation of royal decoration], *Royal Gazette*, vol. 136, section 56 *kho*, 23 October 2019, http://www.ratchakitcha.soc. go.th/DATA/PDF/2562/B/056/T_0001.PDF (accessed 7 November 2019).

70. "Prakat samnak nayokratthamontri hai taengtang kharatchakan phonlaruean nai phra-ong" [Announcement of Prime Minister's Office on appointment of civil servant in royal service], *Royal Gazette*, vol. 123, section 9 *ngo*, 31 January 2006, http://www.ratchakitcha.soc.go.th/DATA/ PDF/2549/00181020.PDF (accessed 12 November 2019).

71. "Prakat samnak nayokratthamontri hai taengtang kharatchakan phon-laruean nai phra-ong" [Announcement of Prime Minister's Office on appointment of civil servant to royal service], *Royal Gazette*, vol. 126, special section 22 *ngo*, 11 February 2009, http://www.ratchakitcha.soc. go.th/DATA/PDF/2552/E/022/12.PDF (accessed 12 November 2019); and

"Prapprung kankamnot tamnaeng lae taengtang kharatchakan nai phra-ong" [Adjustment of position and appointment of official to royal service], *Royal Gazette*, vol. 126, special section 172 *ngo*, 26 November 2009, http://www.ratchakitcha.soc.go.th/DATA/PDF/2552/E/172/22.PDF (accessed 12 November 2019).

72. "Prakat samnak nayokratthamontri rueang phraratchathan yot thahan tam kwa chan naiphon" [Announcement of Prime Minister's Office on royal bestowal of military rank below general], *Royal Gazette*, vol. 134, section 16 *kho*, 22 March 2017, http://www.ratchakitcha.soc.go.th/DATA/PDF/2560/B/014/1.PDF (accessed 30 October 2019).

73. "Prakat samnak nayokratthamontri rueang phraratchathan yot thahan chan naiphon" [Announcement of Prime Minister's Office on royal bestowal of military rank of general], *Royal Gazette*, vol. 134, section 21 *kho*, 24 April 2017, http://www.ratchakitcha.soc.go.th/DATA/PDF/2560/B/021/5.PDF (accessed 12 November 2019).

74. "Prakat hai plot ok lae lai ok thot yot naithahan chan sanyabat phrom riakkhuen khrueangrat itsiriyaphon" [Announcement of removal, dismissal, stripping of military rank and revocation of royal decoration], *Royal Gazette*, vol. 136, section 56 *kho*, 23 October 2019, http://www.ratchakitcha.soc.go.th/DATA/PDF/2562/B/056/T_0001.PDF (accessed 12 November 2019).

75. "Prakat songphrakarunaplotklaoplotkramom hai klap khao rap ratchakan phraratchathan yot naithahan chan sanyabat lae phraratchathan khuen khrueangrat itsiriyaphon thuk chantra" [Announcement on reinstatement, on royal bestowal of military rank and on restoration of all royal decorations to an official in royal service], *Royal Gazette*, vol. 136, section 59 *kho*, 11 November 2019, http://www.ratchakitcha.soc.go.th/DATA/PDF/2562/B/059/T_0001.PDF (accessed 12 November 2019).

76. "Prakat samnak nayokratthamontri rueang phraratchathan phraborommarachanuyat sathapana nuai thahan pen nuai thahan raksa phra-ong" [Announcement of Prime Minister's Office on appointment of military unit as royal guard unit], *Royal Gazette*, vol. 109, section 158, 15 December 1992, http://www.ratchakitcha.soc.go.th/DATA/PDF/2535/D/158/14087.PDF (accessed 5 February 2020).

77. "Pharatchabanyat chat rabiap ratchakan krasuang kalahom chabap this ong pho so 2556" [Ministry of Defence Organisation Act of 2013], *Royal Gazette*, vol. 130, section 109 *kho*, 20 November 2013, http://www.ratchakitcha.soc.go.th/DATA/PDF/2556/A/109/1.PDF (accessed 5 November 2020).

78. "Phraratchakritsadika baeng suanratchakan lae kamnot nathi khong suanratchakan nuai banchakan raksa khwamplotphai raksa phra-ong krasuang kalahom pho so 2557" [Royal decree on Royal Security Command of 2014], *Royal Gazette*, vol. 131, section 38 *kho*, 5 April 2014, http://

www.ratchakitcha.soc.go.th/DATA/PDF/2557/A/038/1.PDF (accessed 5 February 2020).

79. During the reign of Rama IX, the security code 901 referred to King Bhumibol, 902 to Queen Sirikit, and 903 to Princess Ubolratana, while 904 was a reference to Crown Prince Vajiralongkorn. The king maintained his code designation after ascending the throne.

80. Marwaan Macan-Markar, "All the King's Men: Thai Military Power Shifts Away from Prayuth", *Nikkei Asian Review*, 2 July 2019, https://asia.nikkei.com/Spotlight/Asia-Insight/All-the-king-s-men-Thai-military-power-shifts-away-from-Prayuth (accessed 5 December 2019).

81. "Phraratchabanyat rabiap borihan ratchakan nai phra-ong" [Royal Service Administration Act of 2017], *Royal Gazette*, vol. 134, section 88 *ko*, 1 May 2017, http://www.ratchakitcha.soc.go.th/DATA/PDF/2560/A/048/1.PDF (accessed 31 October 2019).

82. Ibid., p. 5.

83. "Phraratchakritsadika chat rabiap ratchakan lae borihan ngan bukkhon khong ratchakan nai phra-ong pho so 2560" [Royal decree on Administration and Personnel in Royal Service of 2017], *Royal Gazette*, vol. 134, section 51 *ko*, 10 May 2017, http://www.ratchakitcha.soc.go.th/DATA/PDF/2560/A/051/1.PDF (accessed 31 October 2019).

84. Ibid, p. 3.

85. "Prakat rabiap suanratchakan nai phra-ong waduai thong chaichaloemphon nuai banchakan thawai khwamplotphai raksa phra-ong pho so 2562" [Announcement on regulations concerning *chaichaloemphon* flag of Royal Security Command of 2019], *Royal Gazette*, vol. 136, special section 303 *ngo*, 12 December 2019, http://www.ratchakitcha.soc.go.th/DATA/PDF/2562/E/303/T_0001.PDF (accessed 13 December 2019). The *chaichaloemphon* flag is a standard granted to military units by the king for them to use in showing loyalty to the monarchy. The flag represents and symbolizes royal blessing of military units. The tradition of oath-taking in front of the flag dates from the reign of King Chulalongkorn, and in the Sarit the strongman gave instructions to all military units that had been granted the *chaichaloemphon* flag to perform the ceremony of oath-taking in front of it annually to uplift the stature of the royal institution and strengthen ideological ties between the monarchy and the military. King Bhumibol granted the flag occasionally to battalions of the three branches of the armed forces and to royal guard units starting in 1953.

86. "Kot krasuang baeng suanratchakan pen kong bangkhapkan rue suanratchakan yang uen nai samnakngan tamruat haengchat (chabap thi 11) pho so 2562" [Ministerial regulation on division of command on other functions in the National Police Office, 2019], *Royal Gazette*, vol.

136, section 12 *ko*, 27 January 2019, http://www.ratchakitcha.soc.go.th/DATA/PDF/2562/A/012/T_0006.PDF (accessed 14 February 2020).

87. "Song to ro mahatlek 904 ruam la chon amanut kha khon ching thong" [Dispatch of royal guard police 904 to joint manhunt for inhumane and murderous gold thieves], *Deli niu*, 11 January 2020, https://www.dailynews.co.th/crime/751316 (accessed 14 February 2020); "Chop pharakit! wisaman khon rai kratying khorat" [End of mission! Extra-judicial killing of mass shooter in Khorat], Thai News Agency, 9 February 2020, https://www.mcot.net/viewtna/5e3f779ae3f8e40af441b5ad (accessed 14 February 2020); and "'Tamruat rajawallop 904' bukthalai 'sep-hao umbun' phop 7 sao rapchang tangkan" ["Rajawallop 904 police" break into "safe house", find seven pregnant-for-hire women], Amarin TV, 13 February 2020, https://www.amarintv.com/news/detail/21803 (accessed 9 June 2020).

88. "Sarup khao kanprachum khanaratthamontri 14 karakadakhom 2563" [News summary of cabinet meeting of 14 July 2020], Royal Thai Government, n.d., https://www.thaigov.go.th/news/contents/details/33356 (accessed 22 July 2020).

89. "2019 Survey of Thai Political Landscape in Transition", *Prachatai English*, 17 February 2020, https://prachatai.com/english/node/8365 (accessed 21 February 2020).

90. Nipat Thonglek, "Phap kao lao tamnan: nuai thahan raksa phra-ong" [Old pictures tell story of royal guards], *Matichon*, 12 February 2019, https://www.matichon.co.th/news-monitor/news_1360525 (accessed 1 November 2019). *Nueng roi pi rongrian nairoi phrachulachomklao*, vol. 2, pp. 14–45; Colonel Worakanbancha, *Tamnan thahan mahatlek* [Chronicle of aides-de-camp] (Bangkok, 15 June 1953), the cremation volume for General Phraworawongthoe Krommamuen Adison Udomsak and a work on which *Nueng roi pi rongrian nairoi phrachulachomklao* draws; and Thep Boontanont, *Kanmueang nai kanthahan samai ratchakan thi hok* [Politics in the Thai military during the reign of Rama VI] (Bangkok: Matichon Books, 2016), pp. 110–11, indicate that Rama V himself set up the "scarecrow" aides-de-camp. But this chapter follows General Nipat, as he offers a specific timeline, while the other texts do not.

91. The oldest announcement seeking applications to serve in the Crown Prince's Rajawallop Guard was found on the internet in July 2015. It was signed by Lieutenant General Jakkraphob Bhuridej, commander of the Crown Prince's Rajawallop Guard. In recent years, the Interior Ministry has circulated the letter of announcement to provincial authorities; see http://www.gad.moi.go.th/nsk-21-12-61-7445.pdf (accessed 4 November 2019). This announcement later appeared on the official websites of provinces including Nakhon Pathom in Central Thailand (see http://www.nakhonpathom.go.th/files/com_news/2018-07_e96d9b59e13cd15.pdf, accessed 4 November

2019), Narathiwat in the Deep South (see http://www2.narathiwat.go.th/nara2016/files/com_order/2018-07_461d8eef923957b.pdf, accessed 4 November 2019), and Nan in the Upper North (see http://www.nan.go.th/webjo/attachments/1920_soger.pdf, accessed 4 November 2019). Provincial authorities also forwarded the announcement to officials at lower levels of local administration—districts, municipalities and subdistricts.

92. Pavin Chachavalpongpun, "Dhaveevatthana Prison: Hell on Earth in Thailand", *Japan Times*, 2 June 2017, https://www.japantimes.co.jp/opinion/2017/06/02/commentary/world-commentary/dhaveevatthana-prison-hell-earth-thailand/#.Xb-4n5ozaUk (accessed 4 November 2019).

93. "Prakat samnak nayokratthamontri rueang taengtang ratcha-ongkharak" [Announcement of Prime Minister's Office on appointment of royal guard], *Royal Gazette*, vol. 134, special section 76 *ngo*, 12 March 2017, http://www.ratchakitcha.soc.go.th/DATA/PDF/2560/E/076/21.PDF (accessed 5 February 2020), p. 21, announced the appointment of just one officer as a bodyguard to the king, while "Prakat samnak nayokratthamontri rueang taengtang ratcha-ongkharak" [Announcement of Prime Minister's Office on appointment of royal guards], *Royal Gazette*, vol. 134, special section 137 *ngo*, 22 May 2017, http://www.ratchakitcha.soc.go.th/DATA/PDF/2560/E/137/1.PDF (accessed 5 February 2020), announced the appointment of as many as 548 officers as bodyguards to the king.

94. "Prakat samnak nayokratthamontri rueang taengtang ratcha-ongkharak" [Announcement of Prime Minister's Office on appointment of royal guards], *Royal Gazette*, vol. 133, special section 250 *ngo*, 2 November 2016, http://www.ratchakitcha.soc.go.th/DATA/PDF/2559/E/250/2.PDF (accessed 4 November 2019).

95. "Prakat taengtang ratcha-ongkharak wen lae naitamruat ratchasamnak wen" [Announcement of appointment of duty royal guards and duty royal guard police], *Royal Gazette*, vol. 134, special section 195 *ngo*, 31 July 2017, http://www.ratchakitcha.soc.go.th/DATA/PDF/2560/E/195/1.PDF (accessed 4 November 2019).

96. Interview with General Sonthi Boonyaratglin, Bangkok, 18 December 2019.

97. King's Guard School, *Khumue kanfuek waduai baepfuek bukkhon tha mue plao* [Handbook of physical training without weapons], n.d., http://www.policeubon.go.th/download/23.pdf (accessed 12 June 2020).

98. Ibid.; in preface, n.p.

90. Ibid.; in frontmatter, n.p.

100. Ibid.

101. Ibid.

102. "Prakat samnak nayokratthamontri rueang hai naithahan rap ratchakan" [Announcement of Prime Minister's Office on appointment of military officer into government service], *Royal Gazette*, vol. 131, special section 132 *ngo*,

16 July 2014, http://www.ratchakitcha.soc.go.th/DATA/PDF/2557/E/132/3. PDF (accessed 8 November 2019).

103. "Prakat taengtang kharatchakan nai phra-ong" [Announcement of appointment of official in royal service], *Royal Gazette*, vol. 135, special section 141 *ngo*, 19 June 2018, http://www.ratchakitcha.soc.go.th/DATA/PDF/2561/E/141/1.PDF (accessed 8 November 2019).

104. Ibid.

105. "Poet thap 14 khunphon kho daeng 'Bik Daeng-Bik Bi-Bik Kaeo-Bik Nui' kap pharakit sut khopfa" [14 red-striped t-shirt commanders unveiled: "Big Daeng", "Big Bi", "Big Kaeo", "Big Nui" and their duties at the end of the horizon], *Matichon sutsapda*, 11–17 October 2019, pp. 14–15.

106. "Prakat taengtang kharatchakan nai phra-ong" [Announcement of appointment of royal officials], *Royal Gazette*, vol. 136, section 239 *ngo*, 25 September 2019, http://www.ratchakitcha.soc.go.th/DATA/PDF/2562/E/239/T_0001.PDF (accessed 5 January 2021).

107. "Prakat taengtang kharatchakan nai phra-ong hai damrong tamnaeng" [Announcement on appointment of royal official to take up position], *Royal Gazette*, vol. 137, section 81 *ngo*, 8 April 2020, http://www.ratchakitcha.soc.go.th/DATA/PDF/2563/E/081/T_0001.PDF (accessed 5 January 2021).

108. "Phon akat ek Sathitphong Sukwimon nai wai 72 pi sitkao diden suan kulap - mo chiangmai lae kharatchaboriphan phurapchai bueang yukhonlabat yangklaichit" [ACM Sathitphong Sukwimon, outstanding alumnus of Suan Kularb School and Chiangmai University who has served the king closely], *BBC Thai*, 2 January 2021, https://www.bbc.com/thai/thailand-55505134 (accessed 7 January 2021).

109. "Senthang dao charatsaeng 'cho ko kho daeng' ma ruchak 'khun phon raksa phra-ong' sutpe!" [Career path of rising star "red collar" King's Guard task force], *Thai Post*, 4 September 2019, https://www.thaipost.net/main/detail/44994 (accessed 7 November 2019).

110. "Kongthap bok triam nam phonthahan tonbaep tam neaothang phraratchadamri nuai thahan mahatlek rajawallop raksa phra-ong fuek thahan mai thua phrathet" [Army to send royal prototype soldiers of the Rajawallop Royal Guard to train newly recruited soldiers across the country], Thai News Bureau, 17 August 1992, http://thainews.prd.go.th/th/news/print_news/TCATG190817193711396 (accessed 7 November 2019).

111. "Tha kaekhoen su yok ok laksutphraratchathan fuek thahanken" [Posture in raising the chest: royally granted curriculum for training military conscripts], *Khom chat luek*, 3 November 2019, https://www.komchadluek.net/news/scoop/396759 (accessed 5 November 2019).

112. "Phraratchakamnot on attra kamlangphon lae ngoppraman bang suan khong kongthap bok kongthap thai krasuang kalahom pai pen khong

nuai banchakan thawai khwamplotphai raksa phra-ong sueng pen nuai ratchakan nai phra-ong" [Royal decree on transfer of some part of the personnel and budget of Army, Armed Forces Headquarters and Ministry of Defence to Royal Security Command, which is a government unit in royal service], *Royal Gazette*, vol. 136, section 103 *ko*, 30 September 2019, http://www.ratchakitcha.soc.go.th/DATA/PDF/2562/A/103/T_0001.PDF (accessed 5 November 2019).

113. Ibid.

114. "King Vajiralongkorn Gains Two Infantry Regiments by Emergency Degree", *Prachatai English*, 3 October 2019, https://prachatai.com/english/node/8230 (accessed 7 February 2020). This news website reported that the estimated strength of the two regiments was between 2,000 and 3,000 troops. There was no official figure for the strength of the king's bodyguard.

115. "Prachum sapha: sapha mi mati 374 siang anumat pho ro ko penpho ro bo on kromthahan rap 1- rap 11 pai pen nuai thawai khwamplotphai raksa phra-ong" [Parliament meets, 374 votes to pass the royal decree into law to transfer army units to Royal Security Command], *BBC Thai*, 17 October 2019, https://www.bbc.com/thai/thailand-50078306 (accessed 10 June 2020).

116. "'Srinual' poet chai pom wot suan mati phak yan mai chai nguhao si som lan tha rap ngoen ching cha la-ok" ["Srinual" gives her account on the vote against party's line, she is not an orange cobra, if really accepted money will resign], *Khao sot*, 1 November 2019, https://www.khaosod. co.th/politics/news_3022576 (accessed 5 November 2019). The orange cobra is an expression for a traitor derived from Aesop's fables. On a winter's day, a farmer found a snake stiff and frozen. He picked it up and placed it under his coat to give it warmth. As the snake revived, it followed its natural instinct and fatally bit the farmer.

117. "Prachum sapha: phuea thai-wip faikhan mai titchai pho ro ko on nuai thahan triam wot rap pen pho ro bo" [Phuea Thai, opposition whip have no problem with the decree, ready to vote to allow transfer military units to become law], *BBC Thai*, 16 October 2019, https://www.bbc.com/thai/ thailand-50071002 (accessed 5 November 2019).

118. "Senate Backs Army Transfer Decree", *Bangkok Post*, 21 October 2019, https://www.bangkokpost.com/thailand/politics/1776454/senate-backs-army-transfer-decree (accessed 5 November 2019).

119. Interview with Lieutenant General Pongsakorn Rodchompoo, Bangkok, 20 December 2019.

120. "Prakat samnak nayokratthamontri rueang kananumat phraratchakamnot kanon attra kamlangphon bang suan khong kongthap bok kongthap thai krasuang kalahom pai pen khong nuai banchakan thawai khwamplotphai raksa phra-ong" [Announcement of Prime Minister's Office approving

transfer of some part of personnel and budget of Army, Armed Forces Headquarters and Defence Ministry to Royal Security Command], *Royal Gazette*, vol. 136, section 111*ko*, 21 October 2019, http://www.ratchakitcha. soc.go.th/DATA/PDF/2562/A/111/T_0001.PDF (accessed 5 November 2019).

121. "Thailand's King Puts Key Army Units under Palace Authority", Associated Press, 1 October 2019, https://apnews.com/ 96144d07efe149ba8a8f7c7d3491962b (accessed 5 November 2019).

122. Interview with Pongsakorn.

123. Interview with General Sonthi.

124. Interview with Pongsakorn.

125. "BBC 100 Women 2020: Who is on the list this year 2020", *BBC*, 23 November 2020, https://www.bbc.com/news/world-55042935 (accessed 7 January 2021).

126. "[Full Statement] The Demonstration At Thammasat Proposes Monarchy Reform", *Prachatai English*, 11 August 2020, https://prachatai.com/english/ node/8709 (accessed 7 January 2021).

127. Ibid.

128. "Mop chu sam nio han lang rawang khabuansadet phan" [Protestors flash three-finger salute and turn their backs to passing royal motorcade], *Krungthep thurakit*, 14 November 2020, https://www.bangkokbiznews.com/ news/detail/907842 (accessed 7 January 2021).

129. "'Penkwin' prakat chaichana nam mop thueng rap 11—an thalaengkan thai-on kamlang thahan khuen sangkat" [Penguin announced victory, leads the protesters to 11th Infantry Regiment—reads statement demanding the return of the unit to Army], *Sanook*, 29 November 2020, https://www. sanook.com/news/8306070/ (accessed 7 January 2021).

130. Thai Lawyers for Human Rights, "Sathiti phu thukdamnoen khadi matra 112 minpramat kasat pi 2563–2564" [Statistics on those charged with *lèse majesté* under section 112 for defamation of monarchy], 6 January 2021, https://tlhr2014.com/archives/23983 (accessed 7 January 2021).

131. Jonathan Miller, Kocha Olarn and Helen Regan, "Thai King addresses protesters in rare public comments, saying he 'loves them all the same'", CNN, 1 November 2020, https://edition.cnn.com/2020/11/01/ asia/thailand-king-vajiralongkorn-protests-intl-hnk/index.html (accessed 7 January 2021).

4

THE MONARCHIZED MILITARY

Unlike the late King Bhumibol, King Vajiralongkorn stays connected to the Thai armed forces through his own network, created after his succession to the throne in late 2016. Studies on the relationship between monarchy and military in Thailand, such as Duncan McCargo's work on the "network monarchy"[1] and Paul Chambers and Napisa Waitoolkiat's article on the resilience of the "monarchized military"[2] have suggested that the late king remained connected to the military through his network, at the centre of which was the late president of the Privy Council, General Prem Tinsulanonda. This network, which Chambers and Napisa regard as a "parallel state", was "an asymmetrical nexus between a powerful monarch (King Bhumibol) and Privy Council and a military leadership".[3] As the chief adviser to the king, Prem used his relations with the monarchy as the source of the legitimacy needed for him to exercise influence over the military. He acted as a power broker who helped cement ties between the monarchy and the military during the last decades of the previous reign.

With such a relationship and the position of Privy Council president, Prem managed to secure a smooth royal transition during the critical period after King Bhumibol passed away in October 2016. The ageing Prem was appointed as regent *pro tempore* on 14 October 2016,[4] a day after King Bhumibol's passing, since the then crown prince—who was supposed to take the throne immediately after the death of his father, for the sake of continuity—said he wanted to take time to grieve with the nation before accepting the invitation to become Thailand's new king.[5] The crown prince realized that there could be some confusion or undesirable difficulties during such a critical period, and he therefore told the regent Prem and the junta chief and Prime Minister Prayut Chan-ocha during an audience that the two should help prevent public confusion over the administration and over the process of succession to the throne.

The crown prince noted that people should have no confusion over the administration or the succession to the throne since the latter process was clearly stated in the constitution and the Palace Law, according to Prayut. The crown prince said that all people, all sectors of society and he personally were suffering great sorrow. All must therefore join hands and help one another before any steps regarding the succession were taken, Prayut said. "Everyone should use this moment to preserve the beautiful memory of the seventy-year reign [of the late king]," the prime minister quoted the crown prince as saying.[6]

Regent Prem, then ninety-six years old, held the position of head of state for three months, after which the crown prince decided to ascend the throne on 1 December 2016. He thus became Rama X of the Chakri Dynasty. Prem offered his resignation from the position of chief adviser to the king, who later reinstated him as president of the Privy Council on 2 December 2016.[7]

The new monarch told Prem and other newly reappointed members of the Privy Council during their first royal audience that he drew confidence from Prem's reappointment. Referring to the Privy Council president as "papa" or "daddy", as did many others in the military, the new king told him and his fellow councillors, "Having Pa as the president of Privy Council is so reassuring. Everybody served the previous reign, and is reliable."[8] However, Prem was assigned mostly to attend royal ceremonies such as making merit for the late King Bhumibol and his brother King Ananda in May and June 2017, as well as offering sacred water to the king during the coronation in May 2019, before his death a few weeks later.

The End of the (Old) Network Monarchy

Prem passed away because of heart failure on 25 May 2019 at the age of ninety-eight. The king appointed Prem's protégé, General Surayud

Chulanont, who had served as prime minister after the 2006 coup, as the chief of the royal advisory body on 2 January 2020.[9] Surayud had served in that role in an acting capacity since 27 May.[10]

Prem held the position of the new king's chief adviser for two and a half years, with considerably less influence than before because of a lack of close personal ties to the new monarch and their cold relations in the past.[11] Likewise, the king's advisory body under Surayud could not be regarded as a powerhouse, above all in its influence over the military. For a number of reasons, the Privy Council could not play the same role that it had played in Prem's time of conveying "unspoken" messages from the palace to the military. First, the king himself gave a less important role to the Privy Council. Rather than tasking it with advisory work for the benefit of his reign, he assigned its members to represent him at public events, such as in offering people basic necessities during natural disasters, with the goal of earning publicity for the palace. Their main job was taking care of royal projects initiated by the late King Bhumibol. Members of the Privy Council were reportedly seen visiting and inspecting projects through the country.[12]

Second, Surayud had less influence in military circles, given that he had climbed the military career ladder under Prem's shadow. Like many others, he graduated from the Armed Forces Academies Preparatory School (AFAPS) and the Chulachomklao Royal Military Academy, where he was a member of Class 12 in 1965, before receiving further training in the United States. But, because of his humble and quiet character, his family background and his colleagues' envy of his American orientation, Surayud had few close friends in the military.[13] His family background in fact led to suspicion within the Thai military establishment. Surayud's maternal grandfather was *Phraya* Srisitthisongkhram (Din Tharap), a royalist officer who was an active participant in the Boworadet Rebellion of 1933, which sought to restore Siam's absolute monarchy. But his father Colonel Payom Chulanont had joined Thailand's communist insurgency. Secret agents had therefore been instructed to keep tabs on Surayud from the time that he was a student at the cadet school, and he was initially prohibited from being posted to the border, until he could prove that he had no connection to his father and did not subscribe to leftist ideology.[14] Ironically, Surayud's eventual service on secret missions in an isolated and small Special Forces command in border areas adjacent to the Khmer Rouge's Cambodian strongholds during the mid-1980s also prevented him from having the kind of influence in military circles that would have come with service in larger units and less clandestine roles.

Third, the Eastern Tiger (*Burapha phayak*) clique has dominated key positions in the Army since its "big brother" General Prawit Wongsuwan served as Army chief in 2004–5. Prem and Surayud managed to have two members of the Special Forces' top brass, General Sonthi Boonyaratglin and General Chalermchai Sitthisart, serve as Army chief in 2005–7 and 2016–18, respectively. However, these commanders did not build strong networks inside the Army. While the generals in the Eastern Tigers faction expressed respect for Prem as a charismatic military leader, Prawit was apparently never on good terms with Surayud, who had sidelined him when Surayud was Army chief in 1998–2002.[15]

Fourth, while some other members of the Privy Council are retired military commanders, they are either Prem's men or less influential officers. They include former Air Force chief Air Chief Marshal Chalit Phukpasuk, former Army deputy chief General Daopong Rattanasuwan, former deputy chief of defence forces General Paiboon Kumchaya, former Army chief Chalermchai,[16] former commander of the Army's 1st Division General Kampanat Ruddit,[17] and former deputy permanent secretary of the Ministry of Defence Admiral Pongthep Nouthes.[18] Former Army chief and key Eastern Tigers figure General Theerachai Nakwanich was supposed to have strong ties to the officers in that faction, but he served on the Privy Council only nineteen months before his resignation in June 2018.[19]

The Rearrangement of Royal Guard Units

The Thai military has long claimed that one of its main duties is to protect the monarchy and that the armed forces as a whole are supposed to provide security for the members of the royal family. In reality, the three service branches—the Army, Navy and Air Force—together with the National Police Office arranged for specific personnel and units to provide security for the monarchy. More than 100 units in the armed forces are dedicated to serve as royal guard units, or *nuai thahan raksa phra-ong*. They have various functions in relation to the monarchy, including rotations to provide security for the crown, participating in parades on the occasion of royal ceremonies, and serving as guards of honour for the monarch, the queen and members of the royal family. However, there are different layers of units serving the monarchy. The units attached to the palace or directly subject to the monarch provide personal security for the members of the royal family and are responsible for palace security. Other units in the armed forces designated as royal guard units are also obligated to protect members of the monarchy in their respective areas of responsibility and occasionally called upon to provide security in the palace or nearby to members of the royal family.

Many of these units have served the royal family for a long time. The Army's 1st Division in Bangkok has, for example, served as the King's Guard unit for more than a century; its roots can be traced back to the time when King Chulalongkorn created the modern Thai army in the second half of the nineteenth century. On the other hand, some units were named as royal guard units only recently.

It became customary from the time of Field Marshal Sarit Thanarat's regime in the late 1950s for the military to arrange for specific units designated as royal guard units to have direct links to particular persons in the royal institution. The 21st Infantry Regiment, for example, was assigned for palace duties, and Queen Sirikit became its honorary commanding colonel in the 1950s. King Bhumibol, who was already constitutionally legitimated as head of armed forces, was specifically named to the position of honorary commandant of the Chulachomklao Royal Military Academy, the 1st Infantry Regiment, the 11th Infantry Regiment, the 1st Cavalry Regiment, the 1st Artillery Regiment, and the 1st Engineers Regiment, even though each of them was already part of the royal guard.[20]

Among the units appointed as royal guard units during the later years of the previous reign were the 5th Cavalry Regiment in 2001,[21] the Air Force Security Command in 2001,[22] the 2nd Cavalry Division in 2001,[23] the Anti-Aircraft Regiment under the Air Force Security Command in 2005,[24] and the 1st Battalion of the Marines Command in 2007.[25] Another three battalions under the Air Force Security Command and the Anti-Aircraft Command were named royal guard units in September 2014,[26] a few months after the 22 May coup.

As the new reign began, Prime Minister Prayut asked permission from King Vajiralongkorn to rearrange the royal guard units in April 2019.[27] The announcement in the *Royal Gazette* did not explain the need for the change, and the new arrangement did not really make any difference. Senior military officials said that all royal guard units would, as a general matter, perform their duty of protecting the monarchy. The new arrangement did not mean that units would serve only the members of the crown for whom those units were named.[28]

As mentioned in a previous chapter, King Vajiralongkorn took two Bangkok-based combat-ready infantry regiments into the Royal Security Command, which was directly subject to his command. Those units added *mahatlek ratchawanlop raksa phra-ong* after their names.[29] Other units left under the jurisdiction of the armed forces but designated as royal guard units simply bore *raksa phra-ong* after their names. They were available for performing duties such as joining parades for royal functions and providing security for the monarchy on rotation. However, some units were dedicated to honour specific members of the crown such as the *Krom thahanrap thi sam sip et raksa phra-ong nai phrabatsomdetphraparaminthara Maha Bhumibol Adulyadej*, which is the 31st Infantry Regiment named to honour the king's late father. Further, some units were not designated as royal guard but were nevertheless dedicated to specific members of the monarchy such as the 6th Cavalry Squadron of the 6th Cavalry Regiment. It bore after its name *nai somdetphra Sri Bajarindra Borommarachininat*, meaning in honour of Queen Sri Bajarindra—one of Rama V's wives.

King Vajiralongkorn granted permission to the government to rearrange and rename royal guard units in April 2019. Subsequently, in December 2019, he renamed 26 military units in accordance with the new royal titles that he had given to King Bhumibol and Queen Sirikit after his coronation.[30] The remaining units retained the names given to them in April 2019, as reflected in Tables 4.2–4.5.

TABLE 4.1
Number of Royal Guard Units during the Reigns of Rama IX and Rama X

Rama IX	Rama X
Army: 87	Army: 57 (+2)
Navy: 9	Navy: 7
Air Force: 15	Air Force: 13

Source: *Royal Gazette*, 23 April 2019.

TABLE 4.2
Royal Guard Units under the Direct Command of Rama X

1. 1st Infantry Regiment *mahatlek rajawallop raksa phra-ong*
   1.1 1st Infantry Battalion *krom thahan mahatlek rajawallop raksa phra-ong thi nueng*
   1.2 2nd Infantry Battalion *krom thahan mahatlek rajawallop raksa phra-ong thi nueng*
   1.3 3rd Infantry Battalion *krom thahan mahatlek rajawallop raksa phra-ong thi nueng*

2. 11th Infantry Regiment *mahatlek rajawallop raksa phra-ong*
   2.1 1st Infantry Battalion *krom thahan mahatlek rajawallop raksa phra-ong thi sip et*
   2.2 2nd Infantry Battalion *krom thahan mahatlek rajawallop raksa phra-ong thi sip et*
   2.3 3rd Infantry Battalion *krom thahan mahatlek rajawallop raksa phra-ong thi sip et*

Source: *Royal Gazette*, various announcements, as cited in the notes to this chapter.

TABLE 4.3
Royal Guard Units under the Army

Unit	Location
31st Infantry Regiment *raksa phra-ong nai phrabatsomdetphraparaminthara Maha Bhumibol Adulyadej Maharat Borommanatbophit* (King Bhumibol)	Lopburi
1st Battalion of 31st Infantry Regiment *raksa phra-ong nai phrabatsomdetphraparaminthara Maha Bhumibol Adulyadej Maharat Borommanatbophit*	Lopburi
2nd Battalion of 31st Infantry Regiment *raksa phra-ong nai phrabatsomdetphraparaminthara Maha Bhumibol Adulyadej Maharat Borommanatbophit*	Lopburi
3rd Battalion of 31st Infantry Regiment *raksa phra-ong nai phrabatsomdetphraparaminthara Maha Bhumibol Adulyadej Maharat Borommanatbophit*	Lopburi
29th Cavalry Squadron *raksa phra-ong nai phrabatsomdetphraparaminthara Maha Bhumibol Adulyadej Maharat Borommanatbophit*	Bangkok
2nd Infantry Division *raksa phra-ong nai somdetphraborommaratchonni phan pi luang* (Queen Sirikit)	Prachinburi

TABLE 4.3 (*cont'd*)

2nd Infantry Regiment *raksa phra-ong nai somdetphraborommaratchonni phan pi luang*	Prachinburi
1st Battalion of 2nd Infantry Regiment *raksa phra-ong nai somdetphraborommaratchonni phan pi luang*	Prachinburi
2nd Battalion of 2nd Infantry Regiment *raksa phra-ong nai somdetpraborommanaratchonni phan pi luang*	Prachinburi
3rd Battalion of 2nd Infantry Regiment *raksa phra-ong nai somdetpraborommaratchonni phan pi luang*	Prachinburi
12th Infantry Regiment *raksa phra-ong nai somdetphraborommaratchonni phan pi luang*	Sakaew
1st Battalion of 12th Infantry Regiment *raksa phra-ong nai somdetphraborommaratchonni phan pi luang*	Sakaew
2nd Battalion of 12th Infantry Regiment *raksa phra-ong nai somdetphraborommaratchonni phan pi luang*	Sakaew
3rd Battalion of 12th Infantry Regiment *raksa phra-ong nai somdetphraborommaratchonni phan pi luang*	Sakaew
21st Infantry Regiment *raksa phra-ong nai somdetphraborommaratchonni phan pi luang**	Chonburi
1st Battalion of 21st Infantry Regiment *raksa phra-ong nai somdetphraborommaratchonni phan pi luang*	Chonburi
2nd Battalion of 21st Infantry Regiment *raksa phra-ong nai somdetphraborommaratchonni phan pi luang*	Chonburi
3rd Battalion of 21st Infantry Regiment *raksa phra-ong nai somdetphraborommaratchonni phan pi luang*	Chonburi
2nd Cavalry Squadron of 2nd Infantry Regiment *raksa phra-ong nai somdetphraborommaratchonni phan pi luang*	Prachinburi
30th Cavalry Squadron of 2nd Infantry Regiment *raksa phra-ong nai somdetphraborommaratchonni phan pi luang*	Prachinburi
2nd Artillery Battalion of 2nd Artillery Regiment *raksa phra-ong nai somdetphraborommaratchonni phan pi luang*	Prachinburi
12th Artillery Battalion of 2nd Artillery Regiment *raksa phra-ong nai somdetphraborommaratchonni phan pi luang*	Prachinburi
21st Artillery Battalion of 2nd Artillery Regiment *raksa phra-ong nai somdetphraborommaratchonni phan pi luang*	Chonburi

TABLE 4.3 (*cont'd*)

102nd Artillery Battalion of 2nd Artillery Regiment *raksa phra-ong nai somdetphraborommaratchonni phan pi luang*	Prachinburi
2nd Engineer Battalion of 2nd Infantry Regiment *raksa phra-ong nai somdetphraborommaratchonni phan pi luang*	Chachoengsao
2nd Cavalry Division *raksa phra-ong nai phrabatsomdet Phra Mongkutklao Chaoyuhua* (King Vajiravudh)	Bangkok
1st Cavalry Squadron of 1st Cavalry Regiment *raksa phra-ong nai phrabatsomdet Phra Mongkutklao Chaoyuhua*	Bangkok
3rd Cavalry Squadron of 1st Cavalry Regiment *raksa phra-ong nai phrabatsomdet Phra Mongkutklao Chaoyuhua*	Bangkok
17th Cavalry Squadron of 1st Cavalry Regiment *raksa phra-ong nai phrabatsomdet Phra Mongkutklao Chaoyuhua*	Saraburi
5th Cavalry Regiment *raksa phra-ong nai phrabatsomdet Phra Mongkutklao Chaoyuhua*	Saraburi
20th Cavalry Squadron of 5th Cavalry Regiment *raksa phra-ong nai phrabatsomdet Phra Mongkutklao Chaoyuhua*	Saraburi
23rd Cavalry Squadron of 5th Cavalry Regiment *raksa phra-ong nai phrabatsomdet Phra Mongkutklao Chaoyuhua*	Saraburi
24th Cavalry Squadron of 5th Cavalry Regiment *raksa phra-ong nai phrabatsomdet Phra Mongkutklao Chaoyuhua*	Saraburi
27th Cavalry Squadron of 2nd Cavalry Regiment *raksa phra-ong nai phrabatsomdet Phra Mongkutklao Chaoyuhua*	Saraburi
4th Cavalry Squadron of 1st Regiment *raksa phra-ong*	Lopburi
1st Artillery Regiment *raksa phra-ong*	Bangkok
1st Battalion of 1st Artillery Regiment *raksa phra-ong*	Bangkok
11th Battalion of 1st Artillery Regiment *raksa phra-ong*	Lopburi
31st Battalion of 1st Artillery Regiment *raksa phra-ong*	Lopburi
1st Engineer Battalion of 1st Regiment *raksa phra-ong*	Bangkok

1st Anti-Aircraft Artillery Battalion of 2nd Anti-Aircraft Artillery Regiment *raksa phra-ong*	Bangkok
1st Engineer Regiment *raksa phra-ong*	Ratchaburi
52nd Engineer Battalion of 1st Regiment rak*sa phra-ong*	Ratchaburi
112th Engineer Battalion of 1st Regiment *raksa phra-ong*	Ratchaburi
3rd Special Force Regiment *raksa phra-ong*	Lopburi
Ranger Battalion *raksa phra-ong*	Lopburi
Special Operation Battalion *raksa phra-ong*	Lopburi
6th Cavalry Squadron of 6th Cavalry Regiment *nai somdetphra Sri Bajarindra Borommarachininat* (Queen Sri Bajarindra; Saovabha Phongsri, consort of Rama V)	Khon Khaen
14th Cavalry Squadron of 7th Cavalry Regiment *nai somdetphra Sri Bajarindra Borommarachininat*	Khon Khaen

Note: *This was the original Queen's Guard unit.
Source: Royal Gazette, 23 April 2019 and 12 December 2019.

TABLE 4.4
Royal Guard Units under the Navy

Unit	Location
Royal Thai Naval Academy *raksa phra-ong*	Samut Prakan
1st Battalion of Royal Thai Naval Academy *raksa phra-ong*	Samut Prakan
2nd Battalion of Royal Thai Naval Academy *raksa phra-ong*	Samut Prakan
3rd Battalion of Royal Thai Naval Academy *raksa phra-ong*	Samut Prakan
4th Battalion of Royal Thai Naval Academy *raksa phra-ong*	Samut Prakan
1st Infantry Battalion of 1st Infantry Regiment of Marine Division of Marine Command *raksa phra-ong*	Chanthaburi
9th Infantry Battalion of 3rd Infantry Regiment of Marine Division of Marine Command *raksa phra-ong*	Narathiwat

Source: Royal Gazette, 23 April 2019 and 12 December 2019.

TABLE 4.5
Royal Guard Units under the Air Force

Unit	Location
Navaminda Kasatriyadhiraj Royal Thai Air Force Academy *raksa phra-ong*	Bangkok
1st Battalion of Royal Thai Air Force Academy *raksa phra-ong*	Bangkok
2nd Battalion of Royal Thai Air Force Academy *raksa phra-ong*	Bangkok
3rd Battalion of Royal Thai Air Force Academy *raksa phra-ong*	Bangkok
4th Battalion of Royal Thai Air Force Academy *raksa phra-ong*	Bangkok
5th Battalion of Royal Thai Air Force Academy *raksa phra-ong*	Bangkok
Royal Thai Air Force (RTAF) Security Force Command *raksa phra-ong*	Bangkok
1st Battalion of RTAF Security Force *raksa phra-ong*	Bangkok
2nd Battalion of RTAF Security Force *raksa phra-ong*	Bangkok
3rd Battalion of RTAF Security Force *raksa phra-ong*	Bangkok
Anti-Aircraft Department of RTAF Security Force Command *raksa phra-ong*	Pathum Thani
1st Battalion of Anti-Aircraft Regiment *raksa phra-ong*	Pathum Thani
2nd Battalion of Anti-Aircraft Regiment *raksa phra-ong*	Pathum Thani

Source: Royal Gazette, 23 April 2019 and 12 December 2019.

The Construction of a New Network

Shortly after ascending the throne, King Vajiralongkorn set up a special task force. It comprised fifteen select senior military officers led by General Apirat Kongsompong, who was then assistant Army chief. These officers were granted a special three-month training course at Daveevatthana Palace in Thawiwatthana District in the western part of Bangkok. With Apirat as its top commander, this exclusive ad hoc unit was known as *nuai chaphokit thahan mahatlek raksa phra-ong 904*, or the King's Guard Task Force 904. Its roles and functions were unclear, but it is likely that it was meant to perform duties upon assignment from the king and to connect the monarch directly with the Army, bypassing the normal line of command within the national defence forces. The elite squad included all of Apirat's favourites, mostly members of the *Wongthewan* faction from the 1st Infantry Division such as General Narongphan Jitkaewthae, Lieutenant General Thammanoon Withee, Major General Charoenchai Hinthao and Major General Songwit Noonpakdi. These men had many things in common, beyond the shared experience of climbing the career ladder within Royal Guard units in the capital. Some, such as Narongphan and Thammanoon, were members of the same Class 22 at the AFAPS. As for Apirat and Songwit, each was the son of a leading participant in the February 1991 coup that seized power from the elected government of Prime Minister Chatichai Choonhavan. Their respective fathers were General Sunthorn Kongsompong and General Isarapong Noonpakdi. While many members of this new task force were infantry officers, some others were cavalry officers, such as General Chalermpol Srisawasdi, former commander of the 2nd Cavalry Division, and Major General Suwit Ketsri and Major General Kantapot Settharasami, each of whom was also from the 2nd Cavalry Division. Some, such as Major General Suksan Nongbualang and former National Council for Peace and Order (NCPO) junta spokesman Major General Piyapong Klinphan, could be regarded as Eastern Tigers as they had been stationed at the 2nd Infantry Division in the eastern part of the country. Among all these officers, Songwit did stand out for having graduated from Virginia Military Institute in the United States, not the Chulachomklao Royal Military Academy in Thailand.

There were no clear criteria for the selection of members for this new task force or for the decision to choose Apirat and his close associates to join it. It was reported that the king had consolidated his personal bodyguard unit 904 with a battalion of the 1st Infantry Division (King's Guard) in November 2016, when Apirat was the commander of the 1st Army Region, which supervised the unit.[31] Apirat also had a personal link to the king through his father, Sunthorn, a former supreme commander and a former military pilot. Sunthorn had helped train the then crown prince to fly helicopters in the 1980s—a basic skill that led the king to become a licensed pilot later. "It was then that [King] Vajiralongkorn first became acquainted with Apirat, a relationship they say endured and deepened after Sunthorn's death from cancer in the 1990s", according to the *Asia Times*.[32] Sunthorn's son was appointed a special officer attached to the King's Guard while serving as a colonel in December 2011,[33] and became one of the king's favourite bodyguards, or Rajawallop, in July 2018.[34] He participated in the special training course and became the top commander of the king's new task force before assuming the position of Army chief a few months later, in October 2018. The king appointed him as a member of the board of Crown Property Bureau in January 2019,[35] in an indication of the trust that the king had in Apirat's ability to participate in the management of royal wealth. Apirat also signalled to the public that he was one of the king's men by pinning the image of Prince Dipangkorn Rasmijoti, the king's son, on the left chest of his deep green military uniform. It was an image that only a small group of people were allowed to wear.[36] That group included other officers who could be regarded as *thahan sai wang*, or the palace's soldiers, such as Narongphan.

Apirat and the Return of *Wongthewan*

Like many others in the Thai military elite, Apirat was born in Bangkok to parents who were both Army military officers. His father, Sunthorn, was a career military officer, and his mother, Orachon Kongsompong, a colonel. His grandfather, Group Captain Supachai Kongsompong, was an Air Force officer. Apirat was born in 1960. Prior to beginning his military education, he attended secondary school at St Gabriel's College, an elite school for the children of well-to-do families, like the Suan Kularb School from which his father had graduated. Apirat received his commission as a second lieutenant upon graduation from the Chulachomklao Royal Military Academy in 1985 before beginning his military career as a helicopter pilot at the Army Aviation Centre, which his father had served as commander in 1983–84. Unlike his father, Apirat had no experience in major combat at home or abroad, as he began his military career at the end of the Cold War and of anti-communist counter-insurgent warfare in the country. Prior to becoming a commander of King's Guard combat units in the capital in 2000, Apirat received training as a helicopter pilot in the United States and was appointed as the assistant logistics officer in the office of the military attaché at the Thai embassy in Washington, D.C., in

1990. He also received a master's degree in business administration from Southeastern University in that same city. Apirat has said that he was a close friend of former massage parlour king Chuwit Kamolvisit, a controversial politician-cum-media figure and businessman whom the general had known since his school days at St Gabriel's.

Apirat was categorized as a *Wongthewan* soldier for having climbed the military career ladder exclusively within King's Guard units during the past two decades—since the time of his assignment as the commander of the 2nd Battalion of the 11th Infantry Regiment in 2000–2, when he was a lieutenant colonel. He became the 11th Regiment's commander five years later. He remained in that position for another five years, undertaking a mission in the predominantly Muslim region of the Deep South and participating in the crackdown against Red Shirt protesters in Bangkok in 2010. He then won promotion to the positions of commander of the 1st Infantry Division (King's Guard) in 2014 and commander of the 1st Army Region, overseeing forces in the entire central region of Thailand, two years later.

Wongthewan literally means divine progeny, but its figurative meaning is offspring of the elite[37] in the armed forces who were put into service at the 1st Infantry Division (King's Guard), stationed in the capital. As already noted, the King's Guard unit evolved from the royal pages (*mahatlek luang*) or king's bodyguard of over a century ago. It was, therefore, a place of work for members of the Thai elite from the beginning. So that the division would be a role model and example of efficiency for the modern military, and because the offspring of the elite were not always smart or capable enough to play such a role, those who graduated with high scores from the military academy or from institutions abroad mostly served in King's Guard units. "It's the custom in the Army to put Grade A officers, meaning those who got high scores, like top ten, in the 1st division [which is located in the capital], while tier two officers would be posted in the 2nd division in the eastern provinces", said former Army chief General Sonthi, who began his career at the Infantry Centre in the southern province of Prachuap Khirikhanand and later took charge of the Special Forces Command in Lopburi before assuming the top position in the Army, and was thus neither a *Wongthewan* soldier nor an Eastern Tiger.[38]

Although he was considered the rising star of the *Wongthewan* faction, Apirat was said to have grown under the patronage of Prayut—one of the Eastern Tigers' top trio—as he had helped Prayut handle many important jobs.[39] In addition to playing a crucial role in the military crackdown on Red Shirt protesters in 2010, Apirat showed his loyalty to Prayut by leading his men to harass media outlets that strongly criticized the top Army boss.[40] He played a key role in the 22 May 2014 coup when he was in charge of the 1st Division, a crucial unit in the putsch.[41] For his role in the coup and for the risk that he took by participating in it, he was rewarded with appointment as the chairman of the National Lottery Office, as a member of the board of directors of Bangchak Petroleum and as adviser to the Office of Small and Medium Enterprises Promotion.[42] Posts like these were sources of extra income for military officers and senior civil servants.

There was some doubt whether Prayut indeed wanted to support Apirat's appointment to the top position in the Army. The former Army chief had many favourites, notably among members of his Eastern Tigers faction such as General Theppong Thipayachan and General Kukiat Srinaka.[43] The two Army commanders who followed Prayut in the 2014–16 period were Generals Udomdej Sitabutr and Theerachai Nakwanich. Each was a member of the Eastern Tigers faction. A member of the *Wongthewan* clique thus seemed to have relatively little chance of breaking the Eastern Tigers' hold on that post.

But the appointment of Chalermchai Sitthisart as Army chief in 2016 was the end of the Eastern Tigers' perpetuation of their power in the Army. The general was Surayud's favourite protégé from the Special Forces. It was reported that then Prime Minister Prayut permitted Chalermchai's appointment because he wanted to show his respect to Prem and Surayud. He also wanted, reports suggested, to maintain unity in the Army by giving chances to other cliques and factions to take the top job, even though this decision upset his mentor and Eastern Tigers big brother Prawit. The latter wanted to secure the government by having trusted men in the position of Army commander during the transition period and to make sure that the government would have strong backing for staying in power after the March 2019 elections.[44] Chalermchai was in the position for two years, before his appointment to the Privy Council upon retirement in 2018.[45] Like Surayud and Sonthi before him, Chalermchai left none of his favourites to sustain his connections and influence in the Army when he retired.

While Prayut and Prawit reserved some say in the military reshuffle after the start of the new reign, Apirat—by then widely and officially known as the commander of the King's Guard Task Force 904—played a significant role in the annual reshuffles of 2017 and 2018. Army chief Chalermchai had no doubt that Apirat, then an assistant Army chief, would be his "designated" successor.[46] Hence, close associates and classmates of Apirat from AFAPS Class 20 and the *Wongthewan* were installed in the key positions in the Army.[47] They included Thammanoon as 1st Army Corps commander, Charoenchai as deputy commander of the 1st Army Region, Songwit as 1st Infantry Division commander, and Suwit as 2nd Cavalry Division commander. Apirat's AFAPS classmates and close associates also occupied the key positions in the Navy and the Air Force.

With Apirat as the Army commander as of October 2018, the *Wongthewan* faction made a comeback to assume the dominant position in the Army that it had not had since General Somtat Attanand left the post in 2003. (See Table 4.6.) This was not the ordinary return of a faction to power in the military. Rather, it was the return of the *Wongthewan* in a new quality, led by an elite squad under Apirat that was specially trained and indoctrinated by King Vajiralongkorn in order to mark the beginning of the new reign.

The 2019 military reshuffle was seen as a consolidation of power and a strengthening of the new monarchical network. Apirat, who had full authority as Army commander, placed senior officers from the King's Guard Task Force 904 into all key positions of military power. He promoted one of his favourites, Narongphan, who had initially served in Eastern Tiger units but was later mostly groomed under the *Wongthewan* faction, from commander of the 1st Army Region to assistant Army chief, a position that made him a potential successor to Apirat after the latter's retirement in 2020.[48] Apart from this position in the Army, Narongphan, also a deputy commander of Task Force 904, took an even more important position as the head of the task force's office. Another of Apirat's favourites, dear "brother" Thammanoon, took the position of 1st Army Region commander. He was Narongphan's classmate in AFAPS Class 22 and is due to retire from the service in the same year, 2023. The position of 1st Army Region commander could then possibly go to either Charoenchai, who was promoted in 2019 to 1st Army Corps commander, or to Songwit, who was made deputy commander of the 1st Army Region. Both of these officers were also deputy commanders of Task Force 904.

TABLE 4.6
Thai Army Chiefs and the Factions to Which They Belonged,
1998–Present

Reign	Army Commander	Faction	Term
Rama IX	Surayud Chulanont	Special Forces	1998–2002
Rama IX	Somtat Attanand	*Wongthewan*	2002–2003
Rama IX	Chaiyasit Shinawatra	none; Thaksin's cousin	2003–2004
Rama IX	Prawit Wongsuwan	Eastern Tigers	2004–2005
Rama IX	Sonthi Boonyaratglin	Special Forces	2005–2007
Rama IX	Anupong Paochinda	Eastern Tigers	2007–2010
Rama IX	Prayut Chan-ocha	Eastern Tigers	2010–2014
Rama IX	Udomdej Sitabutr	Eastern Tigers	2014–2015
Rama IX	Theerachai Nakwanich	Eastern Tigers	2015–2016
Rama IX/ RamaX	Chalermchai Sitthisart	Special Forces	2016–2018
Rama X	Apirat Kongsompong	*Wongthewan*	2018–2020
Rama X	Narongphan Jitkaewthae	Mixed Eastern Tiger/Special Force/*Wongthewan* background	2020–

Source: Compiled by the author.

The 2019 reshuffle was regarded by the media and other observers as the beginning of a new chapter for the new reign. Apirat had a free hand in determining the command line-up, without intervention from the government. Prime Minister Prayut, who also served as defence minister, told the public that he had not interfered in the military reshuffle.[49] Prayut might not have needed to do so as Apirat was not only his trusted protégé but also, more importantly, the king's man. While the *Wongthewan* faction was seen as the dominant clique in the reshuffle, Apirat also showed his respect to Prayut by picking Eastern Tigers officer Charoenchai, Prayut's loyal follower, as the commander of the 1st Army Corps.[50]

The Army chief used the reshuffle to change all important commanders not only in Bangkok-based units such as the 1st Army

Region, the 1st Army Corps and the 1st Division, which had historically played significant roles in political power plays; he also reassigned posts in other units across the entire Army, including cavalry divisions, engineering, logistics, Special Forces and intelligence units as well as military schools. All commanders fit his specifications, in accordance with Task Force 904's guidelines, and had close association with him. "It could be said that the Army is now under Apirat's full control", one news report suggested.[51] Unless the government had close connections in the military, such concentration of power arrangements in the hands of a single faction could be considered a major threat to the elected government.

The 2019 reshuffle was also seen as smoothly steering the Royal Thai Armed Forces Headquarters, the Navy and the Air Force. General Pornpipat Benyasri, chief of defence forces, managed to promote his men to leading positions. General Piraphong Muangboonchoo became commander of the Armed Forces Development Command, and General Nathee Wong-isares commander of the Military Intelligence Department. King's man Chalermpol was in the crucial position of armed forces chief of staff, the brain of the Royal Thai Armed Forces. Also seen for some time as a potential candidate to become the chief of national defence forces in 2020,[52] he did in fact assume that post in the 2020 reshuffle.[53]

The 2020 reshuffle substantially strengthened the king's network in the Army as it saw *thahan kho daeng*, or red-rim soldiers, taking all key positions. (See Table 4.7.) As widely expected, Narongphan replaced Apirat as Army chief. The latter retired from military service and was recruited into the inner circle of the monarch as deputy secretary general of the palace.[54] Army chief Narongphan was regarded by the media as a genuine loyalist to the monarchy.[55] Like Apirat, he had been hand-picked by the king for special training before becoming a member of Task Force 904. He served as that unit's deputy commander and was later promoted to be its commander, replacing Apirat in 2020. If the rivalry between the *Wongthewan* and Eastern Tigers factions mattered, Narongphan was a perfect choice for all. He had begun his military career in the late 1980s at the 2nd Infantry Regiment in the eastern province of Prachinburi, the home of the Eastern Tigers faction. He could at the same time be considered a Special Forces officer after his service in the rapid deployment force of the 31st Infantry Regiment in Lopburi, home of the Thai Special Forces. He also gained experience in peacekeeping activities in Timor Leste in

2000–1. Further, he shared a similar experience with Apirat when he served as a field commander in the predominantly Muslim province of Yala in 2004. And the *Wongthewan* too could claim Narongphan as a member, for he had served as deputy commander of the 1st Division (King's Guard) in 2012 before his promotion to the position of the unit's commander in 2015.

Unlike Apirat, Narongphan refrained from offering political comments to the media, notably during the 2020 student protests calling for reform of the monarchy and changes in monarchy-military relations. He invariably remarked, "I am a soldier who has the duties of defending the country, helping the people and protecting the crown."[56] The Army chief also distributed portraits of King Vajiralongkorn to troops whenever he visited them in the field in the Deep South and in border areas, reminding them that the monarch had done great work for the country and the people.[57] The annnual Army reshuffle for 2021 brought no drastic changes. Narongphan retained his position as Army chief, and others among the king's men retained their posts the same positions, while a number received promotions. (See Table 4.7.)

Unlike the Army, the Thai Air Force is not terribly politicized although Air Chief Marshal Kaset Rojananil and the Air Force played a crucial role in capturing Prime Minister Chatichai and his cabinet members at Don Mueang Airport during the 1991 coup. In shows of unity, the chiefs of the Air Force and Navy, as well as the chief of defence forces, also played along in both the September 2006 and May 2014 coups, but their participation did not make their branches significant political threats to anybody.

In the 2019 Air Force reshuffle, Apirat's close associate Air Chief Marshal Manat Wongwat replaced retiring Air Chief Marshal Chaiyapruek Didyasarin as chief in a move that was widely expected. After graduating from the Royal Thai Air Force Academy, Manat obtained a master's degree in aeronautical engineering and space in Germany. He once served as Thailand's air attaché in Berlin. He has had close ties to many previous Air Force commanders, including Air Chief Marshal Prajin Juntong, a key member of the NCPO junta that seized power in the 2014 coup, and Air Chief Marshal Chalit Pukbhasuk, who served as the commander in 2005–8 and thus at the time of the 2006 coup. Chalit later became a member of the Privy Council. Manat was the key person in commissioning Swedish-made Gripen jet fighters for the Thai air defence system.

However, the 2020 Air Force reshuffle made clear that former jet fighter pilot King Vajiralongkorn had his men in the branch. It saw Air Chief Marshal Airbull Suttiwan being elevated from an inactive post as a special-qualification officer to become the commander of the Royal Thai Air Force. Airbull, whose name was chosen by his father to commemorate a Thai-US joint air exercise named Air Bull held in 1961 under the auspices of the now long-defunct Southeast Asia Treaty Organization, was regarded by the media and other observers as a dark horse candidate for the job. Traditionally, only officers who either had experience in one of five key positions in the Air Force—the two deputy commander positions, the two assistant commander positions, and the post of chief of staff—or were jet fighter pilots were considered eligible for promotion to the branch's top post. Airbull flew C-130 royal transport planes. He formerly served as Thai air attaché and deputy defence attaché in Singapore before taking command of Wing 6 at Don Mueang Air Force Base. Airbull reportedly won the Air Force's top position not because of his qualifications but because of a "special signal". Prime Minister Prayut, who also served as defence minister, apparently objected to his nomination after a protest in the Air Force suggesting other appropriate candidates.[58] Former Air Force Chief Manat defended his decision to make Airbull his successor by stating that there had been "no order" from above to make the appointment.[59] Airbull owed nobody an explanation for his promotion to Air Force commander, but his crew-cut hairstyle—similar to that of other prototype soldiers—had already called attention to his connection to the palace. The 2021 Air Force reshuffle brought no surprises. The retiring Airbull chose jet fighter pilot Air Chief Marshal Napadej Dhupatemiya, chief adviser to the Air Force commander, as his replacement. Napadej, whose name litterrally means "sky power", is a son of former Air Force commander Praphan Dhupatemiya, who held that position from 1983 to 1987. Napadej's experience includes service as deputy defence attaché in Beijing and an education and training course in jet fighter combat readiness in the United States.[60] (See Table 4.8.)

The Navy has not played significant roles in Thai politics since it was undermined and sidelined from politics after the Manhattan Rebellion in 1951—a failed coup attempt by junior naval officers against the government of Field Marshal *Luang* Plaek Phibunsongkhram mounted on the day of a ceremony transferring the United States Navy dredge

TABLE 4.7
Career Paths of the King's Men, 2017–21

Name	2017	2018	2019	2020	2021
Apirat Kongsompong	Assistant Army Chief	Army Chief	Army Chief	Deputy Secretary General of the Palace, after retirement from military service	Deputy Secretary General of the Palace
Narongphan Jitkaewthae	Deputy Commander of 1st Army Region	1st Army Region Commander	Assistant Army Chief	Army Chief	Army Chief
Chalermpol Srisawasdi	Director of Army Operations Department	Army Special Adviser	Army Chief of Staff	Chief of Defence Forces	Chief of Defence Forces
Charoenchai Hinthao	2nd Infantry Division Commander	1st Army Region Deputy Commander	1st Army Corps Commander	1st Army Region Commander	Assistant Army Chief
Ekarat Changkaew	1st Army Corps Chief of Staff	Deputy Commandant of Chulachomklao Royal Military Academy	Deputy Commandant of Chulachomklao Royal Military Academy	Deputy Commander of Army Training Command	Army Deputy Chief of Staff
Kantapot Settharasami	Deputy Commander of 2nd Cavalry Division	Deputy Commander of 2nd Cavalry Division	2nd Cavalry Division Commander	Deputy Commander of 1st Army Region	Deputy Commander of 1st Army Region
Phumjai Chaiyaphan (a former Air Force officer)	Deputy Commander of Air Force Security Command	Commander of Air Force Security Command	Attached to King's Bodyguard Command	Head of Office of the Commander of Aides-de-Camp	Head of Office of the Commander of Aides-de-Camp

Name	Position 1	Position 2	Position 3	Position 4	Position 5
Piyapong Klinphan	11th Military Circle Commander	2nd Infantry Division Commander	Deputy Commandant of Chulachomklao Royal Military Academy	Deputy Commandant of Chulachomklao Royal Military Academy	Commandant of Chulachomklao Royal Military Academy
Songphon Sadsaongern	Deputy Commander of 1st Infantry Division	Deputy Commander of 1st Infantry Division	1st Infantry Division Commander	1st Infantry Division Commander	1st Infantry Division Commander
Songwit Noonpakdi	Deputy Commander of 1st Infantry Division	1st Infantry Division Commander	1st Army Region Deputy Commander	Deputy Army Chief of Staff	Chief Staff Officer Attached to the Army Chief
Suwit Ketsri	Deputy Commander of 2nd Calvary Division	2nd Cavalry Division Commander	1st Army Region Deputy Commander	Deputy Commander of Joint War College and Commanding General of Counter Terrorist Operations Centre	Director of Royal Development Projects and Security Coordination Centre
Suksan Nongbualang	2nd Infantry Division Commander	1st Army Region Deputy Commander	1st Army Region Deputy Commander	1st Army Corps Commander	1st Army Region Commander
Thammanoon Withee	Deputy Commander of 1st Army Region	1st Army Corp Commander	1st Army Region Commander	Assistant Army Chief	Assistant Army Chief
Tharapong Malakham	Deputy Commander of 11th Military Circle	11th Military Circle Commander	2nd Infantry Division Commander	Deputy Commander of 1st Army Region	1st Army Corps Commander
Thawatchai Tangpithakkul	31st Infantry Regiment Commander	Deputy Commander of 2nd Infantry Division	11th Military Circle Commander	11th Military Circle Commander	11th Military Circle Commander

Source: Compiled by the author.

TABLE 4.8
**Top Commanders in the Armed Forces in the New Reign,
since October 2016**

Name	Service Branch	Term
Surapong Suwan-art	Royal Thai Armed Forces Headquarters	2016–2017
Thanchaiyan Srisuwan	Royal Thai Armed Forces Headquarters	2017–2018
Pornpipat Benyasai	Royal Thai Armed Forces Headquarters	2018–2020
Chalermpol Srisawasdi	Royal Thai Armed Forces Headquarters	2020
Chalermchai Sitthisart	Army (Special Forces)	2016–2018
Apirat Kongsompong	Army (Wongthewan)	2018–2020
Narongphan Jitkaewthae	Army	2020
Narit Prathumsuwan	Navy	2017–2018
Luechai Rutdit	Navy	2018–2020
Chatchai Sriworakhan	Navy	2020–2021
Somprasong Nilsamai	Navy	2021
Johm Rungsangwan	Air Force	2016–2018
Chaiyapruek Disyasarin	Air Force	2018–2019
Manat Wongwat	Air Force	2019–2020
Airbull Suttiwan	Air Force	2020–2021
Napadej Dhupatemiya	Air Force	2021

Source: Compiled by the author.

Manhattan to the Thai Navy. Although Admiral Sangad Chaloryu, then supreme commander of the armed forces, took leadership of the October 1976 coup after the massacre in Thammasat University, the Navy as a service branch had no role. It was never considered a political threat to any institution.

Admiral Luechai Rutdit retained his position in the 2019 reshuffle. He was also able to put his men in line for succession to leadership of the Navy without any reports of political intervention. Luechai sealed a deal on the acquisition of submarines from China in 2017, when he was the Navy's chief of staff. With backing from Prayut's government and notably from Deputy Prime Minister Prawit, Luechai tilted hardware procurement to the Chinese defence industry. The Thai Navy eyed the purchase of frigates and a landing platform dock (LPD) from Beijing. Luechai promoted Admiral Chorchat Krathes, who took charge of the LPD project, from the post of special adviser to that of deputy commander of the Navy[61]—so that Chorchat could potentially to replace him after his retirement in 2020. While the shake-up in the Navy seemed to reflect Apirat's influence, among those promoted to key positions only Chorchat was not a member of Apirat's AFAPS Class 20. Admiral Somchai Na Bangchang, the chief adviser; Admiral Chatchai Sriworakhan, the assistant Navy commander; and Vice Admiral Sitthiporn Maskasem, the chief of staff, were all classmates of the Army commander.[62] Luechai's favourite and most trusted subordinate in the Navy was Rear Admiral Prachachart Sirisawasdi, whom he promoted to the post of deputy chief of staff in the 2019 reshuffle. Prachachart, a member of AFAPS Class 21, will remain in service until 2023. As a former naval attaché to France, he also has experience in foreign affairs.

Seeing Chatchai become the branch's commanding officer, the 2020 Navy reshuffle also reflected Leuchai's influence, and in particular his ambition to see the completion of the acquisition of three submarines for the fleet, even though Prayut's cabinet decided to delay the purchase of an additional two submarines from China because of budget constraints after the economic slowdown resulting from the COVID-19 pandemic. Chatchai failed to accomplish this mission in 2021, however. The submarine project was halted for another year because of the continuing pandemic. He was also unable to see to it that his favourite, Admiral Theerawut Kanchana, replace him as Navy chief to carry on the project after his retirement. The Defence Council—on which the defence minister, the deputy minister, the ministry's permanent secretary and his deputy, the chief of defence forces and the heads of the three service branches settle on military reshuffles—rejected Chatchai's choice. It recommended that Admiral Somprasong Nilsamai, deputy permanent secretary of the Ministry of Defence, take the Navy's top position. There was no report of an outside "signal" on the reshuffle of naval posts. Rather, a power game within the ministry seems to have determined its outcome. Somprasong had served in the ministry's deputy permanent secretary post to pave the way for Chatchai's promotion to Navy chief. While

Somprasong had the qualifications to become permanent secretary, out-going permanent secretary General Nat Intracharoen insisted that the position was traditionaly reserved for an Army officer and that Somprasong deserved the top job in the Navy.[63]

Strengthening Monarchism

As the monarchy was the source of ideology and legitimacy that enabled the military to maintain its roles in governance, Army chief Apirat took steps to indoctrinate the force with monarchist ideology and to strengthen the asymmetrical relationship between the monarchy and the military. Judging from his publicly expressed opinions, Apirat sought to reaffirm the national narrative concerning the position and roles of the monarchy as Thailand's soul and spirit and as the source of all that was righteous. While he realized that ideological warfare with the communists had ended when he commenced his military career and that contemporary security threats could come in both conventional and non-conventional forms, he regarded former communist insurgents and left-leaning intellectuals, politicians and activists as dangers to the throne. Like the narrative of his predecessor General Sonthi, Apirat's narrative was seemingly a hangover from the Cold War era. "Propaganda in Thailand is severe and worrying. There is a group of communists who still have ideas to overthrow the monarchy, to turn Thailand to communism", the general told an auditorium of military officers, policemen and uniformed students during a high-profile public lecture in October 2019.[64] The idea of communists might have been too vague for the younger generations among the public to imagine them as enemies of the nation and the royal institution. But during his lecture Apirat seemed to suggest that the leader of the soon to be dissolved Future Forward Party, Thanathorn Jungroongruangkit, had such tendencies. He also linked Thanathorn with Hong Kong activist Joshua Wong, showing a picture taken of the two of them standing together that had been posted on Facebook. But Apirat showed a version of the photograph in which Thanathorn's image appeared only in outline. The commander accused Wong, who was blacklisted in Thailand years ago, of conspiring to cause unrest in Thailand. "Let me ask students here if one day somebody used social media to call for an uprising [like that in Hong Kong], would you guys come out to join?", Apirat asked his audience. Urging those present in the audience to "remember what happened in 2010 when our country was inflamed", the commander referred to a military crackdown against Red Shirt protesters in 2010, when he was seen firing a gun at members of the group during an operation.[65]

Apirat took the mission to protect and promote the monarchy as a personal matter. He humiliated, harassed and threatened politicians, activists and dissidents whom he considered threats to the pillar of the nation. In his first press conference after assuming the Army top post in October 2018, Apirat said that the Army was the servant of the monarchy and that its main duty was to protect this beloved institution.

> Insult and disrespect mostly come from people who have mental disorders. Like recently, one person tried to petition [the King] and was later found to be a mental patient. So the authorities sent him to the [mental asylum at] Srithanya Hospital. Anti-monarchists also include sound people with "strange thoughts" that would not be tolerated. These people can't be in Thailand. We have always been protected by the monarchy, since the time of our ancestors. Why can't they [the anti-monarchists] be grateful for that? Everybody is patriotic here. Governments change, but the monarch will always stay with Thailand. I will protect the monarchy with everything I have, it's the Army's duty.[66]

To set a new standard and style for the military under the new reign, Apirat had a clear intention and policy to train Army conscripts in accordance with royal guidelines and with the curriculum set by King Vajiralongkorn for the King's Guard Task Force 904. Apirat and other commanders who were members of this task force were to teach and train a hundred prototype soldiers and trainers for ten weeks before the launch of the new curriculum in November 2019.[67] The commanders sometimes demonstrated the content of the training themselves. The new curriculum included physical and weapons training as well as martial arts, mental exercises and emotional control as means of developing strong and smart soldiers. "The main objective is to have disciplined and patriotic soldiers with the minds of volunteers (*chit asa*) who are ready to serve the country for security and development", according to a public relations website of the 27th Military Circle.[68]

In addition to professional soldiers in the Army, Apirat eyed the 300,000 students who obtained military education and mind training for a minimum of three years in order to be exempted from conscription.

In a meeting with sixty-two students from nineteen educational institutions in June 2019, the commander said that he wanted them to become active citizens with the minds of volunteers by joining the royally initiated volunteer project known officially as "Good Deeds from Our Hearts" or *chit asa 904*. The project sought to mobilize mass support for royal activities. "Students must be conscious and aware of the importance of the [royal] institution. Those who are not grateful to the benevolent monarchy should not live in Thailand", Apirat said on this same occasion.[69]

If monuments, memorials and symbols could shape the perception of military personnel and members of the public, the Army sent a message with that purpose in October 2019. Prime Minister Prayut, who also served as defence minister, presided over the opening of a renovated building and room of the museum at the Army Headquarters in Bangkok. The newly renovated precincts were named in honour of the royalist military officers Prince Boworadet, a cousin of King Prajadhipok, and the prince's commander, *Phraya* Srisitthisongkhram, who led a failed revolt in October 1933 seeking to restore the absolute monarchy.[70] Prayut had had the idea of honouring these men since he was Army commander in 2010–14, and the project was realized when Apirat took the helm as Army chief.

While it was a tradition of the military to honour its heroic commanders by naming buildings, sites, camps and locations after them, glorifying the leadership of the Boworadet Rebellion—considered the last-ditch effort by arch-royalists to reimpose the monarchy after the 1932 revolution in Siam—was interpreted as a promotion of loyalty to the monarchy within the military.[71] The media could trace the links between the bloody incident more than eighty years ago and today's Thai establishment. Srisitthisongkhram, who died in the fighting that ensued as a result of the rebellion,[72] was, as noted above, the maternal grandfather of Surayud Chulanont, formally the chief adviser of the king and a former Army commander.[73] And the decision to honour men involved in the Boworadet Rebellion was widely understood as being of a piece with the disappearance of the Defence of Democracy Monument from the Lak Si intersection in the north of Bangkok a year earlier.[74] The monument had been erected in 1936 at the site of the fighting to beat back the rebellion and was intended to celebrate the government's victory. In 2018, it was quietly removed in order to make room for the construction of the elevated sky train mass transit project intended to ease traffic congestion at one of Bangkok's busiest intersections. Authorities offered no clear explanation for the decision or information about the whereabouts of the monument.

The military is likely to have had the clear intention of continuing its work to reshape historical memory, at least among soldiers, when it removed statues of military leaders who helped topple the absolute monarchy in 1932. Statues of Colonel *Phraya* Phahon Phonphayuhasena and of Field Marshal *Luang* Plaek Phibunsongkhram were removed quietly from two military camps in Lopburi Province as well as from the National Defence College in Bangkok in January 2020. Initially, relatives of the two were informed by the artillery centre that a religious ceremony for the removal of the statues due to take place on 29 December 2019 would be postponed indefinitely, with no clear reason offered. However, local media reported that the statues in fact disappeared without notice a month later.

Major Phutthinat Phahonphonhayuhasena, son of former Prime Minister Phahon, said that the statue of his father had been erected in the artillery centre within the Phahonyothin military camp—which was named after Phahon—in 1960 to honour the officer. Phahon, the second prime minister of Thailand, was also regarded as the father of the Thai artillery. A memorial building had also been built within the camp to display his belongings. "I don't know what they would do with the statue and his belongings displayed in the small museum, but the centre's chief offered reassurance that he would not destroy them", the son said.[75]

Retired career diplomat Pradap Pibulsonggram, a nephew of the late Prime Minister Phibun, said that he had initially intended to attend the ritual ceremony for the removal of the statues. "I don't know why they cancelled it but hope that the military will conduct it properly", he said.[76] Phibun succeeded Phahon as prime minister. His nationalism and militarist ideology were widely admired in the armed forces. The first statue of Phibum to be removed had stood in front of the 2nd Wing Division within the camp at Lopburi. The second had stood in front of the National Defence College in the Thai capital. Both of them were removed around the same time.[77]

The military removed not only the statues of the two military officers who helped topple the absolute monarchy in 1932 but also their names from the two military camps in Lopburi. An announcement in March 2020 said that the king on 29 December 2019 bestowed the name "Bhumibol Camp" onto the artillery centre located at Tambon Khao Phrangam in Lopburi that had previously been known as "Phahonyothin Camp" and the name "Sirikit Camp" onto the field artillery division base in Tambon Thakhae in the same province, which had previously been called "Phibunsongkhram Camp".[78]

These moves could be part of the same series of events that saw royalist military officers honoured and their opponents erased from history, as the removal of the statues of the two leaders took place after the renaming of a room in the museum at Army Headquarters for the royalist Boworadet in October 2019. Phahon was prime minister at the time of the prince's rebellion, and it was Phibun who led the government's troops to defeat that rebellion. Most of the royalist officers who remained in the armed forces were purged or marginalized during Phibun's subsequent terms as premier (1938–44 and 1948–57), which also de-emphasized the place of the monarchy in Thai life.[79]

Relevant agencies offered no official explanation for the removal of the statues of Phahon and Phibun. Phuttthinat said that Major General Wisanti Srasida, then commander of the artillery centre, had called him to explain that the Army wanted to erect a statue of the late King Bhumibol at the same location in Lopburi where the statues stood and to rename the camp after King Bhumibol. "A monument to a commoner could not be there", he said.[80]

This was the third instance of symbols of the end of royal absolutism vanishing mysteriously under the new reign. In April 2017, a small plaque commemorating the 1932 Revolution, which was embedded in the asphalt at Bangkok's Royal Plaza, was replaced with one lauding the monarchy.[81] The plaque had in fact been pulled out in 1960, during Sarit's regime, and re-installed in 1968, five years after the dictator's death.[82] That earlier removal of the plaque could be interpreted as an attempt to change public memory of the 1932 Revolution, as Sarit was the dictator who built up the political stature of the monarchy after a quarter century of eclipse. No agency took responsibility for the second removal of the plaque, in 2017. A number of activists who demanded that the authorities provide an explanation and take responsibility for the disappearance of the historical object were either arrested or taken to military camps for "attitude adjustment". Some of them were charged with *lèse majesté*, but the cases were later dropped for reasons that remained unclear.[83]

The new reign also brought changes in military parades. It was a custom of the Thai military to parade in front of the king and take an oath of loyalty. King Vajiralongkorn presided over a grand parade of the Thai armed forces and police for the first time during his reign on 18 January 2020, Thai Armed Forces Day. The monarch regarded this parade as the final part of his coronation ceremonies, which had initially ended with a royal barge procession on the Chao Phraya River on 12 December 2019. The extension of the coronation events to include the military parade confirmed the mutuality in the relationship between the monarchy and the military.

During King Bhumibol's reign, military parades in the king's presence were held mostly in the Royal Plaza two days before his birthday on 5 December. On Armed Forces Day, parades demonstrating loyalty to the crown were generally held in military camps, in front of the *chaichaloemphon* flag. The first parade during the new reign was thus unique in that it was held on Armed Forces Day in front of the king and the queen and outside the capital. A total 6,812 troops from 39 battalions from all branches of the armed forces and from the police participated in the event, held at the cavalry centre within Adisorn Camp, in Saraburi Province 100 kilometres northeast of Bangkok. The parade included soldiers marching and running and a procession of horses, vehicles and heavy weapons including tanks and artillery. Helicopters and jets flew by before celebratory fireworks ended the parade.

While the king, the queen, Princess Bajrakitiyabha and the commanders of the service branches wore royally designed white costumes with new hats inspired by those worn by aides-de-camp in the royal guard during the reign of King Chulalongkorn, troops paraded in dark-green combat uniforms. The event, which was televised live nationwide and worldwide via the military-run global network TV5 and streamed on social media, showed the strength of the Thai armed forces and at the same time their loyalty to the head of state.

The king's message to the soldiers was simple: he praised their loyalty to the crown and asked them to keep their word and to perform their duty honestly. "The country will be stable and secure as long as all Thais in unison fulfil their obligations for the same ideal and objective, which is the happiness of the people in the country."[84]

Billions of Baht to Laud the Monarchy

While the Thai government allocated billions of baht from the national budget to the Royal Office, other agencies—and notably the military—also allocated huge budgets to glorifying, uplifting and providing security to the royal institution. The budget for the Royal Office alone has grown significantly in recent years, from 6.3 billion baht in 2018 to 8.9 billion baht in 2021.[85] (See Table 4.9.) Separately, more than 37 billion baht out of a total national budget of 3.2 trillion baht for 2021 was allocated to government agencies for matters related to the monarchy, increasing from 29 billion baht in 2020.[86] This chapter focuses only on the funds allocated to the military for the purpose of glorifying and providing security to the monarchy.

TABLE 4.9
Royal Office and Total Thai Government Budgets, 2018–21
(in billions of baht)

	2018	2019	2020	2021
Budget for Royal Office	6.391	6.800	7.685	8.980
Total government budget	2,900	3,000	3,200	3,285

Source: Bureau of the Budget, Thailand.

The military deemed it necessary to allocate budgetary resources for the protection and promotion of the royal institution and to facilitate royal activities. According to the national budgetary strategy, the military budget for activities related to the monarchy fell into three clusters: the basic plan on security, the strategic plan on enhancing the principal institution of the nation, and the strategic plan on enhancing the national defence capacity. Projects and activities drawing on the national budget included supporting members of the monarchy, dispatching personnel and managing systems to provide for their security, and promoting the image and reputation of the royal institution.

Prior to the restructuring of royal security arrangements in 2017, the Ministry of Defence was responsible for the budget allocation covering protection and promotion of the royal institution. Agencies under the jurisdiction of the ministry, including its Office of the Permanent Secretary, Aide-de-Camp Department, the Armed Forces Headquarters and each of the three branches of the armed forces, were all required to have their own plans, projects and activities for the protection and promotion of the monarchy, as well as for responding to offences against the monarchy. Tables 4.10–4.14[87] show the budgets for these agencies for the fiscal year 2017, which was prepared during the reign of the late King Bhumibol. They also show the figures for subsequent fiscal years up to 2021, when the Aide-de-Camp Department had been transferred to the Royal Office and that office was required to submit its spending plans to parliament.

Thailand's fiscal year begins on 1 October and ends on 30 September. In the 2017 fiscal year, the junta-backed government under General Prayut allocated more than a billion baht to the Ministry of Defence for protection and promotion of the monarchy. Most of this amount was budgeted to the Aide-De-Camp Department, while the Army received the second largest share of this allocation for units under its jurisdiction to spend on activities relating to the monarchy. (See Table 4.10.)

TABLE 4.10
Defence Ministry Budget for Promotion and Protection of the Monarchy, 2017–21 Fiscal Years (in millions of baht)

Agency	2017	2018*	2019*	2020	2021
Aide-de-Camp Department	859				
Office of the Permanent Secretary	17.9			21.7	28.6
Royal Thai Armed Forces Headquarters	26.7			61.8	61.8
Army	106			336	296
Navy	6.8			50.5	50.5
Air Force	3.5			41.3	41.3
Total budget for monarchy-related matters	1,019.9			511.3	478.2
Total budget of the ministry	210,777	104,335	106,640	124,400	107,740

Note: *There are no details on budgetary allocations for activities relating to the monarchy in the Royal Gazette in 2018 and 2019.
Source: Compiled by the author from the announcements on the national budget published in the Royal Gazette on 23 September 2016, 2 October 2017, 17 September 2018, 26 February 2020 and 7 October 2020.

While the Thai government's budgetary arrangements may be examined and scrutinized by the parliament, the budget for matters relating to the royal institution is relatively opaque. The published announcements on the budget bills approved by the NCPO junta's rubber-stamp National Legislative Assembly (NLA) for the 2018 and 2019 fiscal years provided no details on allocations for the royal institution during the transition period between the reigns of King Bhumibol and King Vajiralongkorn. As earlier chapters have noted, this transition saw the transfer to palace jurisdiction of a number of government agencies, including military units, and of their budgets. Budgetary arrangements during the period were confused, as the Royal Office had no experience in preparing its own budget proposals. Notably, too, while the junta held power, the NLA did not trouble itself with scrutiny of the budget for royal activities.

In marked contrast, April 2021 saw the opposition Move Forward Party set a precedent in moving to look into the budget for matters relating to the monarchy and calling for cuts of 15 to 40 per cent in the budget for the Royal Office in the 2022 fiscal year. The party noted that the funds might be needed for other, more important, matters during the COVID-19 pandemic. Reuters quoted one of the party's members of parliament saying, "The royal agencies did not send a representative to explain the budget … there is only a seven-page document that did not explain much", during the debate on the budget bill in the House of Representatives.[88] The party based its proposed cuts on the budgets for agencies including the Aide-de-Camp Department and the Royal Security Command prior to their transfer to palace jurisdiction in 2017. "The merger and transfer of royal agencies were supposed to help save budgetary resources. On the contrary, the royal budget remained a huge amount, while the agencies under the defence ministry still require budgetary allocations for royal security and other activities to glorify the monarchy", said another among the party's lawmakers, Rangsiman Rome.[89]

Move Forward failed to trim even a single baht from the budget for the Royal Office, as lawmakers on the government side disagreed with its move to touch the royal budget. Nevertheless, the budget relating to royal matters proposed by the defence ministry could still be subject to adjustment during consideration of the budget bill in parliament.

Budget proposals prepared by the three service branches of the Thai military and by the armed forces headquarters between 2016 and 2021, made available by the Budget Bureau, shed light on the military's budgetary allocations for and spending on activities relating to the monarchy. The figures in Tables 4.11–4.14 were proposed by the four military entities to indicate their plans for expenditures on the protection and promotion of the royal institution. The total sums approved by the parliament, as seen in Table 4.10, did not differ from those in the following tables, as the parliament rarely exercised its authority to adjust those sums.

The Army's proposed annual budget for monarchy-related matters hovered between 269 million baht and 306 million baht between 2017 and 2021. (See Table 4.11.) Full details on projects and activities undertaken are not provided, although in fiscal year 2020 the Army divided its budget for activities relating to the monarchy into four categories of spending: defence against offences to the monarchy, provision of security for the monarchy, activities to honour the crown, and developing security systems for the monarchy.

The Navy proposed only 12.2 million baht in budgetary allocations for the protection and promotion of the monarchy in 2017 and 2018. However, this figure more than doubled, to 27.2 million baht, in 2019 and then nearly doubled again to 50.5 million baht in both 2020 and 2021. The branch's budget proposals provided details on planned spending for the 2020 and 2021 fiscal years. Of the total 50.5 million baht requested in each of those years, the Navy planned to spend 28.8 million for activities requested by the palace, 13 million baht for contributions to and participation in the new king's royally initiated volunteer project (*chit asa*), and only 4.9 million baht to provide security to the crown. (See Table 4.12.) The Navy did not specify planned spending on the defence of the monarchy against offences to it in 2020 and 2021, but it did allocate a total of 3.8 million baht in each year for activities to honour the royal institution.

It is likely that the Air Force has wanted to expend more budgetary resources on the provision of security for the monarchy than on honouring it and defending it against offences during the 2017–21 period. The branch's budget proposals indicated that expenditures on royal security were to go mostly toward facilitating domestic and foreign travel for members of the royal family. Of the total 3.5 million

TABLE 4.11

The Army's Proposed Budget for Promotion and Protection of the Monarchy, 2017–21 Fiscal Years (in millions of baht)

Item	2017	2018	2019	2020	2021
Providing Security/Honouring the monarchy	182	182	182	212	117.5
Defending the monarchy against offences	106	106	106	30	30
Projects/activities to revere the monarchy*				76	70.5
Developing security systems for the monarchy	18	18	18	18	18
Total budget for monarchy-related matters	306	306	306	336	296

Note: *A new item in the breakdown as of 2020.
Source: Budget Bureau, Thailand.

TABLE 4.12

The Navy's Proposed Budget for Promotion and Protection of the Monarchy, 2017–21 Fiscal Years (in millions of baht)

Item	2017	2018	2019	2020	2021
Providing security to the monarchy	5.4	5.4	5.4	4.9	4.9
Honouring the monarchy and defending it against offences to it	6.8	6.8	21.8	3.8	3.8
Activities undertaken on the palace's request				28.8	28.8
Contributions to the royally initiated *chit asa* volunteer project				13.0	13.0
Total budget for monarchy-related matters	12.2	12.2	27.2	50.5	50.5

Source: Bureau of the Budget, Thailand.

TABLE 4.13
**The Air Force's Proposed Budget for Promotion and Protection
of the Monarchy, 2017–21 Fiscal Years
(in millions of baht)**

Item	2017	2018	2019	2020	2021
Providing security	20.0	20.0	20.0	37.8	37.8
Honouring the monarchy and defending it against offences	3.5	3.5	3.5	3.5	3.5
Total budget for monarchy-related matters	23.5	23.5	23.5	41.3	41.3

Source: Bureau of the Budget, Thailand.

TABLE 4.14
**Royal Thai Armed Forces Headquarters' Proposed Budget
for Promotion and Protection of the
Monarchy, 2017–21 Fiscal Years
(in millions of baht)**

Item	2017	2018	2019	2020	2021
Providing security for the monarchy	30.0	30.0	30.0	20.0	20.0
Honouring the monarchy	16.0	16.0	37.6	30.0	30.0
Defending the monarchy against offences	10.7	10.7	11.8	11.8	11.8
Promoting better understanding of the monarchy					
Total budget for monarchy-related matters	56.7	56.7	79.4	61.8	61.8

Source: Bureau of the Budget, Thailand.

baht for honouring and defending the monarchy each fiscal year, the Air Force sought 3.0 million baht for projects to honour or glorify the institution, while the remainder was for activities to defend it against offences. (See Table 4.13.)

Table 4.14 displays budget proposals for activities relating to the monarchy on the part of the Royal Thai Armed Forces Headquarters in recent fiscal years. These expenditures were to be made in addition to those made by the Army, Navy and Air Force.

****

While King Vajiralongkorn can neither replicate nor utilize all the networks and instruments developed in the reign of his father, King Bhumibol, the new sovereign has chosen not to reject the many things that are useful in maintaining strong influence over the military in order to ensure its loyalty and the security of the crown. During the previous reign, the relationship between monarchy and military operated through the nexus of charismatic monarchy, the king's advisers and the military's leaders. While the late king used his advisers as a broker to deal with the armed forces, the new monarch has attached less importance to the Privy Council and instead strengthened his direct ties with the military. It would be too risky for the new king to rely on old power brokers to connect him with Thailand's armed forces. He cannot place all his trust in brokers who might have links to unknown power cliques. It is safer to have his own men implanted within the military.

This chapter has highlighted the reasons that the Thai monarchy's connections to the military have grown stronger in the new reign. First, the king's men have been placed in all key positions to make sure that they also can control and command their subordinates. Second, led by the king's men, the military has continued to adhere to the monarchist ideology implanted firmly in it since the early 1960s, under the authoritarian Sarit regime. The military has thus simply reproduced the notion of royal supremacy and reemphasized its institutional memory of the role of the military in its relations with the crown. The physical erasure of memorial sites, statues and monuments related to individuals who allegedly showed disloyalty to the monarchy has been necessary to send the message that the military will never betray its master. Finally, the military has spent billions of baht from the budgets that it has received from tax revenues to fulfil the function of not only protecting and providing security to members of the crown but also glorifying and promoting the stature of the monarchy.

NOTES

1. Duncan McCargo, "Network Monarchy and Legitimacy Crises in Thailand", *Pacific Review* 18, no. 4 (2005): 499–519.
2. Paul Chambers and Napisa Waitoolkiat, "The Resilience of Monarchised Military in Thailand", *Journal of Contemporary Asia* 46, no. 3 (2016): 425–44.
3. Ibid, p. 427.
4. "Prem Becomes Regent Pro Tempore", *Bangkok Post*, 14 October 2016, https://www.bangkokpost.com/thailand/general/1110645/prem-becomes-regent-pro-tempore (accessed 26 November 2019).
5. "Privy Council President Prem Regent Pro Tempore: Wissanu", *The Nation*, 16 October 2016, https://www.nationthailand.com/news/30297739 (accessed 26 November 2019).
6. "Crown Prince Urges Regent and PM to Prevent Confusion", *The Nation*, 16 October 2016, https://www.nationthailand.com/politics/30297810 (accessed 26 November 2019).
7. "Prakat taengtang ongkhamontri" [Announcement on appointment of member of Privy Council], *Royal Gazette*, vol. 133, special section 280 *ngo*, 2 December 2016, http://www.ratchakitcha.soc.go.th/DATA/PDF/2559/E/280/1.PDF (accessed 26 November 2019).
8. "Phraratchadamrat ratchakan thi sip 'dai pa ma pen prathan ko unchai laeo' phon ek Prem tham nathi thawai ngan khrang sutthai" [Speech of Rama X, "Having Pa as president is reassuring", Prem performs his final duty], *Matichon*, 26 May 2019, https://www.matichon.co.th/heading-news/news_1510670 (accessed 26 November 2019).
9. "Prakat taengtang ongkhamontri" [Announcement on appointment of member of Privy Council], *Royal Gazette*, vol. 137, special section 3 *ngo*, 4 January 2020, http://www.ratchakitcha.soc.go.th/DATA/PDF/2563/E/003/T_0001.PDF (accessed 6 January 2020).
10. "Prakat taengtang phuraksakan prathan ongkhamontri" [Announcement on appointment of acting Privy Council President], *Royal Gazette*, vol. 136, special section 137 *ngo*, 28 May 2019 http://www.ratchakitcha.soc.go.th/DATA/PDF/2562/E/137/T_0001.PDF (accessed 26 November 2019).
11. Andrew Macgregor Marshall, *A Kingdom in Crisis: Thailand's Struggle for Democracy in the Twenty-First Century* (London: Zed Books, 2015), pp. 174, 188.
12. "Banthuek khrongkan angmachak phraratchadamri" [Notes on royally initiated projects] (Bangkok: Royal Development Projects Bureau, 2020).
13. Wassana Nanuam, *Senthang lek phon ek Surayud Chualanont* [The iron path of General Surayud Chulanont], 4th ed. (Bangkok: Matichon Books, 2006).
14. Ibid., pp. 59–68.

15. Wassana Nanuam, *Senthang phayak Prayut Chan-ochacha thahan suea su lang suea* [The path of Eastern Tiger Prayut Chan-ocha from tiger soldier to tiger's back] (Bangkok: Matichon Books, 2014), p. 298.

16. "Prakat taengtang ongkhamontri" [Announcement on appointment of member of Privy Council], *Royal Gazette*, vol. 133, special section 281 *ngo*, 6 December 2016, http://www.ratchakitcha.soc.go.th/DATA/PDF/2559/E/281/1.PDF (accessed 10 February 2020).

17. "Prakat taengtang ongkhamontri" [Announcement on appointment of member of Privy Council], *Royal Gazette*, vol. 133, special section 305 *ngo*, 24 December 2016, http://www.ratchakitcha.soc.go.th/DATA/PDF/2559/E/305/2.PDF (accessed 10 February 2020).

18. "Prakat taengtang ongkhamontri" [Announcement on appointment of member of Privy Council], *Royal Gazette*, vol. 134, special section 154 *ngo*, 8 June 2017, http://www.ratchakitcha.soc.go.th/DATA/PDF/2560/E/154/1. PDF (accessed 26 February 2020).

19. "Prakat rueang hai ongkhamontri phon chak tamnaeng" [Announcement on resignation of member of Privy Council], *Royal Gazette*, vol. 135, special section 143 *ngo*, 21 June 2018, http://www.ratchakitcha.soc.go.th/DATA/PDF/2561/E/143/1.PDF (accessed 10 February 2020).

20. Thak Chaloemtiarana, *Thailand: The Politics of Despotic Paternalism*, 2nd ed. (Ithaca, New York: Cornell Southeast Asia Program Publications, 2007), p. 210.

21. "Prakat samnak nayokratthamontri rueang phraratchathan phraborom-marachanuyat sathapana nuai thahan pen nuai thahan raksa phra-ong" [Announcement of Prime Minister's Office on the appointment of military unit as royal guard unit], *Royal Gazette*, vol. 118, Section 2 *ngo*, 4 January 2001, http://www.ratchakitcha.soc.go.th/DATA/PDF/2544/D/002/7.PDF (accessed 27 November 2019).

22. "Prakat samnak nayokratthamontri rueang phraratchathan phraborom-marachanuyat sathapana nuai thahan pen nuai thahan raksa phra-ong" [Announcement of Prime Minister's Office on the appointment of military unit as royal guard unit], *Royal Gazette*, vol. 118, Section 14 *ngo*, 14 February 2001, p. 1, http://www.ratchakitcha.soc.go.th/DATA/PDF/2544/D/014/1. PDF (accessed 27 November 2019).

23. "Prakat samnak nayokratthamontri rueang phraratchathan phraborom-marachanuyat sathapana nuai thahan pen nuai thahan raksa phra-ong" [Announcement of Prime Minister's Office on the appointment of military unit as royal guard unit], *Royal Gazette*, vol. 119, Section 5 *ngo*, 15 January 2002, http://www.ratchakitcha.soc.go.th/DATA/PDF/2545/D/005/7.PDF (accessed 27 November 2019).

24. "Prakat samnak nayokratthamontri rueang phraratchathan phraborom-marachanuyat sathapana nuait thahan pen nuai thahan raksa phra-ong"

[Announcement of Prime Minister's Office on appointment of military unit as royal guard unit], *Royal Gazette*, vol. 122, Section 75 *ngo*, 20 September 2005, http://www.ratchakitcha.soc.go.th/DATA/PDF/2548/00171178.PDF (accessed 27 November 2019).

25. "Prakat samnak nayok ratthamontri rueang phraratchathan phraborommarachanuyat sathapana nuai thahan pen nuai thahan raksa phra-ong" [Announcement of Prime Minister's Office on appointment of military unit as royal guard unit], *Royal Gazette*, vol. 124, Section 44 *ngo*, 24 May 2007, http://www.ratchakitcha.soc.go.th/DATA/PDF/2550/D/044/20.PDF (accessed 27 November 2019).

26. "Prakat samnak nayokratthamontri rueang phraratchathan phraborommarachanuyat sathapana nuai thahan pen nuai thahan raksa phra-ong" [Announcement of Prime Minister's Office on appointment of military unit as royal guard unit], *Royal Gazette*, vol. 131, special section 200 *ngo*, 6 October 2014, (http://www.ratchakitcha.soc.go.th/DATA/PDF/2557/E/200/4.PDF (accessed 27 November 2019).

27. "Prakat samnak nayokratthamontri rueang phraratchathan phraborommarachanuyat plianplaeng nuai thahan raksa phra-ong lae nuai thahan nai phra-ong" [Announcement of Prime Minister's Office on change of royal guard units], *Royal Gazette*, vol. 136, special section 100 *ngo*, 23 April 2019, http://www.ratchakitcha.soc.go.th/DATA/PDF/2562/E/100/T_0027.PDF (accessed 27 November 2019).

28. Interviews with General Sonthi Boonyaratglin, 18 December 2019, and Lieutenant General Pongsakorn Rodchompoo, 20 December 2019, Bangkok. As Table 4.3 indicates, two of the royal personages whose names royal guard units now bear were historical figures.

29. Note that this volume generally follows the palace's preferred Romanization of *ratchawanlop* as *rajawallop*.

30. "Prakat song phrakarunaplotklaoplotkramomphraratchathan phraborommarachanuyat plian nam nuai thahan raksa phra-ong" [Announcement on change of name of royal guard units], *Royal Gazette*, vol. 136, special section 303 *ngo*, 12 December 2019, http://www.ratchakitcha.soc.go.th/DATA/PDF/2562/E/303/T_0004.PDF (accessed 13 December 2019).

31. Shawn W. Crispin, "New Reign Takes Hold in Thailand", *Asia Times*, 25 January 2017, https://www.asiatimes.com/2017/01/article/new-reign-takes-hold-thailand/ (accessed 28 November 2019).

32. Ibid.

33. "Prakat samnak nayokratthamontri rueang taengtang naithahan phiset" [Announcement of Prime Minister's Office on appointment of special military officer], *Royal Gazette*, vol. 129 special section 17 *ngo*, 17 January 2012, http://www.ratchakitcha.soc.go.th/DATA/PDF/2555/E/017/8.PDF (accessed 29 November 2019).

34. "Prakat taengtang naithahan phiset" [Announcement on appointment of special military officer], *Royal Gazette*, vol. 135, special section 171 *ngo*, 17 July 2018, (http://www.ratchakitcha.soc.go.th/DATA/PDF/2561/E/171/T1.PDF (accessed 26 February 2020).

35. "Prakat taengtang khanakammakan sapsin suanphramahakasat lae thiphrueksa samnakngan sapsin suanphramahakasat" [Announcement on appointment of Crown Property Board of Directors and adviser to Crown Property Bureau], *Royal Gazette*, vol. 136, special section 4 *ngo*, 6 January 2019, http://www.ratchakitcha.soc.go.th/DATA/PDF/2562/E/004/T_0001.PDF (accessed 4 December 2019).

36. Marwaan Macan-Markar, "All the King's Men: Thai Military Power Shifts Away from Prayut", *Nikkei Asian Review*, 2 July 2019, https://asia.nikkei.com/Spotlight/Asia-Insight/All-the-king-s-men-Thai-military-power-shifts-away-from-Prayuth (accessed 5 December 2019).

37. In Thai, *luk phuyai* or *luk than lan thoe*.

38. Interview with General Sonthi.

39. Wassana Nanuam, *Senthang phayak Prayut Chan-ocha*, pp. 107–8.

40. "Maethap khong thoranong 'Apirat Kongsompong' chok chata fa likhit" ["Apirat Kongsompong" designated commander from the sky], *Khom chat luek*, 15 August 2017, https://www.komchadluek.net/news/people/291961 (accessed 28 November 2019).

41. Wassana Nanuam, "Apirat Tipped as New Army Commander", *Bangkok Post*, 12 August 2017, https://www.bangkokpost.com/thailand/politics/1304603/apirat-tipped-as-new-army-commander (accessed 3 December 2019).

42. Pongpiphat Banchanont, "Luk Jod sami doktoe O senthang chiwit Bik Daeng pho bo tho bo khon mai sai wongthewan" [Jod's son, Dr O's husband: the life path to being new Army chief of Big Daeng from *Wongthewan* clique], *The Matter*, 4 September 2018, https://thematter.co/social/general-apirat-kongsompong/58960?fbclid=IwAR30MHHEhOni-Kp2GYkdlQELeNmtKy3nYItuVcLnVC5I0Brq-2VleiF5RkQ (accessed 5 December 2019).

43. Wassana Nanuam, *Senthang phayak Prayut Chan-ocha*, p. 107.

44. "'Bik Jiab': kha ma khondiao klang dong burapha phayak mong kham chot thot rahat yai 'Bik Tu-Bik Pom' chai thueng" ["Big Jiab": I come alone in the middle of Eastern Tigers, why "Big Tu" and "Big Pom" are so undaunted], *Matichon sutsapda*, 16–22 September 2016, https://www.matichonweekly.com/in-depth/article_7718 (accessed 29 November 2019).

45. "Prakat taengtang ongkhamontri" [Announcement on appointment of member of Privy Council], *Royal Gazette*, vol. 135, special section 244 *ngo*, 2 October 2018, http://www.ratchakitcha.soc.go.th/DATA/PDF/2561/E/244/T_0001.PDF (accessed 29 November 2019).

46. "'Wikhro pho thahan' songthai kho so cho 'Bik Pom-Bik Tu' yuet riap! 'Bik Daeng' khon phiset triam nang pho bo tho bo 'Bik Nat-Bik Kob-Bik Tai' khuen phaeng 'Bik Lue-Bik Tui' biat ching dam maethap ruea" [Analysing military reshuffle; "Big Tu and Big Pom" in full control, special man "Big Daeng" preparing to sit as Army chief, "Big Nat", "Big Kob", "Big Tai" in line, "Big Lue" and "Big Tui" competing to be Navy chief], *Matichon sutsapda*, 20–26 August 2018, https://www.matichonweekly.com/column/article_119148 (accessed 29 November 2019).

47. "Wikhro 'Bik Tu-Bik Pom' khayao pho thahan: chabap fa dan phiset chapta sut lap 'Bik Daeng' klang sathannakan muak daeng" [Analysis: Big Tu, Big Pom in military shake-up, closely watch Big Deang's secret solution in the middle of red beret situation], *Matichon sutsapda*, 27 July–2 August 2018, https://www.matichonweekly.com/column/article_121055 (accessed 29 November 2019).

48. Wassana Nanuam and Wassayos Ngamkham, "Narongpan Tipped to Replace Apirat as Army Chief", *Bangkok Post*, 9 September 2019, https://www.bangkokpost.com/thailand/general/1745729/narongpan-tipped-to-replace-apirat-as-army-chief (accessed 3 December 2019).

49. "Lalai wongthewan-thahan suea-burapha phayak kongthap yuk 'Bik Daeng'" [Dissolution of *Wongthewan*-Eastern Tigers, the Army in Apirat era], *Matichon sutsapda*, 13–19 September 2019, pp. 15–18.

50. "Poet thap 14 khunphon kho daeng 'Bik Daeng-Bik Bi-Bik Kaeo-Bik Nui' kap pharakit sut khopfa" [14 red-striped t-shirt commanders unveiled: "Big Daeng", "Big Bi", "Big Kaeo", "Big Nui" and their duties at the end of the horizon], *Matichon sutsapda*, 11–17 October 2019, p. 14.

51. Ibid.

52. Wassana Nanuam and Wassayos Ngamkham, "Narongpan tipped to replace Apirat".

53. "Prakat samnak nayokratthamontri rueang hai naithahan rapratchakan" [Prime Minister's Office announcement on the appointment of military officers], *Royal Gazette*, vol. 137, special section 218 *ngo*, 18 September 2020, http://www.ratchakitcha.soc.go.th/DATA/PDF/2563/E/218/T_0001.PDF?fbclid=IwAR1dAaRyj7_FynxfRUjqXgDsF7eyxDgec36AZZt1rmZIGqXwVF95-ZHu3FE (accessed 6 January 2021).

54. "Prakat luean kharatchakan nai phra-ong hai sungkhuen lae prap-on kharatchakanthahan lae phonlaruean pen kharatachakan nai phra-ong" [Announcement on the promotion and transfer of military officers and civil servants to be royal officials], *Royal Gazette*, vol. 137, special section 229 *ngo*, 30 September 2020, http://www.ratchakitcha.soc.go.th/DATA/PDF/2563/E/229/T_0001.PDF (accessed 8 January 2021).

55. "Naronghpan Jitkaewthae: 'thahan kho daeng' phuchongrakphakdi phangat nang kao-i pho bo tho bo khon thi 42" [Loyal "red-striped t-shirt soldier" Narongphan Jitkaewthae rises to take the helm as forty-second Army chief], *BBC Thai*, 18 September 2020, https://www.bbc.com/thai/thailand-54077187 (accessed 6 January 2021).

56. "'Narongphan' ning! fa naeokhit 'satharanarat' pat fun '5 dai 7 mai dai' pongpram 'thahan taengmo'" ["Narongphan" remains silent amid growing "republican", dusting off "five yes, seven no", deterring "watermelon soldiers"], *Voice Online*, 24 December 2020, https://voicetv.co.th/read/hPx1yGpUU (accessed 8 January 2021).

57. Ibid.

58. Wassana Nanuam, "Sudden Change to Nomination for New Air Force Chief", *Bangkok Post*, 31 August 2020, https://www.bangkokpost.com/thailand/general/1977491/sudden-change-to-nomination-for-new-air-force-chief (accessed 6 January 2021).

59. Tappanai Boonpradit, "Dark horse: Rise of New Air Force Chief Raises Eyebrows", *Khaosod English*, 6 October 2020, https://www.khaosodenglish.com/politics/2020/10/06/dark-horse-rise-of-new-air-force-chief-raises-eyebrows/ (accessed 6 January 2021).

60. "3 nakbin 'ep-16' suekching kao-i 'pho bo tho o'" [Three "F-16" pilots compete for post as Air Force chief], *Krungthep thurakit*, 28 June 2021, https://www.bangkokbiznews.com/politics/945762 (accessed 24 September 2021).

61. "Navy to Buy B6.1bn Chinese Landing Ship", *Bangkok Post*, 12 September 2019, https://www.bangkokpost.com/thailand/general/1747774/navy-to-buy-b6-5bn-chinese-landing-ship (accessed 2 December 2019).

62. "Changwa kao khong 'Bik Daeng' tangrap ronthoi nai khwamngiapngan kap botbat 'Bik Lue' nai suek maothai lae konlayut chat thapruea muea 'Bik Cho' yu nai wonglom to tho 20" ["Big Daeng's" footsteps, retreating in silence, and the role of "Big Lue" in the Mao Tai battle as "Big Cho" is surrounded by members of AFAPS Class 20], *Matichon sutsapda*, 27 September – 3 October 2019, p. 15.

63. "Khai rahat lap 'Bik Oui' fa khluenlom dan 'Bik Tong' phangat 'pho bo tho ro'" [Decoding secret deal of "Big Oui" to elevate "Big Tong" to Navy chief], *Thai rat*, 26 August 2021, https://www.thairath.co.th/news/politic/2177030 (accessed 24 September 2021).

64. Patpicha Tanakasempipat, "Thai Army Chief Decries Opposition, Hints at Threat to Monarchy", Reuters, 11 October 2019, https://www.reuters.com/article/us-thailand-military/thai-army-chief-decries-opposition-hints-at-threat-to-monarchy-idUSKBN1WQ0WN (accessed 5 December 2019).

65. "'Bik Daeng' sat 'ngao pritsana' dotphop 'Joshua Wong'-to phuak khit kae matra 1 wang lom sathaban" ["Big Daeng" charges that "mysterious

shadow" secretly met "Joshua Wong"-argues that those seeking to amend Article 1 hope to overthrow the institution], *Matichon TV*, 11 October 2019, https://www.youtube.com/watch?v=FIgLa4fmz3o (accessed 6 October 2021, and "'Thanathorn' yoei khae rupkhu 'Joshua Wong' phapdiao chapyong mop hongkong sang khwamkliatchang laeo rue?" ["Thanathorn" derisive, can just a photograph taken with "Joshua Wong" link him with Hong Kong protests and cause hatred towards him?], *Matichon*, 11 October 2019, https://www.matichon.co.th/politics/news_1708540 (accessed 21 September 2021).

66. "Mental Asylum Best Place for 'Cracked' Anti-Monarchists, Says New Army Chief", *The Nation*, 17 October 2018, https://www.nationthailand.com/politics/30356661 (accessed 4 December 2019).

67. "Roem laksut thahantonbaep tam naeothang phraratchathan phruetsachikayon ni" [Royal curriculum for model privates starts this November], *Thai PBS News*, 7 October 2019, https://news.thaipbs.or.th/content/284951 (accessed 4 December 2019).

68. "Khong sutthai kanfuek 'nong khon lek khong kongthapbok' hai pen thahantonbaep" [Last chapter in training of 'youngest Army brothers' to be model soldiers], Website of 27th Military Circle, 3 July 2019, http://mtb27.army2.mi.th/archives/7985 (accessed 4 December 2019).

69. "Apirat yok khamphut no so tho khrai mai rak sathaban mai somkhuan yu nai prathet thai" [Apirat says to military students that those who don't love the institution should not live in Thailand], *Voice Online*, 21 June 2019, https://voicetv.co.th/read/dIzZTs_kO (accessed 4 December 2019).

70. Nikhom Charumanee, "Kabot Boworadet pho so 2476" [The Boworadet Rebellion, 1933], Master's thesis, Chulalongkorn University, 1976.

71. Teeranai Charuvastra, "Royalist Coup Leaders Honoured at Army Hall of Fame", *Khaosod English*, 9 October 2019, http://www.khaosodenglish.com/politics/2019/10/09/royalist-coup-leaders-honored-at-army-hall-of-fame/ (accessed 4 December 2019).

72. Nikhom, "Kabot Boworadet", p. 229.

73. Wassana Nanuam, *Senthang lek phon ek Surayud Chualanont*, pp. 29–35.

74. "Anusawari prap kabot hai kueap pi khana thi chue 'Boworadet-Srisitthisongkhram' plo pen tuek-hong nai tho bo" [As the Defence of Democracy Monument disappears for nearly a year, while the names of Boworadet and Srisitthisongkram emerge at Army headquarters], *Prachatai*, 9 October 2019, https://prachatai.com/journal/2019/10/84685 (accessed 4 December 2019).

75. "Khana ratsadon: sun kanthahan puen yai Lopburi triam buangsuang anusawari chomphon Po – Phraya Phahon kon ruethon" [People's Party: Artillery centre in Lopburi prepares ritual ceremony before removal of Field Marshal Phibun and Phaya Phahon monuments], *BBC Thai*, 27 December

2019, https://www.bbc.com/thai/thailand-50923944 (accessed 11 February 2020).

76. Ibid.

77. "Two Revolutionary Leader Statues Gone Missing", *Prachatai English*, 29 January 2020, https://prachatai.com/english/node/8350 (accessed 11 February 2020).

78. Prakat samnak nayokratthamontri rueang phraratchathanplianplaeng nam khai thahan [Announcement of Prime Minister's Office on renaming of military camps], *Royal Gazette*, vol. 137, special section 68 *ngo*, 24 March 2020, http://www.ratchakitcha.soc.go.th/DATA/PDF/2563/E/068/T_0002. PDF (accessed 5 June 2020).

79. Kobkua Suwannathat-Pian, *Thailand's Durable Premier: Phibun through Three Decades 1932–1957* (Kuala Lumpur: Oxford University Press, 1995), pp. 15, 67–81.

80. "Khana ratsadon: lukchai Phraya Phahon rabu cha mi kananchoen anusawari ro 9 ma pradit sathanthi sun kanthahan puen yai" [People's Party: Rama IX monument to be erected at Artillery Centre, son of *Phraya* Phahon says], *BBC Thai*, 29 December 2019, https://www.bbc.com/thai/thailand-50939914 (accessed 12 February 2020).

81. Phatrawadee Phataranawik, "Disappearing Democracy", *The Nation*, 4 January 2019, https://www.nationthailand.com/news/30361637 (accessed 4 December 2019).

82. "Patikiriya sangkhom to mut khanarat chak pi 2503–2560" [Social reactions to People's Party's plaque from 1960 to 2017], *Matichon sutsapda*, 21–27 April 2017, https://www.matichonweekly.com/column/article_32563 (accessed 6 December 2019).

83. Anna Lawattanaktrakul, "Song pi song duean kanhaipai khong mut khana ratsadon" [Two years and two months since the People's Party plaque went missing], *Prachatai*, 23 June 2019, https://prachatai.com/journal/2019/06/83100 (accessed 6 December 2019).

84. "'Ro 10-rachini' sadet phithi suansanam thawai satpatiyan nai wan kongthap thai" [Rama X and queen preside over parade on Thai Military Day], *Thai rat*, 19 January 2020, https://www.thairath.co.th/news/royal/1750720 (accessed 12 February 2020).

85. The value of the Thai baht fluctuated quite widely during the 2017–21 period, ranging from 29 baht to the US dollar to 35 baht to the US dollar. The average exchange rate during the period was 32 baht to the dollar.

86. "Poet ngoppraman kiaokap sathaban phramahakaksat pi 2564" [Budget for royal institution in 2021], *Prachatai*, 31 August 2020, https://prachatai.com/journal/2020/08/89306 (accessed 6 January 2021).

87. Figures in this section are drawn from reports from Thailand's Budget Bureau, available on the bureau's website, http://www.bb.go.th/topic3.

php?gid=862&mid=545 (accessed 18 January 2021), and on budget
bills announced in the *Royal Gazette*, all accessed 22 August 2021:
"Phraratchabanyat ngoppraman raichai prachampingoppraman pho so 2560"
[2017 Budget Bill], *Royal Gazette*, Volume 133, Section 84 *ko*, 23 September
2016, http://www.ratchakitcha.soc.go.th/DATA/PDF/2559/A/084/1.PDF
(accessed 22 September 2021); "Phraratchabanyat ngoppraman raichai
prachampingoppraman pho so 2561" [2018 Budget Bill], *Royal Gazette*,
Volume 134, Section 101 *ko*, 2 October 2017, http://www.ratchakitcha.
soc.go.th/DATA/PDF/2560/A/101/1.PDF (accessed 21 September 2021);
"Phraratchabanyat ngoppraman raichai prachampingoppraman pho so 2562"
[2019 Budget Bill], *Royal Gazette*, Volume 135, Section 71 *ko*, 17 September
2018, http://www.ratchakitcha.soc.go.th/DATA/PDF/2561/A/071/T1.PDF
(accessed 21 September 2021); "Phraratchabanyat ngoppraman raichai
prachampingoppraman pho so 2563" [2020 Budget Bill], *Royal Gazette*,
Volume 137, Section 15 *ko*, 26 February 2020, http://www.ratchakitcha.soc.
go.th/DATA/PDF/2563/A/015/T_0001.PDF (accessed 21 September 2021);
"Phraratchabanyat ngoppraman raichai prachampingoppraman pho so 2564"
[2021 Budget Bill], *Royal Gazette*, Volume 137, Section 82 *ko*, 7 October
2020, http://www.ratchakitcha.soc.go.th/DATA/PDF/2563/A/082/T_0001.
PDF (accessed 21 September 2021).
88. "Thai Monarchy Budget Survives Rare Calls for Cuts in Parliament",
Reuters, 22 August 2021, https://www.reuters.com/world/asia-pacific/thai-
monarchy-budget-survives-rare-calls-cuts-parliament-2021-08-22 (accessed
22 September 2021).
89. "4 so so 'klao klai' aphiprai 'ngop suanratchakan nai phra-ong" [4 "Move
Forward" MPs speak on "royal budget"], *Prachatai*, 23 August 2021, https://
prachatai.com/journal/2021/08/94603 (accessed 22 September 2021).

Epilogue

ASYMMETRICAL RELATIONS

The relationship between monarchy and military in Thailand has been asymmetrical since the beginning. When King Chulalongkorn's reign gave birth to the modern Thai armed forces in the nineteenth century, their purpose was basically to serve the monarchy. That purpose was much more important than any role they had in national defence, given that fending off armed threats from the British and French empires was always going to be beyond the strength of Siamese forces. Also, the military was then under the command of the absolute monarchy. Thai soldiers took an oath not only to protect the monarchy but also to give loyalty to, to uplift, to glorify and to worship the monarchy as the pillar of the nation and the embodiment of the national spirit. Relations between the two institutions were essentially those of employer and servant, if not sometimes of master and slave. Sometimes in history, no doubt, servants want to have relations of equal partnership with their bosses.

Asymmetrical relations can, however, work to the advantage of both parties. With military protection, the monarchy survives and has the power to govern and to manipulate politics. The military in the meantime draws advantage from those relations in referring to the monarchy as its source of legitimacy as it too manoeuvres politically. This manoeuvring may benefit the military as an institution, one or more of its factions or cliques, or even individual officers. Further, those asymmetrical relations help ensure that the armed forces have no accountability to elected governments.

While the 1932 Revolution saw the monarchy being brought under the constitution, Thai charters—including the current one, sponsored by the military and promulgated in 2017—have positioned the king as the head of the armed forces. King Vajiralongkorn, who enacted the 2017 constitution, has made clear through his actions his intention to go beyond a merely ceremonial role to actually exercise the powers of that position and lead the Thai armed forces as their commander-in-chief.

To that end, the National Council for Peace and Order (NCPO) junta under the leadership of General Prayut Chan-ocha introduced a number of legal instruments to authorize and justify the enhanced role of the monarchy in relation to the armed forces. The 2017 Royal Service Administration Act reorganized the administration of the palace by making the Bureau of the Royal Household, the Privy Council and the Royal Security Command directly subject to the king. More importantly, King Vajiralongkorn took two infantry regiments, numbering a few thousand troops, under his direct command; these were in addition to the royal guard contingents that he had commanded since he was crown prince.

The king has absolute power over his wealth and over the soldiers under palace jurisdiction. Putting this power into the context of military-monarchy relations, the king has a sizeable private army for use in guaranteeing his safety and more. Through the example of the reign of King Vajiravudh, history has revealed the truth that the existence of such a royal private army could be counterproductive. It could alienate the armed forces from the palace. Military leaders and soldiers might feel discriminated against because the head of the armed forces has his own favourite units. Historians have demonstrated that King Vajiravudh created a small army as his toy in order to demonstrate that he had the ability to command military forces and that his small army was well trained and performed better than other units, which were in fact under the command of men who were both his relatives and his rivals.

King Vajiralongkorn apparently favours norms and practices created or promoted by King Vajiravudh, such as the *ratchasawat* discussed in Chapter 3. He may, however, recognize the potential problem in his ties with the military that maintaining what amounts to a private army poses. He has worked to project himself as a well-educated, well-trained and disciplined career military officer, not a man playing with a toy army. Public information has been consistently produced to show that he climbed the career ladder from below, starting as a junior officer and rising to the level of commander, with skill and talent. He also had real experience in the battle against communist insurgents, which were then considered a major threat to the nation. It is hard to say whether Thailand's military leadership does indeed admire the king's military talents, but the monarch has in any case shown that those who resist his commands will be fiercely and sometimes cruelly punished. The armed forces do not need to love the king, but they must fear him. Disloyalty to the monarchy is a crime, and prosecution for that crime is widely known to be unfair. There is no need to ask about justice.

In any case, and as Machiavelli suggested, it is necessary for a prince to employ fear and brutality to control armed forces. "[W]hen a prince is campaigning with his soldiers and is in command of a large army then he need not worry about having a reputation for cruelty; because, without such a reputation, no army was ever kept united and disciplined."[1] However, Machiavelli might have been wrong to some extent. The Thai military is not always united, even if its officers do fear the king. And the palace takes advantage of disunity within the factionalized armed forces to nurture its relations with the military. The king hand-picked officers from the *Wongthewan* faction, led by General Apirat Kongsompong, to receive special training and indoctrination, as well as appointment to the special task force under the name "904". They thus became the king's men, to be positioned in key units in the Army.

The king could make these moves only with the cooperation of his father's men. King Bhumibol's chief adviser, General Prem Tinsulanonda, whom King Vajiralongkorn retained as president of the Privy Council until the end of Prem's life, put an end to the perpetuation of the power of the Army's Eastern Tigers clique in 2016. While that year's military reshuffle was in principle under the authority of the defence minister and the top commander of each branch of the armed forces, Prem in fact exercised his authority as the manager of the "network monarchy" to intervene in the reshuffle in order to place a commander from the Special Forces into the top position in the Army. The government was then under the leadership of the "big brothers" of the Eastern Tigers clique, namely Prime Minister Prayut and Defence Minister General

Prawit Wongsuwan. Without Prem's having spoken for the palace and exerted influence over the military for a long time, it would have been impossible for him to interfere to change the power arrangements within the military during such a period.

While King Vajiralongkorn maintained the palace's alliance with Prem until the death of the aged soldier and palace adviser in 2019, the monarch realized that he might not be able to rely on Prem's protégé General Surayud Chulanont to play the same role. Surayud has had less influence over the military. While the king appointed him to replace Prem as president of the Privy Council and thus as his chief adviser, the council could no longer oversee management of the network monarchy. Instead, King Vajiralongkorn created his own network, run by his men including Apirat and Sathitphong and meant to serve as an instrument to deal with the military.

It is premature to judge whether Apirat or his successor as Army commander, General Narongphan Jitkaewthae, will be able to serve the king as well as Prem served his father in the past, although Apirat obviously tried to take action as the guardian and the leader of military. Apirat had less experience in military operations and leadership than Prem did. He did have many medals decorating his dark-green uniform, but his only experience lies in cracking down on unarmed Red Shirt protesters in 2010 and in a few years spent in the restive Deep South. The Thai military of his era has little or no experience in tough combat. What Apirat could do to serve the king was to bully and to subject to verbal harassment young politicians and activists whom he has labelled threats to national security and to the monarchy. Having replaced Apirat as Army commander in September 2020, Narongphan initially appeared to take a more understated approach.

Apirat and his fellow military leaders have taken a number of measures in the ideological sphere to further the process of monarchization of the armed forces. These measures have included spending money to glorify the monarchy and removing traces of anti-monarchism from military camps and some public places. There has never been a systematic survey to prove whether the average of well more than 500 million baht in budgetary resources that the armed forces have spent annually for activities to protect and promote the monarchy are worth the cost. It is also too early to conclude that the removal of statues and anti-monarchy symbols has really had implications for the military's own and or the public's perception.

Apirat and Narongphan may be different from Prem, and King Vajiralongkorn cannot be another King Bhumibol either. Nevertheless, while the king may not and cannot wear his father's shoes, he can take advantage of the late king's powerful legacy and of the highly monarchized military that he left behind. The armed forces staged numerous coups and attempted coups during the long reign of King Bhumibol—mostly against elected governments and ostensibly "to protect the monarchy". In the cases of the coups of September 2006 and May 2014, and as intensively discussed in this book, it was obvious that the monarchy used the military to intervene in politics for its own survival. Equally obvious was how King Vajiralongkorn was later able to benefit from those actions in smoothly ascending the throne. This history may not absolutely guarantee the safety of the new monarch or even the security of the monarchy itself, but the military will find taking on the monarchy riskier and less appetizing while the latter remains highly revered. Taking a monarch out of the monarchy is not an easy task for the monarchized military of these days, and there is no sign so far that the military wants to do so.

This book does not discuss the political implications of relations between the monarchy and the military in the reign of King Vajiralongkorn. There are two reasons for this. One is that the new monarch is likely to have given priority to securing his ties with the armed forces since the military is the most dangerous among institutions or groups in the country. It has weapons, is well organized and is larger than other institutions. King Vajiralongkorn has thus taken time to secure those ties, and this book simply explains how the two institutions and their personnel have forged relations and cemented links. The second reason is that political arrangements during the transition period from the last reign and in the early years of the new reign have offered a monarchy-friendly setting since it was the military that seized political power to protect the monarchy during such a critical time. The NCPO junta designed a regime meant to empower the monarchy and to secure the royal institution. It also invested considerable effort and resources in raising the stature of the monarchy in Thai society. These considerations notwithstanding, several observations—each informed by the preceding chapters—concerning Thailand's military, monarchy and politics are in order.

First, the consolidation of increased military power under the jurisdiction of the palace may not be equivalent to ensuring the absolute security of the royal institution, as it could cause alienation in and resistance from the armed forces. Chapter 3 notes that a number of police officers have resisted recruitment into the Royal Security Command. While there have been no reports of similar reactions to such transfers among military officers, this does not suggest universal comfort in the armed forces with the current arrangement. Officers' frustration with their units' relationship to the palace could be a threat to the stability of the royal institution and even to the political order.

Second, the monarchy-military nexus might be useful for the two institutions as they seek to manipulate politics. But it may not fit well with the new political developments of these times, when the younger generations have begun to demand the reform of the monarchy as well as more transparency from the military, as a result of which the leaders of the armed forces must show accountability. The nexus faced a major challenge in 2020, when youthful protesters demanded that the royal institution operate under the constitution and that it desisted from endorsing military intervention in Thai politics. As the palace has now taken direct command of a sizeable number of combat-ready troops for its own security, the military therefore needs to explain to the people's representatives who sit in parliament and to the public at large whether it is also worth spending billions of baht in tax revenue to provide additional security to the monarchy, to respond to offences to the royal institution, and to raise the stature of the crown. The country could, after all, devote that revenue to the welfare of its ageing population or even to that of low-ranking and poor soldiers.

Third, the concentration on monarchism within the barracks may not give the military an ideology that will prove useful in dealing with the new security challenges of the twenty-first century, such as non-traditional threats including terrorism, natural disasters and the outbreak of diseases. Faith in the royal institution will never help enhance the military's competency to handle such security threats. The king might feel safe and secure with a loyal and royalist military, but the kingdom itself might not be secure and safe.

NOTE

1. *The Prince by Niccolo Machiavelli*, trans. George Bull (New York: Penguin Books, 2005), p. 72.

Appendix

PRINCIPAL PERSONALITIES AND INSTITUTIONS MENTIONED IN THE TEXT

1. Personalities

Anupong Paochinda: Born on 10 October 1949 in Bangkok, Anupong was the son of Prachao Paochinda, an Army colonel. He received his primary and secondary educations at Panthasueksa and Amnuay Silpa Schools in the capital before enrolling in the Armed Forces Academies Preparatory School in 1967. He continued his military education at the Chulachomklao Royal Military Academy, from which he graduated in 1972. He climbed the ladder in his military career while serving mostly in the 21st Infantry Regiment and the 2nd Infantry Division in Thailand's eastern region before moving to the capital and serving as commander of the 1st Division (King's Guard) starting in 2003 and of the 1st Army Region starting in 2005. Anupong played a crucial role in the September 2006 coup against Prime Minister Thaksin Shinawatra and was rewarded with the post of Army chief in 2007. He became interior minister in the government of General Prayut Chan-ocha following the military coup of May 2014.

Apirat Kongsompong: Apirat was born on 23 March 1960 in Bangkok to General Sunthorn Kongsompong and Colonel Orachorn Kongsompong. He appears to have decided to follow in his parents' footsteps and to become a soldier. He enrolled in the Armed Forces Academies Preparatory School after receiving his secondary education at Saint Gabriel's College in the capital and graduated from the Chulachomklao Royal Military Academy in 1985. He also pursued a civilian education, earning a master's degree in business administration from Southeastern University in Washington, DC. Apirat began his military career as a pilot at the Army Aviation Centre, a unit of which his father had previously served as commander. He undertook several training courses for pilots in the United States, including those at Fort Eustis, Virginia, and Fort Rucker, Alabama. He also attended the United States Army's Infantry Officer Advanced Course at Fort Benning, Gorgia. Apirat served as an assistant logistics officer in the office of Thailand's defence attaché to Washington in the 1990s. He advanced during his military career mostly through service in the 1st Division (King's Guard) in the capital. He also gained experience in counter-insurgency operations in the Deep South, when he served as deputy commander of the 11th Infantry Regiment before returning to the regiment as its commander. Apirat later moved up to the posts of commander of the 1st Division, commander of the1st Army Region, assistant Army commander, and, in 2018, Army chief. He now serves both in a senior position in the palace and on the board of the Crown Property Bureau.

Bhumibol Adulyadej: Thailand's future sovereign was born on 5 December 1927, at Mount Auburn Hospital in Cambridge, Massachusetts, the youngest child of a father studying medicine and a mother studying nursing in the United States. King Bhumibol's father was Mahidol Adulyadej, the Prince of Songkhla and a son of King Chulalongkorn. His mother was a commoner, Sangwan Talapat. "Baby Sonkla", as Bhumibol's American birth certificate read, was qualified to be the president of the United States, but his family settled in Switzerland, where he was raised. King Bhumibol ascended the Thai throne on 9 June 1946, following the mysterious death by gunshot of his brother King Ananda Mahidol. His reign, the longest of the Chakri Dynasty, ended with his demise on 13 October 2016.

Narongphan Jitkaewthae: Born on 1 January 1963, Narongphan obtained his secondary education at Amnuay Silpa School before enrolling in the Armed Forces Academies Preparatory School in 1979. Upon graduation from the Chulachomklao Royal Military Academy in 1986, he served as a second lieutenant at the 2nd Infantry Regiment in Prachinburi Province before joining the Rapid Deployment Force, under the 31st Infantry Regiment in Lopburi Province. Narongphan gained experience in peacekeeping in Timor-Leste in 1999–2000 and in counter-insurgency operations in the Deep South between 2004 and 2005. He became the commander of the 1st Division (King's Guard) in 2015, before being elevated to the posts of deputy commander of the 1st Army Region in 2017, commander of the 1st Army Region in 2018, assistant Army commander in 2019, and Army commander in 2020.

Nattawut Saikua: Born on 4 June 1975 to the family of farmers Samnao and Priya Saikua, in the southern province of Nakhon Si Thammarat, Nattawut has been familiar with politics since he was young. Both his grandfathers served as village heads who dealt with local politicians and bureaucrats for purposes of village administration. Nattawut first gained experience in public speaking as a teenager, when he helped his uncle campaign in a local election campaign. He began his education at Wat Mahathat and Benjamarachuthit Schools in Nakhon Si Thammarat before graduating with a bachelor's degree in communication arts from Dhurakij Pundit University and a master's degree in public administration from the National Institute of Development Administration, both in Bangkok. He formally entered politics for the first time when he joined the Chat Pattana Party in contesting the 2001 parliamentary elections, and then moved to the Thai Rak Thai Party to contest the 2005 polls. He failed in both attempts to win a seat in parliament representing a constituency in his native province. As a skilful orator, Nattawut hosted political talk shows on cable television, first to earn a living and later to counter yellow-clad protesters against Prime Minister Thaksin Shinawatra. Nattawut became a leader of the Red Shirt movement after the September 2006 coup against Thaksin and served as government spokesperson under Prime Ministers Samak Sundaravej and Somchai Wongsawat and as deputy commerce minister in Prime Minister Yingluck Shinawatra's government. In 2020, he was sentenced to two years and eight months in prison for leading protesters who surrounded the residence of the king's chief adviser, Prem Tinsulanonda, in 2010.

Panusaya Sithijirawattanakul: Born on 15 September 1998 in Nonthaburi Province to a middle-class family, Panusaya—better known as "Rung" (rainbow)—is a student activist who set a precedent by publicly challenging the power of the royal institution. She has been interested in politics since her time as a student at Suan Kularb School Nonthaburi (an affiliation of all-boy secondary Suan Kularb School), when she undertook a study to understand the May 2014 military coup. With a plan to become a policy researcher, Panusaya continued her education at Thammasat University's Faculty of Sociology and Anthropology in 2018 and joined many activist groups including radical Dome Revolution Party. The BBC listed her as one of 100 inspiring and influential women in the world in 2020 for her bravery in taking the stage at Thammasat University's Rangsit campus on 10 August 2020 to shock the nation with ten demands for reform of the Thai monarchy, a move that later caused her legal trouble in the form of a *lèse majesté* charge.

Prawit Wongsuwan: Born on 11 August 1945 in Bangkok to a well-to-do family, Prawit is the son of the senior military officer Major General Prasert Wongsuwan. He obtained his education at the elite Saint Gabriel's College before enrolling in the Armed Forces Academies Preparatory School in 1965 and graduating from the Chulachomklao Royal Military Academy in 1974. Like many others in his generation, Prawit gained combat experience in fighting with communist insurgents in Thailand and Vietnam during the 1970s. He began his military career, and mostly climbed through the ranks, in the in 2nd Infantry Division, of which he became the commander in 1996. The post meant that Prawit was regarded as the big brother of the Eastern Tigers faction in the Army. In 1997 he was promoted to the post of deputy commander of the 1st Army Region, which oversees military units in Bangkok and Thailand's central region. He became Army chief in 2004, when Thaksin Shinawatra was prime minister. Prawit was appointed a member of the National Legislative Assembly after the September 2006 coup. He served as defence minister in the 2008–11 government of Prime Minister Abhisit Vejjajiva and again in the 2014–19 junta-backed government of Prime Minister General Prayut Chan-ocha. He was appointed to this post in recognition of his abilities in political management and manipulation during difficult times.

Prayut Chan-ocha: Born on 21 March 1954 in a military camp in Nakhon Ratchasima Province to soldier father Colonel Praphat Chan-ocha and teacher mother Khamphon Chan-ocha, Prayut obtained his primary education in Lopburi Province. He attended secondary school at Wat Nuanradit School in the capital, as his family moved when his father was transferred from post to post. Prayut enrolled in the Armed Forces Academies Preparatory School in 1969 before continuing his military education at the Chulachomklao Royal Military Academy, from which he graduated in 1976. He began his military career in and mostly climbed through the ranks in the 21st Infantry Regiment (Queen's Guard). Prayut became that unit's commander in 1998, and moved on to become the commander of the 2nd Infantry Division in 2003, the commander of the 1st Army Region in 2006, the deputy Army commander in 2009, and the Army chief in 2010. He held that last position for four years before leading a putsch in September 2014 to topple an elected civilian government. This act propelled him to the premiership, where he has remained following the elections of March 2019.

Prem Tinsulanonda: Born in the southern province of Songkhla on 26 August 1925, Prem was a career military officer who assumed the premiership for eight years, starting in 1980, and serving subsequently as chief adviser to King Bhumibol and King Vajiralongkorn. He held that latter position at the time of his death on 26 May 2019. Prem served in the Army for forty years, starting as second lieutenant in a combat vehicle unit (calvary) in 1941 and retiring as Army chief in 1981. He began his political life when, as the commander of the 2nd Army Region, he was tapped in 1977 by Admiral Sangad Chaloryu to join the putsch to topple the ultra-rightist government of Prime Minister Thanin Kraivixian. He was appointed deputy interior minister in the subsequent junta-backed government of Prime Minister General Kriangsak Chamanand in November 1977, when he was an assistant army commander. Kriangsak, who returned to the premiership after elections in April 1979, picked then Army chief Prem to be his defence minister. Prem in turn replaced Kriangsak as prime minister in February 1980, when pressure both from politicians and from a group of young military officers known as the "Young Turks" forced the latter to step down. Prem retained the premiership until August 1988, when Chat Thai Party leader General Chatichai Choonhavan, serving as an elected member of parliament, replaced him as prime minister. Stating that he was done with politics, Prem agreed to step down after internal negotiations led to a deal giving him a seat on the king's advisory body, the Privy Council. He also received the rarely bestowed highest royal decoration, the Ancient and Auspicious Order of the Nine Gems; it had previously been granted to only a few commoners—including Field Marshal Plaek Phibunsongkhram, Regent Pridi Banomyong and Field Marshal Sarit Thanarat. Prem was also officially bestowed the title of "Statesman" that same year.

Sirikit Kitiyakara:　Born on 12 August 1932 into a branch of the royal family, Sirikit bore the honorific *mom ratchawong* in recognition of her descent from King Chulalongkorn. Her father, Prince Nakkhatra Mangala Kitiyakara, was the son of Prince Kitiyakara Voralaksana, the Prince of Chanthaburi and the twelfth of Chulalongkorn's sons. Sirikit's mother was *Mom luang* Bua Snidvongs, a minor member of the extended royal family who served in the Siamese court as a lady-in-waiting to Queen Rambhai Barni, the consort of King Prajadhipok. That queen chose Sirikit's name. Sirikit became engaged to Prince Bhumibol Adulyadej on her birthday in 1949 at the Thai Embassy to London, where her father was serving as ambassador. The couple married on 28 April 1950, a week before the king's coronation on 5 May. Queen Sirikit was granted the title Queen Regent in 1956, becoming only the second consort to have that status under the Chakri Dynasty, for her role in tending to the responsibilities of the throne when the monarch ordained as a Buddhist monk. It is required by tradition and by many Thai constitutions that the king appoint a regent when he cannot perform his duties or must be absent from the kingdom.

Sondhi Limthongkul:　Born in Sukhothai Province on 7 November 1947 to ethnic Chinese parents Wichian and Chaiyong Sae-lim, Sondhi could be regarded as one among the persons who kick-started change in the Thai political landscape in the first decade of the twenty-first century. He completed secondary school at Assumption College in Siracha District, Chonburi Province, before being sent for further studies in Chinese and in engineering at the National Taiwan University. He eventually earned degrees in history from the University of California, Los Angeles, and from Utah State University in 1970s. While Sondhi has experience in many fields of businesses, his involvement in the media business has proved most controversial. He was dubbed a media mogul when his Manager Media Group poured huge investments into print, broadcasting and new media across the region—including in Thailand, Hong Kong and Vietnam—before its bankruptcy in the 1997–98 Asian Financial Crisis. Sondhi was sentenced to twenty years imprisonment in 2016 for misconduct in business affairs committed by him and his associates between 1996 and 1998. He served only three years and one month before benefiting from a royal amnesty granted on the occasion of the coronation of King Vajiralongkorn in September 2019. Sondhi is widely known in Thailand and internationally for his roles in leading yellow-clad protesters against Prime Minister Thaksin Shinawatra and his government in 2005–8; these protests helped precipitate the coup of September 2006.

Sonthi Boonyaratglin: Born on 2 October 1946 in the countryside of Pathum Thani Province and into a mixed Muslim-Buddhist family, Sonthi never imagined that he would become one of the most powerful men in the Thai political arena. Sonthi's father, Colonel Sanan Boonyaratglin, was a Korean War veteran and a Muslim whose roots could be traced to a Persian merchant who served the Siamese court in the Ayutthaya Period. His mother Mani Boonyaratglin was a Buddhist of Mon ethnicity from a farm background. As his father served primarily in Bangkok, and later in Korea, Sonthi was raised mostly by his mother in a Mon community in Pathum Thani. Like many boys during his time, he dreamt of becoming a soldier, in part because he was impressed by the glamorous uniforms of pre-cadet students. Sonthi enrolled in the Armed Forces Academies Preparatory School after completing secondary school at Wat Phra Si Mahathat School in 1963; he graduated from the Chulachomklao Royal Military Academy in 1969. He began his military career as a second lieutenant in an infantry battalion in Prachuap Kirikhan Province. He served as a Thai "volunteer" fighting in support of American forces in Vietnam in 1970–71. He served in the 2nd Infantry Division in Prachinburi Province between 1979 and 1983, before climbing the ranks as a Special Forces officer in Lopburi Province in the period until 2002. Sonthi was later picked to serve as an assistant Army chief in 2004 and as Army chief in 2005, a year before staging the coup that toppled the elected civilian government of Prime Minister Thaksin Shinawatra.

Surayud Chulanont: Born on 28 August 1943, Surayud grew up in a broken family, as his father Colonel Payom Chulanont divorced his mother Amphot Tharap in 1947, after thirteen years of marriage. As a boy Surayud knew very little about his father, who was active in politics—participating in a coup, in elections and in the communist insurgent movement. Nevertheless, Surayud wanted to become a soldier like his father. He enrolled in the Armed Forces Academies Preparatory School after completing secondary school at the prestigious Suan Kularb School in 1958, and he continued his military education at the Chulachomklao Royal Military Academy in 1961. Surayud began his military career in 1965 in an infantry unit in Lopburi Province, the home of the Special Forces. Ironically, the missions that he undertook as a young officer mostly involved countering the communist insurgency, sometimes in areas in which his father was active. Surayud's performance at Thailand's Command and Staff College led to his selection to attend the United States Army's own Command and Staff College at Fort Leavenworth, Kansas, in 1974. Upon returning from the United States, Surayud had the chance to work closely with General Prem Tinsulanonda, whom had known since he was young, as Prem was a classmate of one of his relatives. He was a close aide to Prem before being commissioned as commander the Special Forces and, notably, of the 2nd Army Region, Prem's former stronghold. Surayud was promoted to the post of Army chief in 1998, when Chuan Leekpai was prime minister, before being kicked upstairs to become commander of the Thai Armed Forces in 2002, when Thaksin Shinawatra was prime minister. Upon his retirement in 2003, Surayud joined Prem as a member of the Privy Council, before being granted the premiership by King Bhumibol following the September 2006 coup. Having returned to the Privy Council, Surayud replaced Prem as its president in 2020.

Suthep Thaugsuban: Born on 7 July 1949 in the southern province of Suratthani, Suthep was educated and trained to be a professional politician. With a major in political science, he graduated from the Faculty of Liberal Arts of Chiangmai University, before completing a master's degree in the same field at Middle Tennessee State University in the United States in 1975. Upon returning to Thailand at the age of 26, Suthep won a local election to become the *kamnan* or sub-district head of his native Tha Sathon Sub-district in Suratthani, replacing his father Charat Thaugsuban. From that position, Suthep entered national politics in 1979, when he won election to parliament representing Suratthani on the ticket of the Democrat Party. He held a ministerial post for the first time as deputy agriculture minister in Prem Tinsulanonda's government in 1986, before serving as a minister in every successive cabinet in which the Democrats were represented during the next twenty-five years. Suthep's political career has never been free of controversy and scandal. A notable case involved the "*so po ko* 4-01" land reform scheme during the premiership of Chuan Leekpai in 1995, when plots of land were awarded to rich associates of the Democrat Party rather than to poor farmers as planned. As a deputy prime minister in Abhisit Vejjajiva's 2008–11 government, Suthep played a crucial role in crackdowns on Red Shirt protesters. He left the Democrat Party to lead street the protests against the Yingluck Shinawatra government in 2013–14 that culminated in the military coup of May of the latter year.

Thaksin Shinawatra: Born on 26 July 1949 in Chiangmai to an ethnic Chinese business family, Thaksin is the son of Lert and Yindee Shinawatra. Thaksin has proved a die-hard politician in recent Thai history, managing to combine entrepreneurship and bureaucratic and political skills to shape future of Thailand. He enrolled in the Armed Forces Academies Preparatory School in 1967, after completing secondary school at Montfort College in his native province. Unlike many other future Thai prime ministers, Thaksin then chose the Royal Thai Police Cadet Academy rather than the Chulachomklao Royal Military Academy for his higher education. He joined the police as a second lieutenant upon graduation from the academy in 1973, but he did not begin service until 1978, after the completion of a master's degree and a doctorate in criminal justice from Eastern Kentucky University and Sam Houston State University, in Huntsville, Texas, respectively. As a police officer, Thaksin served as a policy and planning official, teaching at the police cadet academy and attached to a government minister. He also devoted time to helping his wife Potjaman develop various lines of business, including trading silk, operating a cinema, and investing in real estate. Thaksin's business endeavours initially failed, leaving him 50 million baht in debt before he managed to exploit bureaucratic connections to supply computers and equipment to state agencies starting in the early 1980s. Thaksin resigned from the police to do business full time in 1987. In the 1990s, he started a high-flying business in telecommunications and satellites and began to involve himself in politics. His political career officially began in 1994, when he was appointed foreign minister on the quota of the Phalang Tham Party of Major General Chamlong Srimuang, the former secretary to Prime Minister Prem Tinsulanonda and Bangkok governor. Thaksin formed the Thai Rak Thai Party and led it to victory in two elections, serving as prime minister from 2001 until his ouster in the coup of September 2006.

Thanathorn Juangroongruangkit: Born on 25 November 1978 to a billionaire business family in Bangkok, Thanathorn is an activist whose dream to be a politician has proved hard to realize. He attended lower secondary school at Saint Dominic School and upper secondary school at Triam Udomsueksa School, both in Bangkok, before graduating with a joint honours bachelor's degree in engineering from Thammasat University and the University of Nottingham. During his time at Thammasat in the late 1990s, he was a student activist who held the positions of president of the Thammasat University Students Union and, later, of deputy secretary general of the Students Federation of Thailand. He joined street protests by the Assembly of the Poor and other groups supporting workers and the poor. Thanathorn received a master's degree in political economy from Chulalongkorn University, where he built his knowledge on leftist theories and developed an ideological commitment to social democracy. He also received two further master's degrees in business-related subjects from foreign institutions. Initially, Thanathorn wanted to pursue a career in international development, as he was offered a position with a United Nations agency in Algeria. But he was forced to abandon that plan after the death of his father Pattana Juangroongruangkit in 2002. Thanathorn assumed an executive position at the Thai Summit Group, his family's automobile parts manufacturer, at the age of 23. He co-founded the Future Forward Party in 2018 and led it in capturing 81 seats in the March 2019 election, the third highest total of any party. Thanathorn had the chance only to be sworn in as a member of parliament but never to perform the associated duties.

He was disqualified for holding a stake in a media company and for lending funds to his party; the latter charge eventually resulted in the dissolution of the Future Forward Party and to Thanathorn's being barred him from politics for a period of ten years starting in February 2020. He now leads the non-party Progressive Movement, which focuses on local electoral politics and sub-national governance.

Vajiralongkorn: Born in Thailand on 28 July 1952 to King Bhumibol and Queen Sirikit, Vajiralongkorn was groomed from childhood to be the king of Thailand. He enrolled in the elementary programme at the King's Mead School in Sussex and in secondary school at the Millfield School in Somerset, both in the United Kingdom, and he attended the Royal Military College, Duntroon, in Australia. Vajiralongkorn became the heir apparent to the Thai throne when he was bestowed the title of the Crown Prince, the third member of the Chakri Dynasty to hold that title, on 28 December 1972. Vajiralongkorn subsequently pursed a military career and earned certification as a professional pilot, before his accession to the throne on 1 December 2016.

Yingluck Shinawatra: Born on 21 June 1967 in Chiangmai Province to ethnic Chinese merchants Lert and Yindee Shinawatra, Yingluck was the first woman to serve as prime minister of Thailand. She studied at Regina Coeli College and Yupparat Witthayalai School in Chiangmai before earning a bachelor's degree in public administration from Chiang Mai University in 1988 and a master's degree in the same field, with specialization in management information systems, from Kentucky State University in 1991. Yingluck began her business career in 1993 as a sales and marketing intern at Shinawatra Directory, a telephone directory company in which her brother Thaksin Shinawatra was a major stakeholder, before assuming executive positions in the business empire of her family. She officially entered politics when the Phuea Thai Party, the successor to the dissolved Thai Rak Thai Party and People's Power Party, put her at the top of its slate of party-list candidates for Thailand's July 2011 parliamentary elections. Phuea Thai won those elections, and Yingluck served as prime minister until weeks before the May 2014 military coup.

2. Institutions

Administrative Court: The court specializes in administrative law and in contentious cases concerning the exercise of public authority. Its history can be traced to the period in which the country began the modernization of its government in the reign of King Chulalongkorn (1868–1910), who established a Council of State based on European models to give him advice concerning administration. The council has served as governments' legal advisor since the 1932 Revolution. The Administrative Court, in its current form and with its current scope of duties, was established under the 1997 Constitution but officially inaugurated only in March 2001. It is meant to protect the rights of people aggrieved by actions of state agencies or officials. Officials who believe that their rights have been infringed upon by superiors or politicians may also appeal to the Administrative Court to claim fair treatment and justice.

Armed Forces Academies Preparatory School: The school was established on 27 January 1958 in Bangkok to recruit males not older than 18 years old who had completed secondary school to receive military education and training in preparation for higher education at the Army's Chulachomklao Royal Military Academy, the Navaminda Kasatriyadhiraj Royal Thai Air Force Academy, the Royal Thai Naval Academy, or the Royal Thai Police Cadet Academy. The school moved to Nakhon Nayok Province in 2000, as its location near Lumphini Park in the capital was now surrounded by high-density residences and business outlets. The Armed Forces Academies Preparatory School is politically important because of the solidarity and networks among classmates, often spanning service branches, that endure through decades of military and police service. Thaksin Shinawatra, for example, gave priority to promoting his friends in academy's tenth class to key positions when he was prime minister.

Bureau of the Royal Household: The administration of the Siamese and then Thai court has been subject to change over time, following broader patterns of political development. During the reign of King Bhumibol, the court was under jurisdiction of the government. The 2017 Royal Service Administrative Act, promulgated at the beginning of the reign of King Vajiralongkorn, transferred the Bureau of Royal Household from the Prime Minister's Office to the jurisdiction of the Royal Office, thus subjecting it directly to the authority of the monarch. According to the law, there are seven divisions in the Bureau of the Royal Household. These include the Office of the King's Private Secretary and the Office of Royal Family Affairs.

Chulachomklao Royal Military Academy: Established on 5 August 1887 by King Chulalongkorn, the academy aimed to recruit and train young men for a period of five years as professional military leaders and masters of warfighting skills for the modern Thai Army. Its curriculum is now four years, and it has had different names over time: the Cadet School, Saranrom Military School, and the Army School. Its current name, honouring its founder King Chulalongkorn, was granted by King Bhumibol in 1950. Most members of the Thai military elite, and notably prime ministers with military backgrounds, are graduates of the Chulachomklao Royal Military Academy. If education is useful in enabling Thai people to climb the social hierarchy, a military academy like this one is a perfect choice to make one's dream come true. Academy classmates retain strong ties for networking and for the formation of factions and cliques in the Thai military. Rivalries between alumni of different classes caused rifts in the Army in the 1980s and 1990s and led to bloodshed in 1992, when Major General Chamlong Srimuang of Class 7 led street protests against Prime Minister General Suchinda Kraprayoon of Class 5.

Constitutional Court: This court is deemed a constitutional organ, rather than part of Thailand's judicial branch. It performs the duty of legal interpretation, considering whether a law contradicts or is inconsistent with the charter and thus upholding the supremacy of the constitution. The Constitutional Court was established for the first time under the 1997 Constitution. It is empowered to rule on political cases. While Thai constitutions were scrapped after the coups of September 2006 and May 2014, the Constitutional Court survived, as the establishment elite used it as a political tool against the opponents of that elite; since the time of the 2006 coup, the court has ordered the dissolution of numerous political parties.

Privy Council: Established in 1874 by King Chulalongkorn as an advisory body for the monarch, the Privy Council was disbanded after the 1932 Revolution that transformed the country from absolute to constitutional monarchy. It was reactivated in 1947 and initially known in Thai as the *Khana aphiratthamontri* or, in English, the Supreme Council of State. Its original Thai name of *Khana ongkhamontri*, or Privy Council in English, was restored in 1949, and every Thai constitution since that time has authorized the monarch to select its members. Under the 2017 Constitution and the 2017 Royal Service Administrative Act, the king has the authority to appoint no more than nineteen persons to the Privy Council to give advice to the monarch on matters on which he consults it. However, the charter does not give the king complete freedom to choose councilors, as members of parliament, holders of political positions, justices of the Constitutional Court, state or state enterprise officials, and member of political parties may not serve as members of the Privy Council. Members must also, in principle, be politically non-partisan.

Suan Kularb School: Set up in 1882, Suan Kularb—whose name literally means rose garden—is Thailand's oldest all-boys secondary school. Its origins lie in King Chulalongkorn's decision to grant permission to his brother Prince Damrong Rajanubhab to set up a school to educate royal offspring and noble children. Initially, the school also taught military affairs, in order to prepare its students for palace service as aides-de-camp. In 1884, the palace realized that it did not have enough aide-de-camp positions for the school's graduates and that a general education would be more useful for the boys enrolled. The school then became an institution offering basic education for civilian life. Suan Kularb has been involved in politics many times in its history. The People's Party seized the school on 24 June 1932, as it had been founded by Prince Damrong, whom the party had placed under arrest. Boy Scouts from Suan Kularb school were also recruited by the military to help defeat the royalist Boworadet Rebellion in 1933. The prestigious school is still a favourite choice among members of the Thai elite for the education of their sons. Many Thai prime ministers—including Phraya Manopakorn Nititada, Thawi Bunyaket, Pridi Banomyong, Seni Pramoj, Kukrit Pramoj, Thanin Kraivixian and Prem Tinsulanonda—have been Suan Kularb alumni.

Thammasat University: The university was founded on 27 June 1934 by Senior Statesman Pridi Banomyong as an open university at which Thai people could study law and politics. It was intended to lay a foundation for Thai democracy after the 1932 Revolution. Thammasat, known initially as the University of Moral and Political Science, has been a public sphere for political activity for many decades since that time. The successful student uprising of October 1973 against military dictatorship began at Thammasat. It became a killing field when rightist groups and security officials massacred student activists on 6 October 1976, ostensibly for the sake of national security and protection of the monarchy. The university fell under the spotlight again after progressive members of its student body shocked the nation with ten demands for reform of the royal institution in 2020. In publicizing their demands, the students referred to the concept of egalitarianism advanced by the university's founder Pridi—a leading member of People's Party, which transformed the country from absolute to constitutional monarchy.

GLOSSARY OF THAI TERMS

Bik (บิ๊ก): A preface used with the nicknames of prominent Thai military officers, adopted from the English word "big".

Burapha Phayak (บูรพาพยัคฆ์): "Eastern Tigers", a clique of Army officers who began their military careers in the 2nd Infantry Division, headquartered in Prachinburi Province; closely associated with the Queen's Guard.

Chao khun phra (เจ้าคุณพระ): "Royal Noble Consort", a title used to honour the commoner wife of a king. The first woman bestowed the title under the Chakri Dynasty was Lady Mother Pae, a concubine of King Chulalongkorn later known as *Chao khun phra* Prayunrawong. King Vajiralongkorn bestowed the long-unused title on his wife Sineenat, a former military nurse, in July 2019 to indicate that her position in the palace was second only to that of the queen.

Chit asa (จิตอาสา): "Volunteer spirit", the name of a royal project initiated in the reign of King Vajiralongkorn to organize volunteers for public service. Its main function has been one of public relations and propaganda to raise the stature of the monarchy.

Kanpraphruet chua yangrairaeng (การประพฤติชั่วอย่างร้ายแรง): A legal term for gross misconduct, literally meaning "extremely bad behaviour".

Khai phalo (ไข่พะโล้): A boiled egg in a sweet brown sauce, a common Thai dish of Chinese origin.

Khana ratsadon (คณะราษฎร): "The People's Party", a group of senior military officers and civilian officials who seized political power on

24 June 1932 and changed Siam's political regime from absolute to constitutional monarchy. The term was used again in 2020 by a group of young activists and students who staged demonstrations to call for reform of the monarchy.

Lom chao (ล้มเจ้า): "To topple the monarchy", a term used by royalists and other conservatives to charge their opponents with seeking to change Thailand's political system.

Mahatlek (มหาดเล็ก): An aide-de-camp or page in royal service.

Nai luang (ในหลวง): A term for "king". Prior to the reign of King Bhumibol, the term was widely used among members of royal family. Ordinary Thai citizens began to use it to refer to King Bhumibol in the 1970s and 1980s, as a way to express their closeness to a monarch whom they loved like father. People in the North sometimes called him *pho luang*, the same word that they used for their village headmen.

Pa (ป๋า): "Father" or "daddy", usually used to refer to a rich or influential man.

Phrai (ไพร่): Prior to the programme modernization undertaken by King Chualongkorn, the term *phrai* referred to subjects who owed corvée labour service either to the crown or to non-royal patrons. In modern times, the term was used as a pejorative to refer to a servant or a person of low status. After 2006, however, Red Shirts began to adopt the term to describe themselves, as both a mark of pride and a sign of inequality in Thai society.

Rajawallop (ราชวัลลภ): "King's favourite", a term used to designate military units with particularly close ties to the crown.

Raksa phra-ong (รักษาพระองค์): A term meaning "to protect the king, queen or a prince or princess", used to designate royal bodyguard units.

Ratchasawat (ราชสวัสดิ์): An ancient code of conduct rewritten in the form of poetry by King Vajiravudh, prescribing the behaviour of members of royal family and of officials serving the crown.

Suea pa (เสือป่า): "The Wild Tigers Corps", a (pseudo) military unit founded and headed by King Vajiravudh in 1911 as his private army, ostensibly to protect him and to enhance loyalty to the monarchy among members of the armed forces.

Thahan kho daeng (ทหารคอแดง): "Red rim soldiers", military officers who wear t-shirts with red-rim collars under their uniforms. Only officers selected by King Vajiralongkorn as members of the King's Guard Special Task Force 904 can be regarded as *thahan kho daeng*.

Thahan ratcha-ongkharak (ทหารราชองครักษ์): "Royal bodyguard soldiers".

Thahan sai wang (ทหารสายวัง): A soldier who serves the palace, whether formally or informally.

Thahan suea rachini (ทหารเสือราชินี): "Queen's tiger soldiers", military officers who began their careers in or served mostly with the 21st Infantry Regiment, the Queen's Guard, headquartered in Chonburi Province.

Thahan taengmo (ทหารแตงโม): "Water melon soldiers", a metaphor for military officers who helped or had sympathy for Red Shirt protesters. These officers wore green uniforms but were "red" in their hearts.

Wongthewan (วงศ์เทวัญ): "Divine progeny", the name of clique of Army officers who began their careers in the 1st Infantry Division, the King's Guard.

Yok ok uep (ยกอกอึ๊บ): "To raise one's chest up", a posture invented and required by King Vajiralongkorn for soldiers to adopt when saluting their superiors. The word *uep* is also slang for having sex.

BIBLIOGRAPHY

Books and e-books

Atcharaphon Kamutphitsamai. 1997. *Kabot ro so 130: kabot phuea prachathippatai naeokhit thahan mai* [The 1912 rebellion: a rebellion for democracy, new military thinking]. Bangkok: Amarin Printing.

Hoadley, J. Stephen. 2012. *Soldiers and Politics in Southeast Asia: Civil-Military Relations in Comparative Perspective, 1933–1975*. New Brunswick and London: Transaction Publishers.

Khamnoon Sitthisamarn. 2006. *Prakottakan Sondhi chak suea lueang thueng pha phan kho si fa* [The Sondhi phenomenon: From yellow shirt to blue scarf]. Bangkok: Ban Phra Athit Publishing.

Kobkua Suwannathat-Pian, 1995. *Thailand's Durable Premier: Phibun through Three Decades 1932–1957*. Kuala Lumpur: Oxford University Press.

Machiavelli, Niccolo. 2005. *The Prince*. Trans. George Ball. New York: Penguin Books.

McCargo, Duncan, and Ukrist Pathmanand. 2005. *The Thaksinization of Thailand*. Copenhagen: NIAS Press.

Marshall, Andrew Macgregor. 2015. *A Kingdom in Crisis: Thailand's Struggle for Democracy in the Twenty-First Century*. London: Zed Books.

Prayut Sitthipan, *Chao fa* [Prince]. n.d. Bangkok: Ruamkanphim.

Puangthong R. Pawakapan. 2013. *State and Uncivil Society in Thailand at the Temple of Preah Vihear*. Singapore: Institute of Southeast Asian Studies.

Royal Thai Army. 1987. *Nueng roi pi rongrian nai roi phrachulachomklao* [100 Years of Chulachomklao Royal Military Academy]. Three volumes. Bangkok: Royal Thai Army.

Sataporn Books. 2018. *Somdetphrachaoyuhua Maha Vajiralongkorn Bodindrade-bayavarangkun phraphu pen saengsawang klang chai thai* [King Vajiralongkorn: A light in the Thai mind]. Bangkok: Sataporn Books.

Sutthachai Yimprasert. 1991. *Phaen ching chat thai* [The plan to usurp Thailand].
    Bangkok: Samaphan.
Thak Chaloemtiarana. 2007. *Thailand: The Politics of Despotic Paternalism.* 2nd ed.
    Ithaca, New York: Cornell Southeast Asia Program Publications.
Thep Boontanont. 2016. *Kanmueang nai kanthahan thai samai ratchakan thi hok*
    [Politics in the Thai military during the reign of Rama VI]. Bangkok:
    Matichon Books.
Wassana Nanuam. 2006. *Senthang lek phon ek Surayud Chualanont* [The iron
    path of General Surayud Chulanont]. 4th ed. Bangkok: Matichon Books.
———. 2010. *Lap luang phrang phak sam kongthap tang si suek sai lueat cho po ro*
    [Secrets, deceit, camouflage part 3: Armies of different colours and conflict
    among Chulachomklao royal military academy lineages]. 10th ed. Bangkok:
    Matichon Books.
———. 2014. *Awasan Yingluck* [The end of Yingluck]. Bangkok: Matichon Books.
———. 2014. *Senthang phayak Prayut Chan-ocha chak thahan suea su lang suea*
    [The path of Eastern Tiger Prayut Chan-ocha from tiger soldier to tiger's
    back]. Bangkok: Matichon Books.
Worakanbancha, Colonel. 1953. *Tamnan thahan mahatlek* [Chronicle of aides-de-
    camp]. Cremation volume for General Phraworawongthoe Krommamuen
    Adison Udomsak. Bangkok. 15 June 1953.

Theses and Academic Papers

Disathorn Vajarodaya. n.d. "Lak nititham nai nayobai kankamkapdulae ongkon
    thi di" [Rules of law for palace administration]. Constitutional College of
    the Constitutional Court, Thailand. http://www.constitutionalcourt.or.th/
    occ_web/ewt_dl_link.php?nid=8773 (accessed 13 February 2020).
Jackson, Peter A. 2017. "A Grateful Son, a Military King: Thai Media Accounts
    of the Accession of Rama X to the Throne". *ISEAS Perspective* 2017/26, 26
    April 2017. https://www.iseas.edu.sg/wp-content/uploads/pdfs/ISEAS_
    Perspective_2017_26.pdf (accessed 13 July 2019).
Nikhom Charumanee. 1976. "Kabot Boworadet pho so 2476" [The Boworadet
    Rebellion, 1933]. Master's thesis, Chulalongkorn University.

Journal Articles

Chambers, Paul, and Napisa Waitoolkiat. 2016. "The Resilience of Monarchised
    Military in Thailand". *Journal of Contemporary Asia* 46, no. 3: 425–44.
McCargo, Duncan. 2005. "Network Monarchy and Legitimacy Crises in Thailand".
    Pacific Review 4: 499–519.

Chapters in Books

Chambers, Paul. 2013. "A Short History of Military Influence in Thailand". In *Knights of the Realm: Thailand's Military and Politics, Then and Now*, edited by Paul Chambers, pp. 109–446. Bangkok: White Lotus.

Ferrara, Federico. 2014. "Unfinished Business: The Contagion of Conflict over a Century of Thai Political Development". In *Good Coup Gone Bad: Thailand's Political Development since Thaksin's Downfall*, edited by Pavin Chachavalpongpun, pp. 17–46. Singapore: Institute of Southeast Asian Studies.

Montesano, Michael J. 2010. "Four Thai Pathologies, Late 2009". In *Legitimacy Crisis in Thailand*, edited by Marc Askew, pp. 273–302. [King Prajadhipok's Institute Year Book No. 5 (2008/09)]. Chiang Mai: Silkworm Books.

Nattapoll Chaiching. 2010. "The Monarchy and the Royalist Movement in Modern Thai Politics, 1932–1957". In *Saying the Unsayable: Monarchy and Democracy in Thailand*, edited by Søren Ivarsson and Lotte Isager, pp. 147–78. Copenhagen: NIAS Press.

Sulak Sivaraksa. 2007. "Sathaban kasat kap ratthathammanun" [The royal institution and constitutions]. In *Ratthaprahan 19 kanyayon* [The 19 September coup], edited by Thanapol Eawsakul, pp. 20–29. Bangkok: Fadiaokan.

Thanapol Eawsakul. 2007. "Kae roi phanthamit prachachon phuea prachathippatai phu ok batchoen hai khanaratthaprahan" [Tracing the People's Alliance for Democracy, the folks who extended an invitation to the coup makers]. In *Ratthaprahan 19 kanyayon* [The 19 September coup], edited by Thanapol Eawsakul, pp. 288–322. Bangkok: Fadiaokan.

Thongchai Winichakul. 2019. "Thailand's Royal Democracy in Crisis". In *After the Coup: The National Council for Peace and Order Era and the Future of Thailand*, edited by Michael J. Montesano, Terence Chong and Mark Heng, pp. 282–307. Singapore: ISEAS – Yusof Ishak Institute.

Media Reports

Amarin TV. 2020. "'Tamruat rajawallop 904' buk thalai 'sep-hao umbun' phop 7 sao rapchang tangkan" ["Rajawallop 904 police" break into "safe house", find seven pregnant-for-hire women]. 13 February 2020. https://www.amarintv.com/news/detail/21803 (accessed 9 June 2020).

Anna Lawattanaktrakul. 2019. "Song pi song duean kanhaipai khong mut khana ratsadon" [Two years and two months since the People's Party plaque went missing]. *Prachatai*, 23 June 2019. https://prachatai.com/journal/2019/06/83100 (accessed 6 December 2019).

Associated Press. 2019. "Thailand's King Puts Key Army Units under Palace Authority". 1 October 2019. https://apnews.com/96144d07efe149ba8a8f7c7d3491962b (accessed 5 November 2019).

Ban mueang. 1976. "Pho ko ko buk nak ying helikhoptoe ruang rongphukamkap sahat" [Insurgents shoot helicopter down, gravely injure deputy superintendent]. 30 October 1976.

Bangkok Post. 1976. "Battle Rages as Reds Attack Loei Outpost". 31 October 1976.

———. 2015. "Pongpat Sent to Prison for 6 Years in First Case". 30 January 2015. https://www.bangkokpost.com/thailand/general/462642/pongpat-gets-reduced-6-years-in-first-case (accessed 6 November 2019).

———. 2016. "Long Live the King: Military Education". 1 December 2016. https://www.bangkokpost.com/life/social-and-lifestyle/1148940/military-education (accessed 3 February 2020).

———. 2016. "Prem Becomes Regent Pro Tempore". 14 October 2016. https://www.bangkokpost.com/thailand/general/1110645/prem-becomes-regent-pro-tempore (accessed 26 November 2019).

———. 2017. "Six Changes in Constitution". 6 April 2017. https://www.bangkokpost.com/thailand/general/1228183/six-sections-changed-in-constitution (accessed 4 February 2020).

———. 2019. "Army Chief Lashes Communists". 12 October 2019. https://www.bangkokpost.com/thailand/politics/1770189/army-chief-lashes-communists (accessed 3 February 2020).

———. 2019. "Head of State with Heart of Gold: His Majesty the King Has an Illustrious Military Background". 28 July 2019. https://www.bangkokpost.com/thailand/general/1720331/head-of-state-with-heart-of-gold (accessed 30 October 2019).

———. 2019. "Navy to Buy B6.1bn Chinese Landing Ship". 12 September 2019. https://www.bangkokpost.com/thailand/general/1747774/navy-to-buy-b6-5bn-chinese-landing-ship (accessed 2 December 2019).

———. 2019. "Queen Exudes Military Prowess". 3 June 2019. https://www.bangkokpost.com/thailand/general/1688500/queen-exudes-military-prowess (accessed 29 October 2019).

———. 2019. "Senate Backs Army Transfer Decree". 21 October 2019. https://www.bangkokpost.com/thailand/politics/1776454/senate-backs-army-transfer-decree (accessed 5 November 2019).

BBC. 2020. "BBC 100 Women 2020: Who Is on the List This Year 2020". 23 November 2020. https://www.bbc.com/news/world-55042935 (accessed 7 January 2021).

BBC Thai. 2017. "Jumpol Manmai khue khrai?" [Who is Jumpol Manmai?]. 1 March 2017. https://www.bbc.com/thai/thailand-39119559 (accessed 6 November 2019).

———. 2018. "Chamkhuk nueng duean Pongpat Chayaphan khadi thi paet yuen banchi sapsin thet" [Pongpat Chayaphan sentenced to one month in jail in eighth case of false asset declaration]. 27 February 2018. https://www.bbc.com/thai/thailand-43207247 (accessed 6 November 2019).

————. 2019. "Khadi min: Pai Dao Din nam tim ko mo to sak adit mue chaengkhwam kho so cho khadi khwammankhong" [Lèse Majesté: Pai Dao Din leads a team in the House committee to grill military prosecutor in security case]. 27 November 2019. https://www.bbc.com/thai/thailand-50573578 (accessed 10 December 2019).

————. 2019. "Khana ratsadon: lukchai Phraya Phahon rabu cha mi kananchoen anusawari ro 9 ma pradit sathanthi sun kanthahan puen yai" [People's Party: Rama X monument to be erected at Artillery Centre, son of *Phraya* Phahon says]. 29 December 2019. https://www.bbc.com/thai/thailand-50939914 (accessed 12 February 2020).

————. 2019. "Khana ratsadon: sun kanthahan puen yai Lopburi triam buangsuang anusawari chomphon Po-Phraya Phahon kon ruethon" [People's Party: Artillery centre in Lopburi prepares ritual ceremony before removal of Field Marshal Phibun and Phaya Phahon monuments]. 27 December 2019. https://www.bbc.com/thai/thailand-50923944 (accessed 11 February 2020).

————. 2019. "Prachum sapha: phuea thai-wip faikhan mai titchai pho ro ko on nuai thahan triam wot rap pen pho ro bo" [Phuea Thai, opposition whip have no problem with the decree, ready to vote to allow royal to transfer military units to become law]. 16 October 2019. https://www.bbc.com/thai/thailand-50071002 (accessed 5 November 2019).

————. 2019. "Prachum sapha: sapha mi mati 374 siang anumat pho ro ko pen pho ro bo on krom thahan rap 1- rap 11 pai pen nuai thawai khwamplotphai raksa phra-ong" [Parliament meets, 374 votes to pass the royal decree into law to transfer army units to Royal Security Command]. 17 October 2019. https://www.bbc.com/thai/thailand-50078306 (accessed 10 June 2020).

————. 2020. "Naronghpan Jitkaewthae: 'thahan kho daeng' phuchongrakphakdi phangat nang kao-i pho bo tho bo khon thi 42" [Loyal "red-striped t-shirt soldier" Narongphan Jitkaewthae rises to take the helm as forty-second Army chief]. 18 September 2020. https://www.bbc.com/thai/thailand-54077187 (accessed 6 January 2021).

————. 2021. "Phon akat ek Sathiphong Sukwimon nai wai 72 pi sitkao diden suankulap - mo chiangmai lae kharatchaboriphan phurapchai bueang yukhonlabat yangklaichit" [ACM Sathiphong Sukwimon, outstanding alumnus of Suankularb School and Chiangmai Universitty who has served the king closely]. 2 January 2021. https://www.bbc.com/thai/thailand-55505134 (accessed 7 January 2021).

Bild. 2019. "Thai-Geliebteim Horrorknast" [Thai Sweetheart in Prison of Horror]. 30 October 2019. https://www.bild.de/unterhaltung/royals/royals/koenig-rama-x-zeigt-sich-gnadenlos-thai-geliebte-im-horrorknast-65708342.bild.html (accessed 1 November 2019).

Chalathip Thirasoonthrakul. 2008. "Thai Queen Attends Funeral of Anti-Govt Protester". *Reuters.* 13 October 2008. https://uk.reuters.com/article/

thailand-protest/upadte-1-thai-queen-attends-funeral-of-anti-govt-protester-idUKBKK40018720081013 (accessed 13 January 2020).

Crispin, Shawn W. 2017. "New Reign Takes Hold in Thailand". *Asia Times*, 25 January 2017. https://www.asiatimes.com/2017/01/article/new-reign-takes-hold-thailand (accessed 28 November 2019).

Defence Industry Daily. 2007. "Rough Road for Thailand's BRT-3 APC Purchase". 17 October 2007. https://www.defenseindustrydaily.com/rough-road-for-thailands-btr-3-apc-purchase-04028 (accessed 21 February 2020).

Deli niu. 2020. "Song to ro mahatlek 904 ruam la chon amanut kha khon ching thong" [Dispatch of royal guard police 904 to joint manhunt for inhumane and murderous gold thieves]. 11 January 2020. https://www.dailynews.co.th/crime/751316 (accessed 14 February 2020).

Khao sot. 2019. "'Srinual' poet chai pom wot suan mati phak yan mai chai nguhao si som lan tha rap ngoen ching cha la-ok" ["Srinual" gives her account on the vote against party's line, she is not an orange cobra, if really accepted money will resign]. 1 November 2019. https://www.khaosod.co.th/politics/news_3022576 (accessed 5 November 2019).

Khom chat luek. 2017. "Maethap khong thoranong 'Apirat Kongsompong' chok chata fa likhit" ["Apirat Kongsompong" designated commander from the sky]. 15 August 2017. https://www.komchadluek.net/news/people/291961 (accessed 28 November 2019).

———. 2019. "Tha kaekhoen su yok ok laksut phraratchathan fuek thahanken" [Posture in raising the chest: royally granted curriculum for training military conscripts]. 3 November 2019. https://www.komchadluek.net/news/scoop/396759 (accessed 5 November 2019).

Krungthep thurakit. 2014. "'Prayut mop naeothang patirup prathett hai" ["Prayut" lays out reform guidelines for Thailand]. 9 August 2014. https://www.bangkokbiznews.com/news/detail/598041 (accessed 23 January 2020).

———. 2020. "Mop chu sam nio han lang rawang khabuansadet phan" [Protestors flash three-finger salute and turn their backs to passing royal motorcade]. 14 November 2020. https://www.bangkokbiznews.com/news/detail/907842 (accessed 7 January 2021).

———. 2021. "3 nakbin 'ep-16' suekching kao-i 'pho bo tho o'" [Three "F-16" pilots compete for post as Air Force chief] 28 June 2021. https://www.bangkokbiznews.com/politics/945762 (accessed 24 September 2021).

Macan-Markar, Marwaan. 2019. "All the King's Men: Thai Military Power Shifts Away from Prayut". *Nikkei Asian Review*, 2 July 2019. https://asia.nikkei.com/Spotlight/Asia-Insight/All-the-king-s-men-Thai-military-power-shifts-away-from-Prayuth (accessed 5 December 2019).

MacKinnon, Ian. 2008. "Thailand: State of Emergency Declared in Bangkok". *The Guardian*, 3 September 2008. https://www.theguardian.com/world/2008/sep/03/thailand (accessed 13 January 2020).

Manager On-line. 2008. "Khunying Pornthip fan thong san RDX prakop raboet kha nong Bo" [Khunying Pornthip confirms RDX substance killed Nong Bo]. 13 October 2008. https://mgronline.com/crime/detail/9510000121393 (accessed 29 January 2020).

———. 2008. "Rachini sadet ngansop nong Bo songchom dek di rak sathaban kasat" [Queen attends Nong Bo's funeral, praising her as a good girl who loved the monarchy]. 13 October 2008. https://mgronline.com/daily/detail/9510000121836?fbclid=IwAR3mlIwvduav5C60e-oiXM3uNohPS-Nw1MWs3VMouV5FwHu6Lw-HwOUS4H0 (accessed 13 January 2020).

———. 2009. "Ha wan lopsanghan 'Sondhi" mue puen loi nuan-phon ek chua rap ngan kha" [Five days after Sondhi assassination attempt, gunmen have made clean getaway - dirty general took the job of murder]. 22 April 2009. https://mgronline.com/crime/detail/9520000044877 (accessed 29 January 2020).

———. 2009. "Khuk song pi! Kaennam kharawan khon chon-liulo maeo thuean pitlom nechan [Two years in prison! for leaders of caravan of the poor-Thaksin lackeys for blockading *The Nation*]. 30 November 2009. https://mgronline.com/crime/detail/9520000145332 (accessed 24 February 2020).

———. 2012. "'Khangkhok Tu' phon khadi min sathaban thamchai 'Bik Tu' yom dai rue mai" ["Toad Tu" *lèse majesté* case dismissed, is this acceptable to "Big Tu"?]. 11 May 2012. https://mgronline.com/politics/detail/9550000058387 (accessed 20 January 2020).

Matichon. 2017. "Phanraya phon to o Jumpol Manmai khao rap 5 khoha ruk pa thaplan phoei si na khrengkhriat to ro hai prakan wongngoen 2 saen" [Wife of Pol General Jumpol Manmai acknowledges five charges of forest encroachment, released on 200,000 baht bail]. 3 March 2017. https://www.matichon.co.th/local/crime/news_483466 (accessed 6 November 2019).

———. 2019. "Phraratchadamrat ratchakan thi sip 'dai pa ma pen prathan ko unchai laeo' phon ek Prem tham nathi thawai ngan khrang sutthai" [Speech of Rama X, "Having Pa as president is reassuring", Prem performs his final duty]. 26 May 2019. https://www.matichon.co.th/heading-news/news_1510670 (accessed 26 November 2019).

———. 2019. "'Thanathorn' yoei khae rupkhu 'Joshua Wong' phapdiao chapyong mop hongkong sang khwamkliatchang laeo rue?" ["Thanathorn" derisive, can just a photograph taken with "Joshua Wong" link him with Hong Kong protests and cause hatred towards him?]. 11 October 2019. https://www.matichon.co.th/politics/news_1708540 (accessed 21 September 2021).

Matichon sutsapda. 2016. "Banthuek wai pen prawattisat nai luang ratchakan thi kao naeothang kae wikrit kanmueang chat" [The historical record of Rama IX's resolution of national crises]. 16 October 2016.

———. 2016. "'Bik Jiab': kha ma khondiao klang dong burapha phayak mong kham chot thot rahat yai 'Bik Tu-Bik Pom' chai thueng" ["Big Jiab": I come

alone in the middle of Eastern Tigers, why "Big Tu" and "Big Pom" are
so undaunted]. 16–22 September 2016. https://www.matichonweekly.com/
in-depth/article_7718 (accessed 29 November 2019).

———. 2017. "Patikiriya sangkhom to mut khanarat chak pi 2503-2560"
[Social reactions to People's Party's plaque from 1960 to 2017]. 21–27 April
2017. https://www.matichonweekly.com/column/article_32563 (accessed
6 December 2019).

———. 2018. "Wikhro 'Bik Tu-Bik Pom' khayao pho thahan: chabap fa dan phiset
chapta sut lap 'Bik Daeng' klang sathannakan muak daeng" [Analysis: Big
Tu, Big Pom in military shake-up, closely watch Big Deang's secret solution
in the middle of red beret situation]. 27 July-2 August 2018. https://www.
matichonweekly.com/column/article_121055 (accessed 29 November 2019).

———. 2018. "'Wikhro pho thahan' songthai kho so cho 'Bik Pom-Bik Tu'
yuet riap! 'Bik Daeng' khon phiset triam nang pho bo tho bo 'Bik Nat-
Bik Kob-Bik Tai' khuen phaeng 'Bik Lue-Bik Tui' biat ching dam maethap
ruea" [Analysing military reshuffle; "Big Tu and Big Pom" in full control,
special man "Big Daeng" preparing to sit as Army chief, "Big Nat", "Big
Kob", "Big Tai" in line, "Big Lue" and "Big Tui" competing to be Navy
chief]. 20–26 August 2018. https://www.matichonweekly.com/column/
article_119148 (accessed 29 November 2019).

———. 2019. "Changwa kao khong 'Bik Daeng' tangrap ronthoi nai
khwamngiapgnan kap botbat 'Bik Lue' nai suek maothai lae konlayut
chat thapruea muea 'Bik Cho' yu nai wonglom to tho 20" ["Big Daeng's"
footsteps, retreating in silence, and the role of "Big Lue" in the Mao
Tai battle as "Big Cho" is surrounded by members of AFAPS Class 20].
27 September – 3 October 2019.

———. 2019. "Lalai wongthewan-thahan suea-burapha phayak kongthap yuk
'Bik Daeng'" [Dissolution of *Wongthewan*-Eastern Tigers, the Army in Apirat
era]. 13–19 September 2019.

———. 2019. "Poet thap 14 khunphon kho daeng 'Bik Daeng-Bik Bi-Bik Kaeo-Bik
Nui' kap pharakit sut khopfa" [14 red-striped t-shirt commanders unveiled:
"Big Daeng", "Big Bi", "Big Kaeo", "Big Nui" and their duties at the end
of the horizon]. 11–17 October 2019.

———. 2019. "Raingan phiset poet thap 14 khun phon kho daeng Bik Daeng
Bik Bi Bik Kaeo Bik Nui kap pharakit sut khopfa cho suek nok suek nai
thapruea chak khluen tai nam su suenami" [Special report: Revealing the
14 red collar warlords, Big Daeng, Big Bi, Big Kaew, Big Nui and their
mission at the horizon, look into inside and outside naval threats from
undercurrent to tsunami]. 11–17 October 20019.

Matichon TV. 2019. "'Bik Daeng' sat 'ngao pritsana' dotphop 'Joshua Wong'—to
phuak khit kae matra 1 wang lom sathaban" ["Big Daeng" charges that
"mysterious shadow" secretly met "Joshua Wong"—argues that those seeking

to amend Article 1 hope to overthrow the institution]. 11 October 2019. https://www.youtube.com/watch?v=FIgLa4fmz3o (accessed 6 October 2021).

Miller, Jonathan, Kocha Olarn, and Helen Regan. 2020. "Thai King Addresses Protesters in Rare Public Comments, Saying He 'Loves Them All the Same'". *CNN*, 1 November 2020. https://edition.cnn.com/2020/11/01/asia/thailand-king-vajiralongkorn-protests-intl-hnk/index.html (accessed 7 January 2021).

Nation, The (Thailand). 2016. "Crown Prince Urges Regent and PM to Prevent Confusion". 16 October 2016. https://www.nationthailand.com/politics/30297810 (accessed 26 November 2019).

———. 2016. "Privy Council President Prem Regent Pro Tempore: Wissanu". 16 October 2016. https://www.nationthailand.com/news/30297739 (accessed 26 November 2019).

———. 2018. "Mental Asylum Best Place for 'Cracked' Anti-Monarchists, Says New Army Chief". 17 October 2018. https://www.nationthailand.com/politics/30356661 (accessed 4 December 2019).

———. 2019. "Pai Dao Din Released Early on Royal Pardon". 10 May 2019. https://www.nationthailand.com/news/30369158 (accessed 10 December 2019).

New Straits Times. 2019. "Cabin Crew, Body Guard, Thai Queen: Suthida's Meteoric Rise". 4 May 2019. https://www.nst.com.my/world/2019/05/485564/cabin-crew-bodyguard-thai-queen-suthidas-meteoric-rise (accessed 29 October 2019).

Nipat Thonglek. 2019. "Phap kao lao tamnan: nuai thahan raksa phra-ong" [Old pictures tell story of royal guards]. *Matichon*, 12 February https://www.matichon.co.th/news-monitor/news_1360525 (accessed 1 November 2019).

Patpicha Tanakasempipat. 2019. "Thai Army Chief Decries Opposition, Hints at Threat to Monarchy". *Reuters*, 11 October 2019. https://www.reuters.com/article/us-thailand-military/thai-army-chief-decries-opposition-hints-at-threat-to-monarchy-idUSKBN1WQ0WN (accessed 5 December 2019).

Pavin Chachavalpongpun. 2017. "Dhaveevatthana Prison: Hell on Earth in Thailand". *Japan Times*, 2 June 2017. https://www.japantimes.co.jp/opinion/2017/06/02/commentary/world-commentary/dhaveevatthana-prison-hell-earth-thailand/#.Xb-4n5ozaUk (accessed 4 November 2019).

Peck, Grant. "Former Thai Prime Minister Prem Tinsulanonda dies at 98". *Associated Press*, 27 May 2019. https://apnews.com/article/4e5193aa 780e4b32ae34966f647f2fc5 (accessed 15 September 2021).

Phatrawadee Phataranawik. 2019. "Disappearing Democracy". *The Nation*, 4 January 2019. https://www.nationthailand.com/news/30361637 (accessed 4 December 2019).

Pongpiphat Banchanont. 2018. "Luk Jod sami doktoe O senthang chiwit Bik Daeng pho bo tho bo khon mai sai wongthewan" [Jod's son, Dr O's husband: The life path to being new Army chief of Big Daeng from *Wongthewan* clique]. *The Matter*, 4 September 2018. https://thematter.co/social/general-apirat-kongsompong/58960?fbclid=IwAR30MHHEhOni-Kp2GYkdlQELeNm tKy3nYItuVcLnVC5I0Brq-2VleiF5RkQ (accessed 5 December 2019).

Prachatai. 2009. "Prem pat bueanglang patiwat-mai dai nam 'pho o Sonthi' khaofao" [Prem brushes off being behind the 2019 coup, never led General Sonthi to see the king]. 30 March 2009. https://prachatai.com/journal/2009/03/20540 (accessed 15 September 2021).

———. 2011. "Khosok so o cho yomrap taeng phang lom chao phuea topto kansairai than phuying Jarungjit" [CRESs spokesman admits fabrication of anti-monarchist chart to respond to allegations against Lady Jarungjit]. 26 May 2011. https://prachatai.com/journal/2011/05/34974 (accessed 20 January 2020).

———. 2019. "Anusawari prap kabot hai kueap pi khana thi chue 'Boworadet-Sri Sitthisongkhram' plo pen tuek-hong nai tho bo" [As the Defence of Democracy Monument disappears for nearly a year, while the names of Boworadet and Sri Sitthisongkram emerge at Army headquarters]. 9 October 2019. https://prachatai.com/journal/2019/10/84685 (accessed 4 December 2019).

———. 2019. "Kham to kham: chat thai lae phai khwammankhong nai khwamnuekkhit khong phon ek Apirat Kongsompong" [Word by word: The Thai nation and security threats in the thinking of General Apirat Kongsompong]. 12 October 2019. https://prachatai.com/journal/2019/10/84718 (accessed 5 June 2020).

———. 2020. "Poet ngoppraman kiaokap sathaban phramahakaksat pi 2564" [Budget for royal institution in 2021]. 31 August 2020. https://prachatai.com/journal/2020/08/89306 (accessed 6 January 2021).

———. 2021. "4 so so 'klao klai' aphiprai 'ngop suanratchakan nai phra-ong" [4 "Move Forward" MPs speak on "royal budget"]. 23 August 2021. https://prachatai.com/journal/2021/08/94603 (accessed 22 September 2021).

Prachatai English. 2019. "King Vajiralongkorn Gains Two Infantry Regiments by Emergency Degree". 3 October 2019. https://prachatai.com/english/node/8230 (accessed 7 February 2020).

———. 2020. "2019 Survey of Thai Political Landscape in Transition". 17 February 2020. https://prachatai.com/english/node/8365 (accessed 21 February 2020).

———. 2020. "Two Revolutionary Leader Statues Gone Missing". 29 January 2020. https://prachatai.com/english/node/8350 (accessed 11 February 2020).

————. 2020. "[Full Statement] The demonstration at Thammasat proposes monarchy reform". 11 August 2020. https://prachatai.com/english/node/8709 (accessed 7 January 2021).

Reuters. 2019. "Thailand's King Rama X — From Pilot Prince to Powerful Monarch". 2 May 2019. https://www.reuters.com/article/us-thailand-king-vajiralongkorn-profile/thailands-king-rama-x-from-pilot-prince-to-powerful-monarch-idUSKCN1S8114 (accessed 29 October 2019).

————. 2021. "Thai Monarchy Budget Survives Rare Calls for Cuts in Parliament". 22 August 2021. https://www.reuters.com/world/asia-pacific/thai-monarchy-budget-survives-rare-calls-cuts-parliament-2021-08-22 (accessed 22 September 2021).

Romfa. 1976. "Sangkhom phak klang" [Central Thai society]. *Thai rat*. 6 November 1976.

Sanook. 2020. "'Penkwin' prakat chaichana nam mop thueng rap 11-an thalaengkan thai-on kamlang thahan khuen sangkat" [Penguin announced victory, leads the protestors to 11th Infantry Regiment—reads statement demanding the return of the unit to Army]. 29 November 2020. https://www.sanook.com/news/8306070/ (accessed 7 January 2021).

Southgate, Laura. 2017. "The Enduring Influence of Prem Tinsulanonda". *Global Risk Insights*, 1 February 2017. https://globalriskinsights.com/2017/02/asian-power-broker-series-the-enduring-influence-of-prem-tinsulanonda (accessed 15 September 2021).

Taifun. 1976. "Bukkhon nai khao" [People in the news]. *Thai rat*. 9 November 1976.

Tappanai Boonpradit. 2020. "Dark Horse: Rise of New Air Force Chief Raises Eyebrows". *Khaosod English*, 6 October 2020. https://www.khaosodenglish.com/politics/2020/10/06/dark-horse-rise-of-new-air-force-chief-raises-eyebrows/ (accessed 6 January 2021).

Teeranai Charuvastra. 2019. "Royalist Coup Leaders Honoured at Army Hall of Fame". *Khaosod English*, 9 October 2019. http://www.khaosodenglish.com/politics/2019/10/09/royalist-coup-leaders-honored-at-army-hall-of-fame (accessed 4 December 2019).

Thai News Agency. 2020. "Chop pharakit! wisaman khon rai kratying khorat" [End of mission! extra-judicial killing of mass shooter in Khorat]. 9 February 2020. https://www.mcot.net/viewtna/5e3f779ae3f8e40af441b5ad (accessed 14 February 2020).

Thai News Bureau. 1992. "Kongthap bok triam nam phon thahan tonbaep tam neaothang phraratchadamri nuai thahan mahatlek rajawallop raksa phra-ong fuek thahan mai thua phrathet" [Army to send royal prototype soldiers of the Rajawallop Royal Guard to train newly recruited soldiers across the country]. 17 August 1992. http://thainews.prd.go.th/th/news/print_news/TCATG190817193711396 (accessed 7 November 2019).

Thai PBS News. 2019. "Roem laksut thahan tonbaep tam naeothang phraratchathan phruetsachikayon ni" [Royal curriculum for model privates starts this November]. 7 October 2019. https://news.thaipbs.or.th/content/284951 (accessed 4 December 2019).

Thai Post. 2019. "Senthang dao charatsaeng 'cho ko kho daeng' ma ruchak 'khun phon raksa phra-ong' sutpe!" [Career path of rising star "red collar" King's Guard task force]. 4 September 2019. https://www.thaipost.net/main/detail/44994 (accessed 7 November 2019).

Thai rat. 1976. "Sadet naeona" [Royal visit to the front lines]. 8 November 1976.

———. 1976. "Sala chip phuea chat" [They sacrificed their lives for the nation]. 6 November 1976.

———. 1976. "Supsip" [Gossip]. 7 November 1976.

———. 2013. "Yingluck khlia Thaksin, lueak Nipat nang palat kalahom" [Yingluck clears with Thaksin, chooses Nipat as defence ministry permanent secretary]. 30 August 2013. https://www.thairath.co.th/content/366852 (accessed 22 January 2020).

———. 2017. "San chamkhuk Jumpol Manmai hok pi saraphap lot luea sam thot yot chak phon tamruat ek pen nai" [Court sentences Jimpol Manmaito six years, reduced to three after confession, reduced in rank from general to private]. 10 March 2017. https://www.thairath.co.th/news/880615 (accessed 6 November 2019).

———. 2019. "'Ro 10' sadet liap phranakhon ngotngam yingyai somphrakiat saesong songphracharoen kuekkong" [Rama X circles Phranakhon to emphatic cries of "Long live the king!"]. 6 May 2019. https://www.thairath.co.th/news/royal/1561088 (accessed 29 October 2019).

———. 2020. "'Ro 10-rachini' sadet phithi suansanam thawai satpatiyan nai wan kongthap thai" [Rama X and queen preside over parade on Thai Military Day]. 19 January 2020. https://www.thairath.co.th/news/royal/1750720 (accessed 12 February 2020).

———. 2021. "Khai rahat lap 'Bik Oui' fa khluenlom dan 'Bik Tong' phangat 'pho bo tho ro'" [Decoding secret deal of "Big Oui" to elevate "Big Tong" to Navy chief]. 26 August 2021. https://www.thairath.co.th/news/politic/2177030 (accessed 24 September 2021).

Voice Online. 2019. "Apirat yok khamphut no so tho khrai mai rak sathaban mai somkhuan yu nai prathet thai" [Apirat says to military students, those who don't love the institution should not live in Thailand]. 21 June 2019. https://voicetv.co.th/read/dIzZTs_kO (accessed 4 December 2019).

———. 2021. "'Thoni' chae ro bo ho pi 49 sue ang wali 'wang mai ao'-phoei phaen su Sonthi-rap phlat nirathot thukchong yuet amnat samsong" ["Tony" discloses 2006 coup details, media told "palace doesn't want him", unveils a plan to fight back against Sonthi, admits mistake on the amnesty bill, used for second coup]. 14 September 2021. https://www.voicetv.

co.th/read/qd0c-b0wz?fbclid=IwAR2hhtkUWpTnOxI06_MiOdwNal6thQ_-
X8KpW6GTRyuq7ZBfB5gKq0IhLv4 (accessed 15 September 2021).

———. 2020. "'Narongphan' ning! fa naeokhit 'satharanarat' pat fun '5 dai
7 mai dai' pongpram 'thahan taengmo'" ["Narongphan" remains silent
amid growing "republican", dusting off "five yes, seven no", deterring
"watermelon soldiers"]. 24 December 2020. https://voicetv.co.th/read/
hPx1yGpUU (accessed 8 January 2021).

Washington Post. 2019. "Photos of the Thai Consort Shooting a Rifle and Flying
a Jet May Have Crashed a Royal Website". 27 August 2019. https://www.
washingtonpost.com/world/2019/08/27/photos-thai-consort-shooting-rifle-
flying-jet-may-have-crashed-royal-website (accessed 30 October 2019).

Wassana Nanuam. 2017. "Apirat Tipped as New Army Commander".
Bangkok Post, 12 August 2017. https://www.bangkokpost.com/thailand/
politics/1304603/apirat-tipped-as-new-army-commander (accessed
3 December 2019).

———. 2020. "Sudden Change to Nomination for New Air Force Chief".
Bangkok Post, 31 August 2020. https://www.bangkokpost.com/thailand/
general/1977491/sudden-change-to-nomination-for-new-air-force-chief
(accessed 6 January 2021).

———, and Wassayos Ngamkham. 2019. "Narongpan Tipped to Replace Apirat
as Army Chief". *Bangkok Post*, 9 September 2019. https://www.bangkokpost.
com/thailand/general/1745729/narongpan-tipped-to-replace-apirat-as-army-
chief (accessed 3 December 2019).

Official Documents

27th Military Circle, Royal Thai Army. 2019. "Khong sutthai kanfuek 'nong
khon lek khong kongthap bok' hai pen thahan tonbaep" [Last chapter in
training of 'youngest Army brothers' to be model soldiers]. Website of
27th Military Circle. 3 July 2019. http://mtb27.army2.mi.th/archives/7985
(accessed 4 December 2019).

King's Guard School, Thailand. n.d. *Khumue kanfuek waduai baepfuek bukkhon tha
mue plao* [Handbook of physical training without weapons]. http://www.
policeubon.go.th/download/23.pdf (accessed 12 June 2020).

Ministry of Education, Thailand. n.d. "Royal Biography of Her Majesty Queen
Suthida Bajrasudhabimalalakshana". http://www.en.moe.go.th/enMoe2017/
index.php/articles/387-royal-biography-of-her-majesty-queen-suthida-
bajrasudhabimalalakshana (accessed 29 October 2019).

Public Relations Department, Thailand. n.d. "Royal Biography of H.M. Queen
Suthida Bajrasudhabimalalakshana". https://thailand.prd.go.th/ewt_news.
php?nid=8035&filename=index (accessed 29 October 2019).

Royal Development Projects Bureau, Thailand. 2020. "Banthuek khrongkan annueangmachak phraratchadamri" [Notes on royally initiated projects]. Bangkok: Royal Development Projects Bureau.

Royal Gazette, Thailand. 1957. "Prakat phraborommaratcha-ongkan tang phu raksa phranakhon fai thahan" [Announcement on the appointment of a military commander to protect the capital]. Volume 74, Section 76, Special Edition. 16 September 1957. http://www.ratchakitcha.soc.go.th/DATA/PDF/2500/A/076/1.PDF (accessed 1 February 2020).

———. 1986. "Prakat samnak nayokratthamontri rueang taengtang phubangkhapkan phiset" [Announcement of the Prime Minister's Office on appointment of special commander]. Volume 103, Section 64, (special issue). 21 April 1986. http://www.ratchakitcha.soc.go.th/DATA/PDF/2529/D/064/1.PDF (accessed 10 October 2019).

———. 1989. "Phraratchabanyat nirathotsakam kae phu krathamkan an pen khwamphit to khwammankhong khong rat phainai ratchananachak tam pramuan kotmai aya lae khwamphit tam kotmai waduai kanpongkan kankratham an pen khommionit pho so 2532" [The 1989 amnesty law on national security offenders in accordance with the Penal Code and Anti-Communist Law]. Volume 106, Section 142, Special Edition. 30 August 1989. http://www.ratchakitcha.soc.go.th/DATA/PDF/2532/A/142/4.PDF (accessed 22 June 2020).

———. 1991. "Prakat samnak nayokratthamontri rueang taengtang nai thahan phiset" [Announcement of the Prime Minister's Office on appointment of special military officer]. Volume 108, Section 104. 13 June 1991. http://www.ratchakitcha.soc.go.th/DATA/PDF/2534/D/104/5555.PDF (accessed 10 October 2019).

———. 1992. "Prakat samnak nayokratthamontri rueang phraratchathan phraborommarachanuyat sathapana nuai thahan pen nuai thahan raksa phra-ong" [Announcement of prime minister's office on appointment of military unit as royal guard unit]. Volume 109, Section 158. 15 December 1992. http://www.ratchakitcha.soc.go.th/DATA/PDF/2535/D/158/14087.PDF (accessed 5 February 2020).

———. 1999. "Prakat samnak nayokratthamontri hai naithahan rap ratchakan" [Announcement of Prime Minister's Office on the appointment of military officer to government service]. Volume 116, Section 92 *ngo*. 18 November 1999. http://www.ratchakitcha.soc.go.th/DATA/PDF/2542/D/092/51.PDF (accessed 7 January 2021).

———. 2001. "Prakat samnak nayokratthamontri hai naithahan rap ratchakan" [Announcement of Prime Minister's Office on appointment of military officer to government service]. Volume 117, Section 76 *ngo*. 20 September

2001. http://www.ratchakitcha.soc.go.th/DATA/PDF/2544/D/076/2.PDF (accessed 7 January 2021).

———. 2001. "Prakat samnak nayokratthamonthi rueang phraratchathan phraborommarachanuyat sathapana nuai thahan pen nuai thahan raksa phra-ong" [Announcement of Prime Minister's Office on the appointment of military unit as royal guard unit]. Volume 118, Section 2 *ngo.* 4 January 2001. http://www.ratchakitcha.soc.go.th/DATA/PDF/2544/D/002/7.PDF (accessed 27 November 2019).

———. 2001. "Prakat samnak nayokratthamonthi rueang phraratchathan phraborommarachanuyat sathapana nuai thahan pen nuai thahan raksa phra-ong" [Announcement of Prime Minister's Office on the appointment of military unit as royal guard unit]. Volume 118, Section 14 *ngo.* 14 February 2001. http://www.ratchakitcha.soc.go.th/DATA/PDF/2544/D/014/1.PDF (accessed 27 November 2019).

———. 2002. "Prakat samnak nayokratthamontri rueang phraratchathan phraborommarachanuyat sathapana nuai thahan pen nuai thahan raksa phra-ong" [Announcement of Prime Minister's Office on the appointment of military unit as royal guard unit]. Volume 119, Section 5 *ngo.* 15 January 2002. http://www.ratchakitcha.soc.go.th/DATA/PDF/2545/D/005/7.PDF (accessed 27 November 2019).

———. 2005. "Prakat samnak nayokratthamontri rueang phraratchathan phraborommarachanuyat sathapana nuait thahan pen nuai thahan raksa phra-ong" [Announcement of Prime Minister's Office on appointment of military unit as royal guard unit]. Volume 122, Section 75 *ngo.* 20 September 2005. http://www.ratchakitcha.soc.go.th/DATA/PDF/2548/00171178.PDF (accessed 27 November 2019).

———. 2006. "Prakat samnak nayokratthamontri hai taengtang kharatchakan phonlaruean nai phra-ong" [Announcement of prime minister's office on appointment of civil servant in royal service]. Volume 123, Section 9 *ngo.* 31 January 2006. http://www.ratchakitcha.soc.go.th/DATA/PDF/2549/00181020.PDF (accessed 12 November 2019).

———. 2007. "Prakat samnak nayok ratthamontri rueang phraratchathan phraborommarachanuyat sathapana nuai thahan pen nuai thahan raksa phra-ong" [Announcement of Prime Minister's Office on appointment of military unit as royal guard unit]. Volume 124, Section 44 *ngo.* 24 May 2007. http://www.ratchakitcha.soc.go.th/DATA/PDF/2550/D/044/20.PDF (accessed 27 November 2019).

———. 2008. "Phraratchabanyat chat rabiap krasuang kalahom pho so 2551" [Defence Ministry Administration Act 2008]. Volume 125, Section 26 *ko.* 1 February 2008. http://www.ratchakitcha.soc.go.th/DATA/PDF/2551/A/026/35.PDF (accessed 13 January 2020).

———. 2009. "Prakat samnak nayokratthamontri hai taengtang kharatchakan phonlaruean nai phra-ong" [Announcement of prime minister's office on appointment of civil servant to royal service]. Volume 126, Special Section 22 *ngo*. 11 February 2009. http://www.ratchakitcha.soc.go.th/DATA/PDF/2552/E/022/12.PDF (accessed 12 November 2019).

———. 2009. "Prapprung kankamnot tamnaeng lae taengtang kharatchakan nai phra-ong" [Adjustment of position and appointment of official to royal service]. Volume 126, Special Section 172 *ngo*. 26 November 2009. http://www.ratchakitcha.soc.go.th/DATA/PDF/2552/E/172/22.PDF (accessed 12 November 2019).

———. 2010. "Prakat samnak nayokratthamontri hai nai thahan rap ratchakan" [Announcement of prime minister's office on appointment of military officer to government service]. Volume 127, Section 44 *ngo*. 7 April 2010. http://www.ratchakitcha.soc.go.th/DATA/PDF/2553/E/044/27.PDF (accessed 7 November 2019).

———. 2011. "Prakat samnak nayokratthamontri hai banchu lae taengtang kharatchakan phonlaruean nai phra-ong" [Announcement of prime minister's office on appointment of official in royal service]. Volume 128, Special Section 72 *ngo*. 28 June 2011. http://www.ratchakitcha.soc.go.th/DATA/PDF/2554/E/072/10.PDF (accessed 6 November 2019).

———. 2012. "Prakat samnak nayokratthamontri rueang phraratchanthan yot thahan tam kwa chan nai phon" [Announcement of prime minister's office on royal bestowal of military rank below general]. Volume 129, Section 15 *kho*. 27 April 2012. http://www.ratchakitcha.soc.go.th/DATA/PDF/2555/B/015/1.PDF (accessed 29 October 2019).

———. 2012. "Prakat samnak nayokratthamontri rueang taengtang nai thahan phiset" [Announcement of Prime Minister's Office on appointment of special military officer]. Volume 129 Special Section 17 *ngo*. 17 January 2012. http://www.ratchakitcha.soc.go.th/DATA/PDF/2555/E/017/8.PDF (accessed 29 November 2019).

———. 2013. "Pharatchabanyat chat rabiap ratchakan krasuang kalahom chabap thi song pho so 2556" [Ministry of Defence Organisation Act of 2013]. Volume 130, Section 109 *kho*. 20 November 2013. http://www.ratchakitcha.soc.go.th/DATA/PDF/2556/A/109/1.PDF (accessed 5 February 2020).

———. 2013. "Prakat samnak nayokratthamontri rueang phraratchathan khrueangrat itsiriyaphon pen korani phiset" [Announcement of prime minister's office on special bestowal of royal decoration]. Volume 130, Section 28 *kho*. 13 November 2013. http://www.ratchakitcha.soc.go.th/DATA/PDF/2556/B/028/1.PDF (accessed 4 February 2020).

———. 2013. "Prakat samnak nayokratthamontri rueang phraratchathan yot thahan chan nai phon" [Announcement of prime minister's office on royal bestowal of military rank of general]. Volume 130, Section 27 *kho*. 11 November 2013. http://www.ratchakitcha.soc.go.th/DATA/PDF/2556/B/027/1.PDF (accessed 29 October 2019).

————. 2013. "Prakat samnak nayokratthamontri rueang phraratchathan yot thahan tam kwa chan nai phon" [Announcement of prime minister's office on royal bestowal of military rank below general]. Volume 130, Section 3 *kho*. 25 January 2013. http://www.ratchakitcha.soc.go.th/DATA/PDF/2556/B/003/1.PDF (accessed 29 October 2019).

————. 2013. "Prakat samnak nayokratthamontri rueang phraratchathan yot thahan tam kwa chan nai phon" [Announcement of prime minister's office on royal bestowal of military rank below general]. Volume 130, Section 14 *kho*. 17 June 2013. http://www.ratchakitcha.soc.go.th/DATA/PDF/2556/B/014/1.PDF (accessed 29 October 2019).

————. 2014. "Phraratchakritsadika baeng suanratchakan lae kamnot nathi khong suanratchakan nuaibanchakan raksakhwamplotphai raksa phra-ong krasuang kalahom pho so 2557" [Royal decree on Royal Security Command of 2014]. Volume 131, Section 38 *kho*. 5 April 2014. http://www.ratchakitcha.soc.go.th/DATA/PDF/2557/A/038/1.PDF (accessed 5 February 2020).

————. 2014. "Prakat rueang la-ok chak thanandonsak" [Announcement on stepping down from royal status]. Volume 131, Section 29 *kho*. 12 December 2014. http://www.ratchakitcha.soc.go.th/DATA/PDF/2557/B/029/1.PDF (accessed 6 November 2019).

————. 2014. "Prakat samnak nayokratthamontri hai nai thahan rap ratchakan" [Announcement of prime minister's office announcement on military reshuffle]. Volume 131, Special Section 176 *ngo*. 8 September 2014. http://www.ratchakitcha.soc.go.th/DATA/PDF/2557/E/176/1.PDF (accessed 28 January 2020).

————. 2014. "Prakat samnak nayokratthamontri rueang hai nai thahan rap ratchakan" [Announcement of prime minister's office on appointment of military officer into government service]. Volume 131, Special Section 132 *ngo*. 16 July 2014. http://www.ratchakitcha.soc.go.th/DATA/PDF/2557/E/132/3.PDF (accessed 8 November 2019).

————. 2014. "Prakat samnak nayokratthamontri rueang phraratchathan khrueangrat itsiriyaphon pen koraniphiset" [Announcement of prime minister's office on special bestowal of royal decoration]. Volume 131, Section 10 *kho*. 6 May 2014. http://www.ratchakitcha.soc.go.th/DATA/PDF/2557/B/010/3.PDF (accessed 4 February 2020).

————. 2014. "Prakat samnak nayokratthamontri rueang phraratchathan phraborommarachanuyat sathapana nuai thahan pen nuai thahan raksa phra-ong" [Announcement of Prime Minister's Office on appointment of military unit as royal guard unit]. Volume 131, Special Section 200 *ngo*. 6 October

2014. http://www.ratchakitcha.soc.go.th/DATA/PDF/2557/E/200/4.PDF (accessed 27 November 2019).

———. 2014. "Prakat samnaknayokratthamontri rueang taengtang kharatchakan phonlaruean nai phra-ong" [Announcement of prime minister's office on appointment of civilian official in royal service]. Volume 131, Special Section 59 *ngo*. 4 April 2014. http://www.ratchakitcha.soc.go.th/DATA/PDF/2557/E/059/1.PDF (accessed 4 February 2020).

———. 2016. "Prakat samnak nayokratthamontri rueang phraratchathan phraborommarachanuyat hai thot yot thahan" [Announcement of prime minister's office on royal permission to strip military rank]. Volume 133, Section 3 *kho*. 2 February 2016. http://www.ratchakitcha.soc.go.th/DATA/PDF/2559/B/003/8.PDF (accessed 4 February 2020).

———. 2016. "Phraratchabanyat ngoppraman raichai prachampingoppraman pho so 2560" [2017 Budget Bill]. Volume 133, Section 84 *ko*. 23 September 2016. http://www.ratchakitcha.soc.go.th/DATA/PDF/2559/A/084/1.PDF (accessed 22 September 2021).

———. 2016. "Prakat samnak nayokratthamontri rueang phraratchathan yot thahan chan nai phon" [Announcement of prime minister's office on royal bestowal of military rank of general]. Volume 133, Section 44 *kho*. 10 December 2016. http://www.ratchakitcha.soc.go.th/DATA/PDF/2559/B/044/1.PDF (accessed 29 October 2019).

———. 2016. "Prakat samnak nayokratthamontri rueang taengtang ratcha-ongkharak" [Announcement of prime minister's office on appointment of royal guards]. Volume 133, Special Section 250 *ngo*. 2 November 2016. http:// www.ratchakitcha.soc.go.th/DATA/PDF/2559/E/250/2.PDF (accessed 4 November 2019).

———. 2016. "Prakat taengtang ongkhamontri" [Announcement on appointment of member of Privy Council]. Volume 133, Special Section 280 *ngo*. 2 December 2016. http://www.ratchakitcha.soc.go.th/DATA/PDF/2559/E/280/1.PDF (accessed 26 November 2019).

———. 2016. "Prakat taengtang ongkhamontri" [Announcement on appointment of member of Privy Council]. Volume 133, Special Section 281 *ngo*. 6 December 2016. http://www.ratchakitcha.soc.go.th/DATA/PDF/2559/E/281/1.PDF (accessed 10 February 2020).

———. 2016. "Prakat taengtang ongkhamontri" [Announcement on appointment of member of Privy Council]. Volume 133, Special Section 305 *ngo*. 24 December 2016. http://www.ratchakitcha.soc.go.th/DATA/PDF/2559/E/305/2.PDF (accessed 10 February 2020).

———. 2017. "Hai nai thahan sanyabat ok chak yot thahan" [Stripping commissioned officer of military rank]. Volume 134, Section 61 *kho*. 24 November 2017. http://www.ratchakitcha.soc.go.th/DATA/PDF/2560/B/061/1.PDF (accessed 30 October 2019).

————. 2017. "Phraratchabanyat rabiap borihan ratchakan nai phra-ong" [Royal Service Administration Act of 2017]. Volume 134, Section 88 *ko*. 1 May 2017. http://www.ratchakitcha.soc.go.th/DATA/PDF/2560/A/048/1.PDF (accessed 31 October 2019).

————. 2017. "Phraratchakritsadika chat rabiap ratchakan lae borihan ngan bukkhon khong ratchakan nai phra-ong pho so 2560" [Royal Decree on Administration and Personnel in Royal Service of 2017]. Volume 134, Section 51 *ko*. 10 May 2017. http://www.ratchakitcha.soc.go.th/DATA/PDF/2560/A/051/1.PDF (accessed 31 October 2019).

————. 2017. "Prakat samnak nayokratthamontri hai thot yot tamruat" [Announcement of prime minister's office on stripping of police rank]. Volume 134, Section 10 *kho*. 10 March 2017. http://www.ratchakitcha.soc. go.th/DATA/PDF/2560/B/010/1.PDF (accessed 6 November 2019).

————. 2017. "Prakat samnak nayokratthamontri rueang phraratchathan yot thahan tam kwa chan naiphon" [Announcement of prime minister's office on royal bestowal of military rank below general]. Volume 134, Section 16 *kho*. 22 March 2017. http://www.ratchakitcha.soc.go.th/DATA/PDF/2560/B/014/1.PDF (accessed 30 October 2019).

————. 2017. "Prakat samnak nayokratthamontri rueang phraratchathan yot thahan chan nai phon" [Announcement of prime minister's office on royal bestowal military rank of general]. Volume 134, Section 21 *kho*. 24 April 2017. http://www.ratchakitcha.soc.go.th/DATA/PDF/2560/B/021/5.PDF (accessed 12 November 2019).

————. 2017. "Prakat samnak nayokratthamontri rueang phraratchathan yot thahan tam kwa chan nai phon" [Announcement of prime minister's office on royal bestowal of military rank below general]. Volume 134, Section 29 *kho*. 23 June 2017. http://www.ratchakitcha.soc.go.th/DATA/PDF/2560/B/029/1. PDF (accessed 30 October 2019).

————. 2017. "Prakat samnak nayokratthamontri rueang phraratchathan yot thahan tam kwa chan nai phon" [Announcement of prime minister's office on royal bestowal of military rank below general]. Volume 134, Section 29 *kho*. 23 June 2017. http://www.ratchakitcha.soc.go.th/DATA/PDF/2560/B/029/2. PDF (accessed 30 October 2019).

————. 2017. "Prakat samnak nayokratthamontri rueang phraratchathan yot thahan tam kwa chan nai phon" [Announcement of prime minister's office on royal bestowal of military rank below general]. Volume 134, Section 29 *kho*. 23 June 2017. http://www.ratchakitcha.soc.go.th/DATA/PDF/2560/B/029/3. PDF (accessed 30 October 2019).

————. 2017. "Prakat samnak nayokratthamontri rueang taengtang ratcha-ongkharak" [Announcement of prime minister's office on appointment of royal guard]. Volume 134, Special Section 76 *ngo*. 12 March 2017. http://

www.ratchakitcha.soc.go.th/DATA/PDF/2560/E/076/21.PDF (accessed 5 February 2020).

———. 2017. "Prakat samnak nayokratthamontri rueang taengtang ratcha-ongkharak" [Announcement of prime minister's office on appointment of royal guards]. Volume 134, Special Section 137 *ngo*. 22 May 2017. http://www.ratchakitcha.soc.go.th/DATA/PDF/2560/E/137/1.PDF (accessed 5 February 2020).

———. 2017. "Prakat taengtang khanakammakan sapsin suanphramahakasat" [Announcement on the appointment of board of Crown Property Bureau]. Volume 134, Special Section 183 *ngo*. 17 July 2017. http://www.ratchakitcha.soc.go.th/DATA/PDF/2560/E/183/3.PDF (accessed 7 January 2021).

———. 2017. "Prakat taengtang ongkhamontri" [Announcement on appointment of member of Privy Council]. Volume 134, Special Section 154 *ngo*. 8 June 2017. http://www.ratchakitcha.soc.go.th/DATA/PDF/2560/E/154/1.PDF (accessed 26 February 2020).

———. 2017. "Prakat taengtang ratcha-ongkharakwen lae nai tamruat ratchasamnakwen" [Announcement of appointment of duty royal guards and duty royal guard police]. Volume 134, Special Section 195 *ngo*. 31 July 2017. http://www.ratchakitcha.soc.go.th/DATA/PDF/2560/E/195/1.PDF (accessed 4 November 2019).

———. 2017. "Phraratchabanyat ngoppraman raichai prachampingoppraman pho so 2561" [2018 Budget Bill]. Volume 134, Section 101 *ko*. 2 October 2017. http://www.ratchakitcha.soc.go.th/DATA/PDF/2560/A/101/1.PDF (accessed 21 September 2021).

———. 2018. "Prakat phraratchathan yot thahan" [Announcement of royal bestowal of military rank]. Volume 135, Section 25 *kho*. 24 July 2018. http://www.ratchakitcha.soc.go.th/DATA/PDF/2561/B/025/T1.PDF (accessed 8 November 2019).

———. 2018. "Prakat rueang hai ongkhamontri phon chak tamnaeng" [Announcement on resignation of member of Privy Council]. Volume 135, Special Section 143 *ngo*. 21 June 2018. http://www.ratchakitcha.soc.go.th/DATA/PDF/2561/E/143/1.PDF (accessed 10 February 2020).

———. 2018. "Prakat rueang phraratchathan khrueangrat itsiriyaphon chulachomkhlao" [Announcement of bestowal of Chulachomklao royal decoration]. Volume 135, Section 1 *kho*. 4 January 2018. http://www.ratchakitcha.soc.go.th/DATA/PDF/2561/B/001/1.PDF (accessed 29 October 2019).

———. 2018. "Prakat rueang phraratchathan yot thahan" [Announcement of royal bestowal of military rank]. Volume 138, Section 8 *ko*. 5 March 2018. http://www.ratchakitcha.soc.go.th/DATA/PDF/2561/B/008/1.PDF (accessed 8 November 2019).

————. 2018. "Prakat samnak nayok ratthamontri rueang phraratchathan yot thahan tam kwa chan nai phon" [Announcement of prime minister's office on royal bestowal of military rank below general]. Volume 135, Section 21 *kho*. 25 June 2018. http://www.ratchakitcha.soc.go.th/DATA/PDF/2561/B/021/1.PDF (accessed 30 October 2019).

————. 2018. "Prakat taengtang kharatchakan nai phra-ong" [Announcement of appointment of official in royal service]. Volume 135, Special Section 141 *ngo*. 19 June 2018. http://www.ratchakitcha.soc.go.th/DATA/PDF/2561/E/141/1.PDF (accessed 8 November 2019).

————. 2018. "Prakat taengtang lekhathikan phraratchawang lae phu-amnuaykan samnakngan sapsin suanphramahakasat" [Announcement of appointment of secretary general of the palace and director of Crown Property Bureau]. Volume 135, Special Section 55 *ngo*. 16 March 2018. http://www.ratchakitcha.soc.go.th/DATA/PDF/2561/E/055/2.PDF (accessed 7 January 2021).

————. 2018. "Prakat taengtang nai thahan phiset" [Announcement on appointment of special military officer]. Volume 135, Special Section 171 *ngo*. 17 July 2018. http://www.ratchakitcha.soc.go.th/DATA/PDF/2561/E/171/T1.PDF (accessed 26 February 2020).

————. 2018. "Prakat taengtang ongkhamontri" [Announcement on appointment of member of Privy Council]. Volume 135, Special Section 244 *ngo*. 2 October 2018. http://www.ratchakitcha.soc.go.th/DATA/PDF/2561/E/244/T_0001.PDF (accessed 29 November 2019).

————. 2018. "Prakat taengtang thahan ratcha-ongkharak phiset" [Announcement of appointment of special royal guard]. Volume 135, Section 48 *ngo*. 5 March 2018. http://www.ratchakitcha.soc.go.th/DATA/PDF/2561/E/048/1.PDF (accessed 8 November 2019).

————. 2018. "Phraratchabanyat ngoppraman raichai prachampingoppraman pho so 2562" [2019 Budget Bill]. Volume 135, Section 71 *ko*. 17 September 2018. http://www.ratchakitcha.soc.go.th/DATA/PDF/2561/A/071/T1.PDF (accessed 21 September 2021).

————. 2019. "Kot krasuang baeng suanratchakan pen kong bangkhapkan rue suan ratchakan yang uen nai samnakngan tamrua thaengchat (chabap thi 11) pho so 2562" [Ministerial regulation on division of command on other functions in the National Police Office, 2019]. Volume 136, Section 12 *ko*. 27 January 2019. http://www.ratchakitcha.soc.go.th/DATA/PDF/2562/A/012/T_0006.PDF (accessed 14 February 2020).

————. 2019. "Phraratchakamnot on attra kamlangphon lae ngoppraman bang suan khong kongthap bok kongthap thai krasuang kalahom pai pen khong nuai banchakan thawai khwamplotphai raksa phra-ong sueng pen nuai ratchakan nai phra-ong" [Royal decree on transfer of some part of the personnel and budget of Army, Armed Forces Headquarters and Ministry of Defense to Royal Security Command which is a government unit in royal service]. Volume 136, Section 103 *ko*. 30 September 2019. http:// www.ratchakitcha.soc.go.th/DATA/PDF/2562/A/103/T_0001.PDF (accessed 5 November 2019).

———. 2019. "Prakat hai kharatchaboriphan phon wara ratcha-ongkharak nai phra-ong" [Announcement of the end of royal official's term in royal service]. Volume, 136 Special Section 11 *ngo*. 23 April 2019. http://www. ratchakitcha.soc.go.th/DATA/PDF/2562/E/101/T_0001.PDF (accessed 7 November 2019).

———. 2019. "Prakat hai kharatchaboriphan taengtang pen ratcha-ongkharak nai phra-ong" [Announcement of appointment royal official as royal bodyguard]. Volume 136, Special Section 111 *ngo*. 3 May 2019. http://www.ratchakitcha. soc.go.th/DATA/PDF/2562/E/111/T_0001.PDF (accessed 7 November 2019).

———. 2019. "Prakat hai kharatchakan nai phra-ong fai thahan phon chak tamnaeng thot thanandonsak lae yot thahan talot chon riakkhuen khruengrat itsiriyaphon thuk chantra" [Announcement of removal of military officer in royal service from position, stripping royal status and military rank and status, and revocation of all royal decorations]. Volume 136, Section 55 *kho*. 21 October 2019. http://www.ratchakitcha.soc.go.th/DATA/PDF/2562/ B/055/T_0001.PDF (accessed 22 October 2019).

———. 2019. "Prakat hai lai kharatchakan phonlaruean nai phra-ongokchak ratchankan lae thot yot thahan phrom riakkhuen khrueangrat itsiriyaphon" [Announcement on removal from service of civilian officials in royal service, on stripping of military ranks and on revocation of royal decorations]. Volume 136, Section 57 *kho*. 29 October 2019. http://www.ratchakitcha. soc.go.th/DATA/PDF/2562/B/057/T_0001.PDF (accessed 30 October 2019).

———. 2019. "Prakat hai plot nai thahan chan sanyabat ok chak ratchakan lae thot yot thahan phrom riakkhuen khruengrat itsiriyaphon" [Announcement on removal of military officers from service, on stripping of rank and on revocation of royal decorations]. Volume 136, Section 57 *kho*. 29 October 2019. http://www.ratchakitcha.soc.go.th/DATA/PDF/2562/B/057/T_0002. PDF (accessed 30 October 2019).

———. 2019. "Prakat hai plot ok lae lai ok thot yot nai thahan chan sanyabat phrom riakkhuen khrueangrat itsiriyaphon" [Announcement of removal, dismissal, stripping of military rank and revocation of royal decoration]. Volume 136, Section 56 *kho*. 23 October 2019. http://www.ratchakitcha.soc. go.th/DATA/PDF/2562/B/056/T_0001.PDF (accessed 7 November 2019).

———. 2019. "Prakat rabiap suanratchakan nai phra-ong waduai thong chaichaloemphon nuai banchakan thawai khwamplotphai raksaphra-ong pho so 2562" [Announcement on regulations concerning *chaichaloemphon* flag of Royal Security Command of 2019]. Volume 136, Special Section 303 *ngo*. 12 December 2019. http://www.ratchakitcha.soc.go.th/DATA/ PDF/2562/E/303/T_0001.PDF (accessed 13 December 2019).

———. 2019. "Prakat rueang sathapana somdetphranangchao Sutthida Bajrasudhabimalalakshana" [Announcement of installation of Queen Sutthida]. Volume 136, Section 14 *kho*. 4 May 2019. http://www.ratchakitcha.soc.go.th/ DATA/PDF/2562/B/014/T_0002.PDF (accessed 29 October 2019).

———. 2019. "Prakat samnak nayokratthamontri rueang kananumat phraratchakamnot kanon attra kamlangphon bang suan khong kongthap bok kongthap thai krasuang kalahom pai pen khong nuai banchakan thawai khwamplotphai raksa phra-ong" [Announcement of prime minister's office approving transfer of some part of personnel and budget of Army, armed forces headquarters and defence ministry to Royal Security Command]. Volume 136, Section 111 *ko*. 21 October 2019. http://www.ratchakitcha.soc. go.th/DATA/PDF/2562/A/111/T_0001.PDF (accessed 5 November 2019).

———. 2019. "Prakat samnak nayokratthamontri rueang phraratchathan phraborommarachanuyat plianplaeng nuai thahan raksa phra-ong lae nuai thahan naiphra-ong" [Announcement of Prime Minister's Office on change of royal guard units]. Volume 136, Special Section 100 *ngo*. 23 April 2019. http://www.ratchakitcha.soc.go.th/DATA/PDF/2562/E/100/T_0027.PDF (accessed 27 November 2019).

———. 2019. "Prakat songphrakarunaplotklaoplotkramom hai klap khao rapratchakan phraratchathan yot nai thahan chan sanyabat phraratchathan khuen khrueangrat itsiriyaphon thuk chantra hai kharatchakan nai phra-ong" [Announcement on reinstatement, on royal bestowal of military rank and on restoration of all royal decorations to an official in royal service]. Volume 136, Section 59 *kho*. 11 November 2019. http://www.ratchakitcha.soc. go.th/DATA/PDF/2562/B/059/T_0001.PDF (accessed 12 November 2019).

———. 2019. "Prakat songphrakarunaplotklaoplotkramomphraratchathan phraborommarachanuyat plian nam nuai thahan raksa phra-ong" [Announcement on change of name of royal guard units]. Volume 136, Special Section 303 *ngo*. 12 December 2019. http://www.ratchakitcha.soc. go.th/DATA/PDF/2562/E/303/T_0004.PDF (accessed 13 December 2019).

———. 2019. "Prakat taengtang khanakammakan sapsin suanphramahakasat lae thiphrueksa samnakngan sapsin suanphramahakasat" [Announcement appointment of crown property board and advisor to Crown Property Bureau]. Volume 136, Special Section 4 *ngo,* 6 January 2019. http://www. ratchakitcha.soc.go.th/DATA/PDF/2562/E/004/T_0001.PDF (accessed 4 December 2019).

———. 2019. "Prakat taengtang kharatchakan nai phra-ong" [Announcement of appointment of royal officials]. Volume 136, Section 239 *ngo*. 25 September

2019. http://www.ratchakitcha.soc.go.th/DATA/PDF/2562/E/239/T_0001. PDF (accessed 5 January 2021).

———. 2019. "Prakat taengtang phuraksakan prathan ongkhamontri" [Announcement on appointment of acting Privy Council chairman]. Volume 136, Special Section 137 *ngo*. 28 May 2019. http://www.ratchakitcha.soc. go.th/DATA/PDF/2562/E/137/T_0001.PDF (accessed 26 November 2019).

———. 2020. "Prakat luean kharatchakan nai phra-ong hai sungkhuen lae prap-on kharatchakanthahan lae phonlaruean pen kharatachakan nai phra-ong" [Announcement on the promotion and transfer of military officers and civil servants to be royal officials]. Volume 137, Special Section 229 *ngo*. 30 September 2020. http://www.ratchakitcha.soc.go.th/DATA/PDF/2563/ E/229/T_0001.PDF (accessed 8 January 2021).

———. 2020. "Prakat rueang taengtang hai damrong thanandonsak lae phraratchathan khrueangrat itsiriyaphon thuk chantra" [Announcement on appointment to royal status and award of decorations of all classes]. Volume 137, Section 23 *kho*. 29 August 2020. http://www.ratchakitcha. soc.go.th/DATA/PDF/2563/B/023/T_0020.PDF (accessed 5 January 2021).

———. 2020. "Prakat samnak nayokratthamontri rueang hai naithahan rapratchakan" [Prime Minister's Office announcement on the appointment of military officers]. Volume 137, Special Section 218 *ngo*. 18 September 2020. http://www.ratchakitcha.soc.go.th/DATA/PDF/2563/E/218/T_0001. PDF?fbclid=IwAR1dAaRyj7_FynxfRUjqXgDsF7eyxDgec36AZZt1rmZIGqXw VF95-ZHu3FE (accessed 6 January 2021).

———. 2020. "Prakat samnak nayokratthamontri rueang phraratchathan plianplaeng nam khai thahan" [Announcement of Prime Minister's Office on renaming of military camps]. Volume 137, Special Section 68 *ngo*. 24 March 2020. http://www.ratchakitcha.soc.go.th/DATA/PDF/2563/E/068/T_0002. PDF (accessed 5 June 2020).

———. 2020. "Prakat taengtang kharatchakan nai phra-ong hai damrong tamnaeng" [Announcement on appointment of royal official to take up position]. Volume 137, Section 81 *ngo*. 8 April 2020. http://www.ratchakitcha. soc.go.th/DATA/PDF/2563/E/081/T_0001.PDF (accessed 5 January 2021).

———. 2020. "Prakat taengtang ongkhamontri" [Announcement on appointment of member of Privy Council]. Volume 137, Special Section 3 *ngo*. 4 January 2020. http://www.ratchakitcha.soc.go.th/DATA/PDF/2563/E/003/T_0001. PDF (accessed 6 January 2020).

———. 2020. "Phraratchabanyat ngoppraman raichai prachampingoppraman pho so 2563" [2020 Budget Bill]. Volume 137, Section 15 *ko*. 26 February 2020. http://www.ratchakitcha.soc.go.th/DATA/PDF/2563/A/015/T_0001. PDF (accessed 21 September 2021).

————. 2020. "Phraratchabanyat ngoppraman raichai prachampingoppraman pho so 2564" [2021 Budget Bill]. Volume 137, Section 82 *ko*. 7 October 2020 http://www.ratchakitcha.soc.go.th/DATA/PDF/2563/A/082/T_0001. PDF (accessed 21 September 2021).

Royal Thai Government. n.d. "Sarup khao kanprachum khanaratthamontri 14 karakadakhom 2563" [News summary of cabinet meeting of 14 July 2020]. https://www.thaigov.go.th/news/contents/details/33356 (accessed 22 July 2020).

Unofficial Documents

Puangthong R. Pawakapan. 2017. "Voice of the Victims: Truth for Justice". In *Truth for Justice: A Fact-Finding Report on the April–May 2010 Crackdowns in Thailand,* edited by Kwanravee Wangudom, pp. 5–6. 17 May 2017. http://www.pic2010.org/en-report/ (accessed 4 January 2021).

Thai Lawyers for Human Rights. 2021. "Sathiti phu thukdamnoen khadi matra 112 minpramat kasat pi 2563-2564" [Statistics on those charged with *lèse majesté* under section 112 for defamation of monarchy]. 6 January 2021. https://tlhr2014.com/archives/23983 (accessed 7 January 2021).

Interviews

Nattawut Saikua, 17 December 2019, Bangkok.
Lieutenant General Pongsakorn Rodchompoo, 20 December 2019, Bangkok.
Retired Thai Army general, 18 December 2019, Bangkok.
General Sonthi Boonyaratglin, 18 December 2019, Bangkok.

INDEX

Note: Page numbers followed by "n" refer to notes.

ABOUT THE AUTHOR

Supalak Ganjanakhundee is a journalist and author, active both within and outside Thailand and specializing in Thai politics and international relations. Having worked as a reporter in Thai and foreign media, including with the Matichon Group, the Manager Media Group and Kyodo News, he served as chief editor of *The Nation* in 2018–19. Supalak was a Visiting Fellow in the Thailand Studies Programme of the ISEAS – Yusof Ishak Institute, Singapore, between October 2019 and June 2020.

Ingram Content Group UK Ltd.
Milton Keynes UK
UKHW010033130323
418355UK00023B/337